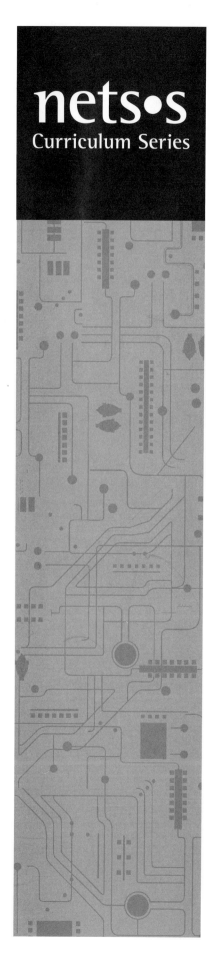

net s•s
Curriculum Series

National Educational Technology Standards for Students

Foreign Language Units for All Proficiency Levels

Carl Falsgraf, Editor

iste

INTERNATIONAL SOCIETY FOR TECHNOLOGY IN EDUCATION
EUGENE, OREGON • WASHINGTON, DC

nets•s
Curriculum Series

Foreign Language Units for All Proficiency Levels

Carl Falsgraf, Editor

ACQUISITIONS AND DEVELOPMENT EDITOR
Scott Harter

DEVELOPMENTAL AND COPY EDITOR
Lynne Ertle

PRODUCTION EDITOR
Lynda Gansel

BOOK DESIGN
Katherine Getta, Tracy Cozzens

GRAPHIC DESIGNER
Signe Landin

COVER DESIGN
Signe Landin

PRODUCTION COORDINATOR
Maddelyn High

LAYOUT AND PRODUCTION
Kim McGovern, Tracy Cozzens

International Society for Technology in Education (ISTE)

Washington, DC, Office:
1710 Rhode Island Ave NW, Suite 900
Washington, DC 20036

Eugene, Oregon, Office:
175 West Broadway, Suite 300
Eugene, OR 97401-3003
Order Desk: 1.800.336.5191
Order Fax: 1.541.302.3778
Customer Service: orders@iste.org
Book Publishing: books@iste.org
Rights and Permissions: permissions@iste.org
Web site: www.iste.org

First Edition
ISBN: 978-1-56484-222-0

about iste

The International Society for Technology in Education (ISTE) is a nonprofit professional organization with a worldwide membership of leaders in education technology. We are dedicated to promoting appropriate uses of technology to support and improve learning, teaching, and administration in PK–12 and teacher education. As part of that mission, ISTE provides high-quality and timely information, services, and materials, such as this book.

ISTE Book Publishing works with experienced educators to develop and produce practical resources for classroom teachers, teacher educators, and technology leaders. Every manuscript we select for publication is carefully peer-reviewed and professionally edited. We look for content that emphasizes the effective use of technology where it can make a difference—increasing the productivity of teachers and administrators; helping students with unique learning styles, abilities, or backgrounds; collecting and using data for decision making at the school and district level; and creating dynamic, project-based learning environments that engage 21st-century learners. We value your feedback on this book and other ISTE products. E-mail us at **books@iste.org**.

ISTE is home of the National Educational Technology Standards (NETS) Project, the National Educational Computing Conference (NECC), and the National Center for Preparing Tomorrow's Teachers to Use Technology (NCPT[3]). To find out more about these and other ISTE initiatives and to view our complete book list or request a print catalog, visit our Web site at **www.iste.org**. You'll find information about:

- ISTE, our mission, and our members
- Membership opportunities and services
- Online communities and special interest groups (SIGS)
- Professional development services
- Research & evaluation services
- Educator resources
- ISTE's National Technology Standards for Students, Teachers, and Administrators
- *Learning & Leading with Technology* magazine
- *Journal of Research on Technology in Education*

about the authors

EDITOR

Carl Falsgraf is founder and Director of the Center for Applied Second Language Studies, a National Foreign Language Resource Center at the University of Oregon. He was president of the Pacific Northwest Council for Languages (PNCFL) and has served on the ACTFL Executive Council, The Association of Teachers of Japanese (ATJ) Board of Directors, and the editorial board of Foreign Language Annals. He has delivered numerous keynote addresses and workshops, and published papers on second language acquisition, functional linguistics, and standards-based language education. He is the lead designer of the STAMP online proficiency assessment and other technology-based tools to help teachers develop and measure student proficiency.

CONTRIBUTING AUTHORS

Chapter 1

Carl Falsgraf, Director, Center for Applied Second Language Studies (CASLS), University of Oregon

Chapter 2

Kyle Ennis, Vice President, Language Learning Solutions, Eugene, Oregon

Chapter 3

Kathleen M. Riordan, Director of Foreign Languages, Springfield, Massachusetts

Rita Oleksak, Foreign Language Director K–12, Glastonbury, Connecticut

Chapter 4

Ann Tollefson, Foreign Language Content Specialist for the Wyoming Department of Education

Chapter 5

Walter McKenzie, Director of Technology, Northborough–Southborough Regional School District, Northborough, Massachusetts

MOSAIC PROJECT: **Content-based Instruction in Spanish** (Units 1–3)

Introduction

Robert Davis, Associate Professor of Spanish, University of Oregon

Unit Authors

Lisa Albrich, Sheldon High School, Eugene, Oregon

Susan Hardwick, Professor of Geography, University of Oregon

Kelly León Howarth, Instructor, Romance Languages, University of Oregon

Brent Mellor, Churchill High School, Eugene, Oregon

Project Directors

Robert L. Davis, Associate Professor of Spanish, University of Oregon (project editor)

Greg Hopper-Moore, Research and Development Coordinator, Center for Applied Second Language Studies, University of Oregon

Sally Hood-Cisar, University of Hawaii

MOSAIC PROJECT: **Content-based Instruction in Japanese** (Units 4–6)

Introduction

Sachiko Kamioka, Assistant Director, Center for Applied Second Language Studies, University of Oregon

Unit Authors

Andrew Goble, Associate Professor of History, University of Oregon

Etsuko Inoguchi, Department of East Asian Language and Literatures, University of Oregon

Fred Lorish, former Japanese immersion school teacher, Eugene, Oregon

Yoko O'Brien, Adjunct Instructor, Chemeketa Community College, Salem, Oregon

Yoshiko Shioya, Sheldon High School, Eugene, Oregon

Project Directors

Robert L. Davis, Associate Professor of Spanish, University of Oregon

Greg Hopper-Moore, Research and Development Coordinator, CASLS, University of Oregon

Evaluator

Atsuko Hayashi, Lecturer, East Asian Languages and Cultural Studies, University of California, Santa Barbara

Editor

Sachiko Kamioka, Assistant Director, Center for Applied Second Language Studies, University of Oregon

COBALTT PROJECT: **Content-Based Language Teaching with Technology**
(Units 7–9)

Introduction

Laurent Cammarata, University of Minnesota; and Diane J. Tedick, Associate Professor, University of Minnesota

Unit Authors

Unit 7. Original unit developed by Barbara C. Anderson, French teacher, Edina High School, Edina, Minnesota. Unit adapted by Laurent Cammarata and Diane J. Tedick for this publication.

Unit 8. Original unit developed by Pam Wesely, middle school French teacher, Breck School, Minneapolis, Minnesota, and Ph.D. student, Second Languages and Cultures Education, University of Minnesota. Unit adapted by Laurent Cammarata and Diane J. Tedick for this publication.

Unit 9. Original unit developed by Mary Bartolini (from Chiclayo, Peru), first grade teacher, Adams Spanish Immersion School, St. Paul, Minnesota. Unit adapted by Laurent Cammarata and Diane J. Tedick for this publication.

IOWA STATE: **The National K–12 Foreign Language Resource Center**
(Units 10–12)

Introduction

Marcia Harmon Rosenbusch, director of the National K–12 Foreign Language Resource Center, Iowa State University

Unit Authors

Unit 10. Nancy Gadbois, department chair, High School of Science and Technology, Springfield, Massachusetts. Foreign Languages

Unit 11. Michele Montás, high school Spanish teacher at Trevor Day School, New York, New York

Unit 12. Karen Willetts-Kokora, foreign language resource teacher, Springbrook High School, Montgomery County Public Schools, Rockville, Maryland

contents

Section 2 • Resource Units 59

The NETS Project

The National Educational Technology Standards (NETS) Project was initiated by the Accreditation and Professional Standards Committee of the International Society for Technology in Education (ISTE). ISTE has emerged as a recognized leader among professional organizations for educators involved with technology. ISTE's mission is to promote appropriate uses of technology to support and improve learning, teaching, and administration. Its members are leaders in educational technology, including teachers, technology coordinators, education administrators, and teacher educators. ISTE supports all subject area disciplines by providing publications, conferences, online resources, and services that help educators combine the knowledge and skills of their teaching fields with the application of technologies to improve learning and teaching.

The primary goal of the NETS Project is to enable stakeholders in PK–12 education to develop national standards for the educational uses of technology that facilitate school improvement in the United States. The NETS Project is developing standards to guide educational leaders in recognizing and addressing the essential conditions for the effective use of technology to support PK–12 education.

The NETS for Students (NETS•S) Curriculum Series Project represents a continuation of ISTE's desire to provide educators with the means to implement the NETS. *Foreign Language Units for All Proficiency Levels* is specifically designed to provide foreign language teachers with curriculum to meet the NETS•S.

NATIONAL EDUCATIONAL TECHNOLOGY STANDARDS FOR STUDENTS

The NETS for Students are divided into six broad categories. Standards within each category are to be introduced, reinforced, and mastered by students. These categories provide a framework for linking performance indicators, listed by grade level, to the standards. Teachers can use these standards and profiles as guidelines for planning technology-based activities in which students achieve success in learning, communication, and life skills.

1. **Basic operations and concepts**
   - Students demonstrate a sound understanding of the nature and operation of technology systems.
   - Students are proficient in the use of technology.

2. **Social, ethical, and human issues**
   - Students understand the ethical, cultural, and societal issues related to technology.

- Students practice responsible use of technology systems, information, and software.
- Students develop positive attitudes toward technology uses that support lifelong learning, collaboration, personal pursuits, and productivity.

3. **Technology productivity tools**
   - Students use technology tools to enhance learning, increase productivity, and promote creativity.
   - Students use productivity tools to collaborate in constructing technology-enhanced models, preparing publications, and producing other creative works.

4. **Technology communications tools**
   - Students use telecommunications to collaborate, publish, and interact with peers, experts, and other audiences.
   - Students use a variety of media and formats to communicate information and ideas effectively to multiple audiences.

5. **Technology research tools**
   - Students use technology to locate, evaluate, and collect information from a variety of sources.
   - Students use technology tools to process data and report results.
   - Students evaluate and select new information resources and technological innovations based on the appropriateness to specific tasks.

6. **Technology problem-solving and decision-making tools**
   - Students use technology resources for solving problems and making informed decisions.
   - Students employ technology in the development of strategies for solving problems in the real world.

THE NETS•S PERFORMANCE INDICATORS

Section 2 provides 12 foreign language resource units. This technology-embedded curriculum is specifically designed to help students meet the following performance indicators, which all students should have opportunities to demonstrate. Numbers in parentheses following each performance indicator refer to the standards category to which the performance is linked.

Prior to completion of Grade 2, students will:

1. Use input devices (e.g., mouse, keyboard, remote control) and output devices (e.g., monitor, printer) to successfully operate computers, VCRs, audiotapes, and other technologies. (1)
2. Use a variety of media and technology resources for directed and independent learning activities. (1, 3)

3. Communicate about technology using developmentally appropriate and accurate terminology. (1)

4. Use developmentally appropriate multimedia resources (e.g., interactive books, educational software, elementary multimedia encyclopedias) to support learning. (1)

5. Work cooperatively and collaboratively with peers, family members, and others when using technology in the classroom. (2)

6. Demonstrate positive social and ethical behaviors when using technology. (2)

7. Practice responsible use of technology systems and software. (2)

8. Create developmentally appropriate multimedia products with support from teachers, family members, or student partners. (3)

9. Use technology resources (e.g., puzzles, logical thinking programs, writing tools, digital cameras, drawing tools) for problem solving, communication, and illustration of thoughts, ideas, and stories. (3, 4, 5, 6)

10. Gather information and communicate with others using telecommunications, with support from teachers, family members, or student partners. (4)

Prior to completion of Grade 5, students will:

1. Use keyboards and other common input and output devices (including adaptive devices when necessary) efficiently and effectively. (1)

2. Discuss common uses of technology in daily life and the advantages and disadvantages those uses provide. (1, 2)

3. Discuss basic issues related to responsible use of technology and information and describe personal consequences of inappropriate use. (2)

4. Use general purpose productivity tools and peripherals to support personal productivity, remediate skill deficits, and facilitate learning throughout the curriculum. (3)

5. Use technology tools (e.g., multimedia authoring and presentation software, Web tools, digital cameras, scanners) for individual and collaborative writing, communicating and publishing activities to create knowledge products for audiences inside and outside the classroom. (3, 4)

6. Use telecommunications efficiently and effectively to access remote information, communicate with others in support of direct and independent learning, and pursue personal interests. (4)

7. Use telecommunications and online resources (e.g., e-mail, online discussions, Web environments) to participate in collaborative problem-solving activities for the purpose of developing solutions or products for audiences inside and outside the classroom. (4, 5)

8. Use technology resources (e.g., calculators, data collection probes, videos, and educational software) in activities for problem-solving, self-directed learning, and extended learning. (5, 6)

9. Determine when technology is useful and select the appropriate tool(s) and technology resources to address a variety of tasks and problems. (5, 6)

10. Evaluate the accuracy, relevance, appropriateness, comprehensiveness, and bias of electronic information sources. (6)

Prior to completion of Grade 8, students will:

1. Apply strategies for identifying and solving routine hardware and software problems that occur during everyday use. (1)

2. Demonstrate knowledge of current changes in information technologies and the effect those changes have on the workplace and society. (2)

3. Exhibit legal and ethical behaviors when using information and technology, and discuss consequences of misuse. (2)

4. Use content-specific tools, software, and simulations (e.g., environmental probes, graphing calculators, exploratory environments, Web tools) to support learning and research. (3, 5)

5. Apply productivity/multimedia tools and peripherals to support personal productivity, group collaboration, and learning throughout the curriculum. (3, 6)

6. Design, develop, publish, and present products (e.g., Web pages, videotapes) using technology resources that demonstrate and communicate curriculum concepts to audiences inside and outside the classroom. (4, 5, 6)

7. Collaborate with peers, experts, and others using telecommunications and collaborative tools to investigate curriculum-related problems, issues, and information, and to develop solutions or products for audiences inside and outside the classroom. (4, 5)

8. Select and use appropriate tools and technology resources to accomplish a variety of tasks and solve problems. (5, 6)

9. Demonstrate an understanding of concepts underlying hardware, software, and connectivity, and of practical applications to learning and problem solving. (1, 6)

10. Research and evaluate the accuracy, relevance, appropriateness, comprehensiveness, and bias of electronic information sources concerning real-world problems. (2, 5, 6)

Prior to completion of Grade 12, students will:

1. Identify capabilities and limitations of contemporary and emerging technology resources and assess the potential of these systems and services to address personal, lifelong learning, and workplace needs. (2)

2. Make informed choices among technology systems, resources, and services. (1, 2)

3. Analyze advantages and disadvantages of widespread use of and reliance on technology in the workplace and in society as a whole. (2)

4. Demonstrate and advocate for legal and ethical behavior among peers, family, and community regarding the use of technology and information. (2)

5. Use technology tools and resources for managing and communicating personal/professional information (e.g., finances, schedules, addresses, purchases, correspondence). (3, 4)

6. Evaluate technology-based options, including distance and distributed education, for lifelong learning. (5)

7. Routinely and efficiently use online information resources to meet needs for collaboration, research, publications, communications, and productivity. (4, 5, 6)

8. Select and apply technology tools for research, information analysis, problem solving, and decision making in content learning. (4, 5)

9. Investigate and apply expert systems, intelligent agents, and simulations in real-world situations. (3, 5, 6)

10. Collaborate with peers, experts, and others to contribute a content-related knowledge base by using technology to compile, synthesize, produce, and disseminate information, models, and other creative works. (4, 5, 6)

Essential Conditions for Technology Integration

Successful learning activities, such as the ones provided in this book, depend on more than just the technology. Certain conditions are necessary for schools to effectively use technology for learning, teaching, and educational management. Physical, pedagogical, financial, and policy dimensions greatly affect the success of technology use in schools.

The curriculum provided in this book will be more effective if a combination of essential conditions for creating learning environments conducive to powerful uses of technology is achieved, including:

- vision with support and proactive leadership from the education system;
- educators skilled in the use of technology for learning;
- content standards and curriculum resources;
- student-centered approaches to learning;
- assessment of the effectiveness of technology for learning;
- access to contemporary technologies, software, and telecommunications networks;
- technical assistance for maintaining and using technology resources;
- community partners who provide expertise, support, and real-life interactions;
- ongoing financial support for sustained technology use; and
- policies and standards supporting new learning environments.

Traditional educational practices no longer provide students with all the necessary skills for economic survival in today's workplace. Students today must apply strategies for solving problems using appropriate tools for learning, collaborating, and communicating. The following chart lists characteristics representing traditional approaches to learning and corresponding strategies associated with new learning environments.

The most effective learning environments meld traditional approaches and new approaches to facilitate learning of relevant content while addressing individual needs. The resulting learning environments should prepare students to:

- communicate using a variety of media and formats;
- access and exchange information in a variety of ways;
- compile, organize, analyze, and synthesize information;
- draw conclusions and make generalizations based on information gathered;
- know content and be able to locate additional information as needed;
- become self-directed learners;
- collaborate and cooperate in team efforts; and
- interact with others in ethical and appropriate ways.

Teachers know that the wise use of technology can enrich learning environments and enable students to achieve marketable skills. We hope that high school educators will find the curriculum and other material provided within helpful in meeting these goals.

ESTABLISHING NEW LEARNING ENVIRONMENTS

Incorporating New Strategies

Traditional Learning Environment————→	New Learning Environments
Teacher-centered instruction————→	Student-centered learning
Single-sense stimulation————→	Multisensory stimulation
Single-path progression————→	Multipath progression
Single media————→	Multimedia
Isolated work————→	Collaborative work
Information delivery————→	Information exchange
Passive learning————→	Active/exploratory/inquiry-based learning
Factual, knowledge-based learning————→	Critical thinking and informed decision-making
Reactive response————→	Proactive/planned action
Isolated, artificial context————→	Authentic, real-world context

How to Use This Book

Foreign Language Units for All Proficiency Levels is divided into two main sections.

SECTION 1 • STRATEGIES FOR GETTING STARTED

Section 1 provides chapters that will help teachers successfully integrate technology into K–12 classrooms. Teachers are provided with guidelines for integrating technology in foreign language instruction. Teachers also are given ideas on integrating technology standards and foreign language standards, the role technology plays in performance assessment, enhancing foreign language education with distance learning, and using search engines effectively.

SECTION 2 • RESOURCE UNITS

Section 2 provides teachers with 12 resource units developed as part of four different projects. For each unit, the following sections are provided:

OVERVIEW — At the start of each unit, an overview provides quick glance information on the unit, including the target age, the language, the ACTFL Proficiency Level, the primary content area, which other disciplines connect through the unit, and the time frame within which the unit can be taught.

DESCRIPTION — This is a brief description of the unit, covering topics such as the unit's development and special resources the unit incorporates.

OBJECTIVES — The unit is designed to meet the objectives listed in this section.

STANDARDS ADDRESSED — The NETS•S and Standards for Foreign Language Learning that are addressed in the unit are listed. Full listings of both sets of standards appear in appendixes B and C.

CONNECTIONS TO OTHER DISCIPLINES — Every unit connects to other disciplines. This section identifies the content that the unit explores as part of the foreign language lessons.

SPOTLIGHT ON TECHNOLOGY — Each unit highlights the use of one or more types of technology. This section explains how the highlighted technology is incorporated into the lesson plan.

TECHNOLOGY RESOURCES NEEDED — Each unit provides a list of all the hardware and software needed to successfully implement the lesson.

SUPPLEMENTARY RESOURCES — This section gives the teacher a list of important Web sites, books, videos, audiotapes, or other resources that can be used to enhance the lesson. The resources are organized in various ways depending on the unit, to best fit the needs of an educator teaching the unit.

TEACHING THE UNIT — This section provides a complete teaching plan for the unit, broken into activities and days. Within each section, you'll find the subsections "Preview" and "Focused Learning," with the frequent addition of "Expansion" ideas.

EXTENSION ACTIVITIES — Sometimes lessons are so good, students and teachers don't want them to end. This section offers additional unit-wide suggestions for extending the lesson for teachers interested in further exploring the topic.

TEACHING TIPS — Many units offer "Teaching Tips" within each activity. This section helps teachers get the most out of the unit as a whole. Provided are implementation suggestions, along with insights into which teaching strategy might be the most effective for you. Some units conclude with unit-wide "Teaching Tips."

ASSESSMENTS — Assessment ideas are included with each unit. Please note that scoring rubrics appear in the appendix A.

CD • RESOURCE UNIT SUPPLEMENTS

Tucked in the back cover is a CD that contains a wealth of resources for educators applying the units. Included are more detailed unit descriptions, along with handouts such as worksheets, vocabulary lists, and illustrations. The units on the CD also include hotlinks to online resources.

APPENDIXES

The appendixes provide the assessment rubrics for the resource units, the full National Educational Technology Standards for students, teachers, and administrators, and the Standards for Foreign Language Learning.

Beyond This Book

Keep in mind that the authors of individual learning activities could not address the needs of every teaching situation. Take the examples presented and modify them to fit your circumstances and needs. The sample lessons also provide a lens for re-examining traditional lessons and discovering ways to infuse technology to enrich teaching and learning.

Be proactive about sharing your good work with others. There are many lesson plan Web sites as well as school, district, professional association, and parent meetings at which to present new lesson plans and the resulting student work. Educators need to learn from their peers. Educators also need to inform parents of their efforts to integrate technology and learning, and to inform the greater public about how schools are meeting the needs of students, parents, and the community.

Reference

International Society for Technology in Education (ISTE). (1998). *National educational technology standards for students.* Eugene, OR: Author. Also available online at http://cnets.iste.org/students/s_stands.html

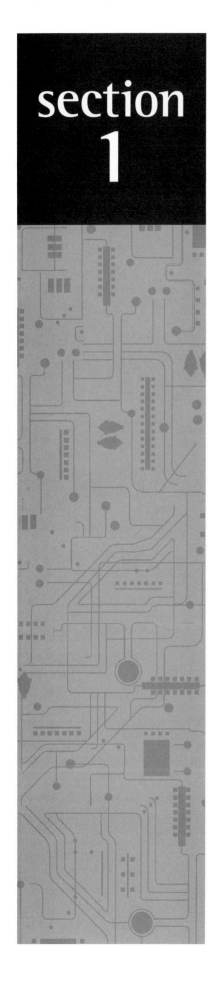

section 1

Strategies for Getting Started

CARL FALSGRAF

Learner-Friendly Technology in a Brain-Friendly Classroom

Appropriate Technology in the Service of Proficiency

Technology can be scary. We have a love/hate relationship with technology along with paradoxical expectations, with the hope that it will solve all our problems and the fear that it will take over our lives. Neither is a real possibility, but it sometimes seems like it when we see a whiz-bang demonstration of the latest gizmo or, conversely, when we feel the abject panic that ensues when the computer lab crashes and we're facing 30 14-year-olds with nothing to distract them from following their basest impulses.

Most language teachers come to the field with training in literature and language, not technology. It makes sense, therefore, to look to literature to tell us about our attitudes toward technology, to review our understanding of how students learn, and then to go from there to explore ways that technology can help us make our classrooms more compatible with our educational goals.

Literature and Technology

As Kyle Ennis points out in this volume, the most critical factor in ensuring effective use of technology in the classroom is the attitude the teacher brings to the technology. Looking at literature written at the dawn of the technological age can tell us a great deal about the love/hate relationship human beings have with the machines they create. Jules Verne and Mary Shelley invented science fiction in the 19th century. Up to that point, ideas about the future had focused on utopian social relations, such as Jefferson's nation of small, independent farmers, or on apocalyptic religious visions, such as Dante's inferno. Verne and Shelley added the notion of technology as the source of that utopia or that hell. Let's start with hell and work upwards.

If you have seen the Hollywood Frankenstein movies, you know that Dr. Frankenstein "created a monster" by playing God and using two cutting-edge technologies of the day—surgery and electricity. His creation then escaped, taking on a life of his own and terrorizing the population. The Frankenstein metaphor has come to symbolize the dangers of scientific hubris and our fear of technological inventions we scarcely understand. This metaphor has become more powerful as the technology that terrifies us has gone from electricity and surgery in Shelley's time, to gas chambers and atom bombs in Boris Karloff's, to the computer databases of today that know which genetically modified foods you bought at the grocery store for dinner last night. Technology has always been scary.

But Shelley's original monster was quite different from Boris Karloff's interpretation. Based on the Karloff movie, you would think that Dr. Frankenstein implanted the brain of a grizzly bear in the monster—lots of roaring, holding out stiff arms, and dismembering innocent people. Shelley's monster, however, clearly has a human brain. There are long passages of the monster's philosophical musings on the notion of identity, the relationship between the individual and society, and the nature of prejudice. The monster is misunderstood and persecuted because of his appearance and the nature of his birth.

Shelley's *Frankenstein* is not just about the terrifying potential of technology—about "creating a monster"—but about us and our irrational fears of the unknown, the new, and the different. Shelley's genius is that she captured both the means of destruction—runaway technology—and the social conditions that enable such horrors to be unleashed—hatred, intolerance, and mob psychology.

Are you a villager, torch in hand, convinced that the monster is a menace on the loose? Or are you the young girl who was able to see past her fear, understand the heart of the monster, and befriend it?

Jules Verne had a different vision of the future. Technology would further the human spirit by allowing new and wonderful experiences. Our curiosity about the nature of the world would lead us to unprecedented knowledge and prosperity. Like Shelley, he was prescient. Technology, whether it be hot-air balloons, automobiles, or spacecraft, can provide us with experiences that expand the mind and feed the spirit.

Jules Verne had the spirit of a teacher. He believed that the human condition could be improved through the expansion of knowledge. He was optimistic about the future—as all teachers need to be. Jules Verne was what would now be called an "early adopter": the kind of guy who rushes out to get the latest model of handheld computer or cell phone, can't wait to upgrade his operating system, and uses Internet dating services.

Are you an early adopter, a latter-day Phileas Phogg willing to get in the balloon and trust that you will come down somewhere safe?

We should be neither villagers giving in to our Philistine instincts of destroying that which is new and unfamiliar nor Vernian heroes setting off in untested contraptions. The model for a healthy approach to technology is—and it pains me deeply to say this—*Star Wars*. While he pales in comparison as a literary figure, George Lucas got it right on our modern relationship with technology.

The *Star Wars* series is best known for its special effects. The audience may be thrilled, but the characters don't even bat an eye. The *Star Wars* heroes are neither fearful nor enamored of the technology at their disposal. Luke Skywalker and his sidekicks prevail against superior technology—such as the Death Star—with their relatively rudimentary spacecraft and weapons. The key to their success—and ours—is a superior sense of spiritual purpose. It is the Force, not the fancy gizmos, that ensures ultimate victory. Parlor tricks such as levitating objects are merely exercises to cultivate spiritual discipline and strength, not ends in themselves. The good guys are as likely to take down an enemy with a club as with a laser gun. Light sabers are cool, but really, they are just high-tech swords. But they do the trick. Just like chalkboards.

Language Teaching and Technology

So let's assume we are neither villagers in the mob bent on killing the monster nor Phileas Phogg willing to try any newfangled gizmo that comes along. We are Luke Skywalkers: We are willing and able to use whatever low-tech or high-tech tools are at our disposal to accomplish our mission. May the Force be with you!

Our mission is proficiency: every student able to communicate meaningful content in realistic contexts. How can we create realistic contexts in our classrooms? Role-plays are great and pair work is wonderful, but at some point, students know that this is playacting. The content of what they are talking about, the cultural context in which they are operating, is contrived. They are not communicating with a community of real people, but a contrived community of personas. The best—the most appropriate—use of technology in the second language classroom is to provide authentic, contextualized interactive tasks with members of a target language speech community. Let's break that down.

AUTHENTIC

The definition of an authentic text is one that is written by native speakers for native speakers. Authentic oral communication can either be speech between native speakers or speech to or from a non-native speaker *for a real-life purpose*. Think about what a student hears from you on a typical day. First, how much of that speech is in English? Clearly not authentic. How much is for pedagogic purpose? Also out the door. Now how much of the target language does the student hear that is for a real-life purpose? Perhaps greetings, some housekeeping matters, an occasional exchange in the hall? How can we expect students to succeed in authentic contexts when they never experience one? Technology can help.

CONTEXTUALIZED

Authentic language always appears in context. Pedagogic language rarely does. We read the paper for information. We read labels to make sure foods don't have anything we are allergic to. We know what we are looking for and context gives us most of the information. You never see stock quotes or poems on the side of a macaroni and cheese box. Context helps us focus on our specific task. Off-task students are a pretty common sight in most of our classrooms. Maybe it is because we just gave them a reading passage called "Jose's Diary," in which he tells us how he gets ready for school in the morning. This may be useful for contrasting the preterit and imperfect, but serves no real-life purpose and has no context. Textbooks are, strictly speaking, a context, but not one that will do you much good in the real world. This is what people mean when they say, "I studied two years of French, but when I went to Paris I couldn't say a thing." Of course not. They had never been in that context, or anything like that context, before. Technology can help.

INTERACTIVE   How often do students get a chance to interact with authentic, contextualized texts—spoken or written—in our classrooms? Not often enough. The major focus of second language acquisition studies over the past 10 years or so has been on the effect of interaction. In study after study, students have been shown to learn better when they are interacting with others. Play a tape of a native speaker describing how to put together a puzzle and about 40% of the new vocabulary contained in the instructions is retained. Have a real person there to describe the same thing and more than 60% is retained. Why? Two reasons:

1. As human beings, our memories are wired to remember more emotionally intense events. Monkey watches the rain fall and forgets it. Monkey gets chased by a lion and never forgets it. Dealing with real human beings is full of emotions that become associated with words, helping us to remember them.

2. Two-way communication allows for back channels (responses such as "Huh?" and "What's that?") and other devices to increase the comprehensibility of a passage. How much interaction happens in the typical language classroom? Not enough. Technology can help.

TASKS   A task is an activity with a concrete, nonlinguistic, realistic goal that requires language to reach that goal. Notice that the goal is not linguistic, but that it requires language to accomplish that goal. In other words, it is authentic. In real life, how often do we say, "I think I need to brush up on my conjugations: 'go, went, gone'; 'come, came, come'; 'amo, amas, amat'?" We have plenty of authentic tasks in our lives that require language, however. You want your kids to do their homework (use imperatives!); you want your principal to give you a bigger classroom next year (use modals and interrogatives!); you want to tell a joke (use narrative past!).

The beauty of tasks is that just as we focus on a goal and let the language take care of itself, students engaged in tasks are focused on the content of what they are doing, not the forms they must use. Consequently, tasks are extremely valuable as a means for building fluency and for making language automatic. A few years ago, my colleagues and I (the Center for Applied Second Language Studies [CASLS] and Language Learning Solutions [LLS]) started doing oral assessment in Oregon. Initially, teachers complained bitterly when students who "knew" the topics of weather or family or food did not pass the oral performance assessment. We showed these teachers the tapes of their students being asked, "So what did you eat for breakfast?" and sitting there tongue-tied. The most common reaction was, "But we covered food in chapter 3!" Yes, it was covered. Yes, the student "had" food words. But it was not automatic, it was not acquired, it was just memorized. Tasks allow us to take language knowledge and develop it into language proficiency. So why in the world would we do anything else when we use technology to teach language?

So, to review, our technology checklist looks something like this:

- Is it authentic?
- Is it contextualized?
- Is it interactive?
- Is it task-oriented?

Conclusion

The proficiency movement began in the 1980s with the publication of the ACTFL Proficiency Guidelines. Its vision was revolutionary: the purpose of language teaching is to prepare students to communicate meaningful content in realistic situations. While "proficiency" is the buzzword that everybody uses, in most classrooms the majority of time is still spent developing formal knowledge through explanations, drills, or worksheets. The same is true of standards: everybody thinks they are great, but standards-based classrooms are few and far between. Why is there such a gap between what we say and what we do?

Although most teachers want to focus on proficiency standards, most lack the time and expertise to develop materials, lesson plans, and assessments, and therefore they continue to follow a textbook. It isn't entirely fair to blame teachers. With growing class sizes, few teachers have the time to create special lessons, materials, and tests.

Technology can help us become efficient enough to individualize instruction, to plan for proficiency, to measure students' progress toward the goal of communicating effectively in realistic situations. This is not a pipe dream: The tools are available today. Many of them are described in this volume. Unlike Phileas Phogg, we know that the balloon works and where it will land. Anybody who can order a book online can use these tools to improve their teaching. There is nothing to be afraid of here. We have not created a monster. Technology in our classrooms is no more likely to take over our lives than vacuum cleaners are. If we remain focused on the goal of proficiency, using these tools to improve student performance, we will surely prevail in our struggle. May the Force be with you!

chapter 2

KYLE ENNIS

The NETS•S and the Five Cs

Integrating Technology and Foreign Language Standards

As accountability in K–12 education has increased over the past several years, state and national standards have been introduced in all content areas to outline high expectations for students and teachers. While most educators view this as a good development, many also feel a bit overwhelmed by all they must know and do to help their students meet these standards. To bring some clarity to this complicated state of affairs, this chapter offers a quick summary of both the foreign language content area standards adopted by the American Council on the Teaching of Foreign Languages (ACTFL; 1991) and ISTE's National Educational Technology Standards for Students (NETS•S; 1998), and suggests ways that foreign language teachers can effectively address both sets of standards in the classroom.

Because the foreign language field is not generally considered to be a core content area, it has not received as much public or political attention as math, science, or language arts. Nevertheless, foreign language standards have been in use for several years—well ahead of standards in these core content areas. In 1993, the ACTFL coordinated a national effort to develop and publish foreign language standards. The five categories of standards that were developed—Communication, Cultures, Connections, Comparisons, and Communities, now known fondly as the "Five Cs"—outline critical areas of student focus in foreign language learning (Figure 2.1).

Figure 2.1 The Five Cs of the Standards for Foreign Language Learning.

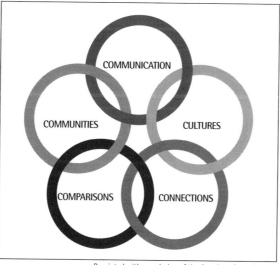

Reprinted with permission of the American Council on the Teaching of Foreign Languages.

K–12 Performance Guidelines were also developed to describe the specific levels of proficiency through which students should progress as they acquire a foreign language. Individual states have subsequently elaborated on these national standards to develop detailed state-level guidelines that clearly articulate expected learner outcomes connected to the Five Cs and the K–12 Performance Guidelines.

When reviewing the Standards for Foreign Language Learning, as we will in just a moment, some may ask: why five Cs, and not six? Why have "Computers" not been added to this model? Shouldn't technology be included in these standards for foreign language learning? These are good questions, and speak to the need for this book on technology integration in the foreign language classroom.

This chapter will outline an integration process that you can easily utilize in your classroom. However, to better understand the attitudes that may surround this issue, it is important that we first tackle the notion that foreign language teachers should concern themselves only with teaching their specialized content—that someone else will need to instruct students on the use of technology or computers. Nothing could be further from the truth. If our goal is to help students gain ever-higher levels of language proficiency, we need to familiarize ourselves and become comfortable using every teaching tool and resource available that can make that happen for our students. And today, that means learning how to integrate technology in our teaching practices.

The ISTE NETS•S identify what students should know and be able to do with technology to accomplish tasks and enhance their learning across the curriculum. The underlying assumption of this book is that foreign language teachers should become familiar with these standards and actively seek to integrate technology in meaningful ways to assist student learning. This does not mean that we think foreign language content should ever take a back seat or be considered less important than the technology that *delivers* that content. Instead, we simply want to help teachers weave technology more seamlessly and effectively into their curriculum, so that they can support student achievement of both the foreign language and the technology standards.

This chapter will introduce the Standards for Foreign Language Learning and discuss ways that technology can enhance these broad areas of study and focus. We will also look at the NETS•S through the lens of the foreign language classroom and explore areas of possible connection. The final section of this chapter presents a convenient series of charts that links these two sets of standards and outlines activities and ideas that can support and improve the teaching and learning of foreign languages. It is important to emphasize at the outset, however, that technology standards should not be considered "extra baggage" that will slow and hinder progress in achieving the Five Cs. Instead, when integrated effectively, technology can make our classrooms more instructive and meaningful places that will foster higher levels of student involvement and language proficiency.

Standards for Foreign Language Learning

In introducing the Standards for Foreign Language Learning, we will look briefly at the language created by the ACTFL and the coalition groups responsible for creating the standards. These standards outline critical focal points for which students should develop skills as they acquire languages. Work on the standards began in 1993 through a grant dedicated for this purpose, with representative groups from each of the national language associations, the American Association of Teachers of French, the American Association of Teachers of German, the American Association of Teachers of Spanish and Portuguese, and the National Council of Secondary Teachers of Japanese (since renamed the National Council of Japanese Language Teachers). Representatives from each of these organizations worked to draft the global areas of the standards and define the scope of each broad goal. They also worked closely with other educational organizations as well as business and community leaders to ensure broad acceptance of the standards.

Once these standards were drafted and approved, other task forces were charged with the mission of creating content requirements and key learning scenarios that more fully detailed the standards in action. Now known as the Five Cs, these standard categories outline key instruction that all students in foreign language education should encounter as part of their learning. The Five Cs are Communication, Cultures, Connections, Comparisons, and Communities.

Communication is at the heart of the standards, underscoring the notion that communication with others is the central goal in learning a foreign language.

Cultures stresses that through study of other languages, students gain a knowledge and understanding of the cultures that use the language. Students can't really master the language until they have mastered the cultural contexts in which the language occurs.

Connections is the idea that learning another language will give students an opportunity to connect with other content areas through the lens of the language they are studying, allowing them to learn new concepts in new ways.

Comparisons focuses upon the idea that learning a foreign language will allow students an opportunity to compare and contrast their immediate world to that of the language they are learning, giving them broadened appreciation for their own language and culture, while also helping them to acquire appreciation and acceptance of other languages and cultures.

Communities focuses on the need to reach outside the classroom to interact with others in meaningful ways, using the language being learned. This challenging standard calls for students and teachers to think creatively about how the language can be used to accomplish real-world tasks and how they can endeavor to use the language in their communities. Focusing on this goal helps teachers motivate students to use the language they are learning, to see applications of the concepts in real-world situations, and to understand that language learning is a lifelong process.

The Five Cs frame the instruction that students should encounter as they progress through language programs. Although the standards do not detail the specifics of what students should be able to do or describe how well they should be able to accomplish those tasks, they serve as guiding principles for language educators and administrators in terms of the broad topics that should be addressed. Each standard can be further defined with progress indicators for grades 4, 8, and 12 (the ACTFL provides sample progress indicators at its Web site, www.actfl.org). Again, although technology is not specifically included in these standards, it is easy to see areas where technology could be used to support their achievement.

STANDARDS FOR FOREIGN LANGUAGE LEARNING

COMMUNICATION

Communicate in Languages Other Than English

Standard 1.1: Students engage in conversations, provide and obtain information, express feelings and emotions, and exchange opinions.

Standard 1.2: Students understand and interpret written and spoken language on a variety of topics.

Standard 1.3: Students present information, concepts, and ideas to an audience of listeners or readers on a variety of topics.

CULTURES

Gain Knowledge and Understanding of Other Cultures

Standard 2.1: Students demonstrate an understanding of the relationship between the practices and perspectives of the culture studied.

Standard 2.2: Students demonstrate an understanding of the relationship between the products and perspectives of the culture studied.

CONNECTIONS

Connect with Other Disciplines and Acquire Information

Standard 3.1: Students reinforce and further their knowledge of other disciplines through the foreign language.

Standard 3.2: Students acquire information and recognize the distinctive viewpoints that are only available through the foreign language and its cultures.

COMPARISONS

Develop Insight into the Nature of Language and Culture

Standard 4.1: Students demonstrate understanding of the nature of language through comparisons of the language studied and their own.

Standard 4.2: Students demonstrate understanding of the concept of culture through comparisons of the cultures studied and their own.

COMMUNITIES

Participate in Multilingual Communities at Home and Around the World

Standard 5.1: Students use the language both within and beyond the school setting.

Standard 5.2: Students show evidence of becoming lifelong learners by using the language for personal enjoyment and enrichment.

To learn more about the Five Cs and the Standards for Foreign Language Learning, visit the ACTFL Web site at www.actfl.org. Reprinted with permission from the National Standards in Foreign Language Education Project.

Performance Guidelines

Beyond these general content standards, the ACTFL has defined proficiency levels for how well students should be able to communicate in the language they are learning, from Novice through Pre-Advanced levels. These levels are described in the K–12 Performance Guidelines and further incorporated into state- and district-level documents.

Technology integration, however, is not fully addressed in these standards. We need to look to the NETS•S to help determine what students should be able to do with technology as they study the language and to define how we as teachers can use technology both to enhance learning and to help students acquire skills that will support them as lifelong learners of the language.

To better understand these technology standards, we will examine the NETS•S and their parameters for student learning. As you review these technology standards, consider ways that each could be addressed as part of your current classroom activities. Reflect also upon your current use of technology and seek ways to enhance instruction through the inclusion of these standards within your instruction.

National Educational Technology Standards

The National Educational Technology Standards for Students describe what students should be able to do with technology within six skill categories. The categories are broad enough to be easily applied across all content areas, yet detailed enough to communicate clear expectations of technology use and integration. Teachers should use the standards as they plan for activities, looking for natural areas of integration that support the standards while at the same time applying technology in a manner that better facilitates teaching and learning. The full text for the standards appears in the Introduction, and can be viewed online at www.iste.org.

Similar to the Five Cs, these standards suggest general areas of student focus. On close investigation of these standards, one learns quickly that they have been written to support learning and education in a very broad sense. No single class or course could incorporate all of these standards. It must be a coordinated collaborative effort across the curriculum if these standards are to be achieved.

As foreign language teachers, we have a shared responsibility to address these standards and seek opportunities to include elements of technology in our lessons that expose our students to the power and purpose of technology in language learning and support our instructional goals. The key to this integration is a clear understanding of the technologies that are available to assist in achieving these standards.

Bringing the Next "C" into Focus

In this section, we will look at how the foreign language standards and NETS•S can be combined to support both the learning of a language and the acquisition of technology skills. We will approach this from the perspective of a foreign language teacher and will include integration strategies that showcase how technology could be used to support both the foreign language standards as well as the NETS•S. The list of ideas is not exhaustive. More than anything else, these ideas should act as a catalyst to expand attitudes about how technology could be used to support teaching and learning in the foreign language classroom.

Communication

TABLE 2.1

STANDARDS FOR FOREIGN LANGUAGE LEARNING	TECHNOLOGY-BASED ACTIVITIES AND NETS•S
Communicate in Languages Other Than English STANDARD 1.1: Students engage in conversations, provide and obtain information, express feelings and emotions, and exchange opinions. STANDARD 1.2: Students understand and interpret written and spoken language on a variety of topics. STANDARD 1.3: Students present information, concepts, and ideas to an audience of listeners or readers on a variety of topics.	• Teachers can incorporate online resources that allow students to record their voice on a computer and immediately listen to their recording. Teachers can use this technology to collect speaking samples without the need for tapes and recorders or dedicated language labs. NETS•S 2, 3, 4 • Teachers can utilize online resources to evaluate student reading, writing, listening, and speaking skills to track progress and identify proficiency levels. The use of technology in this area will allow teachers to collect large amounts of student achievement and proficiency data in an efficient, effective, and powerful way. NETS•S 2, 3, 4 • Teachers can institute e-mail pals/instant messaging relationships with other classes. Students can exchange e-mails and messages with students from around the world in the target language. This activity is a new play on the pen-pals concept with immediate results, rather than lengthy waiting periods between exchanges. This is a great way to teach keyboarding skills in the target language, i.e., the proper use of accented characters and character sets for languages such as Japanese, Chinese, Korean, and Arabic. NETS•S 2, 3, 4 • Students can complete WebQuests that expose them to Web pages from the target language/culture. They will experience realia in the form of Web pages, with guided direction from the teacher or WebQuest creator. NETS•S 2, 3, 4, 5 • Students can research topics connected with learning a foreign language and present them to a class of peers using electronic presentation forms, Web pages, or print publications, including photo, video, and audio elements that better showcase the research topic and enhance the presentation. NETS•S 1, 2, 3, 4, 5 • Teachers can employ the use of video recording equipment and computer editing software to collect speech and presentation samples from students and showcase these to other classes or archive them in electronic portfolio collections that catalog student proficiencies. NETS•S 2, 3, 4, 5

Cultures

TABLE 2.2

STANDARDS FOR FOREIGN LANGUAGE LEARNING	TECHNOLOGY-BASED ACTIVITIES AND NETS•S
Gain Knowledge and Understanding of Other Cultures STANDARD 2.1: Students demonstrate an understanding of the relationship between the practices and perspectives of the culture studied. STANDARD 2.2: Students demonstrate an understanding of the relationship between the products and perspectives of the culture studied.	• Teachers can assign students to research elements of the target culture and then build electronic presentations or Web sites that share what they learned with the class. NETS•S 2, 3, 4, 5 • Students can create online or print surveys that can be delivered to both same-language and target-language individuals and then tabulate results and share findings with their class. This builds a greater understanding of the key cultural components of the target culture. NETS•S 3, 4, 5, 6 • Teachers can construct a Web activity in which students engage in a structured search of the Web for sites that showcase cultural icons or products of the target language/culture. Students can then share their findings in electronic presentations to the class. NETS•S 2, 3, 4, 5

Connections

TABLE 2.3

STANDARDS FOR FOREIGN LANGUAGE LEARNING	TECHNOLOGY-BASED ACTIVITIES AND NETS•S
Connect with Other Disciplines and Acquire Information STANDARD 3.1: Students reinforce and further their knowledge of other disciplines through the foreign language. STANDARD 3.2: Students acquire information and recognize the distinctive viewpoints that are only available through the foreign language and its cultures.	*Note:* This particular standard is a great challenge in any instructional setting. It requires a high degree of language proficiency for both students and teachers, as well as outside experience and access to other content area support. Though challenging, it should not be neglected. Technology will assist in this area in many ways, allowing access to critical content information needed to make these connections possible for the students. • Students can utilize online resources to access content for other disciplines in the target language/culture. This can be done by locating educational support sites for these content areas, developed for speakers of the target language. NETS•S 2, 3, 4, 5, 6 • Teachers can direct student projects in which students research a content area of their choice by utilizing a variety of electronic resources and then present their projects in the form of mini-lessons to the entire class. NETS•S 2, 3, 4, 5

Comparisons

TABLE 2.4

STANDARDS FOR FOREIGN LANGUAGE LEARNING	TECHNOLOGY-BASED ACTIVITIES AND NETS•S
Develop Insight into the Nature of Language and Culture STANDARD 4.1: Students demonstrate understanding of the nature of language through comparisons of the language studied and their own. STANDARD 4.2: Students demonstrate understanding of the concept of culture through comparisons of the cultures studied and their own.	• Through the use of video and audio resources, teachers can showcase sociolinguistic elements of the target language/culture. Students can also access a variety of online resources that utilize video and audio elements as components of their delivery system. Many news and information sites on the Internet now include short video elements that can be viewed on a regular basis. This allows an almost endless resource of real-world language, which can be used in a variety of ways. NETS•S 3, 4, 5 • Teachers can direct student projects in which students research a specific social or cultural issue. Students can create survey or interview sessions that will allow them to gather information from individuals and then transfer the information to spreadsheets. This will allow comparisons and contrasts of the viewpoints of those surveyed or interviewed. NETS•S 3, 4, 5

Communities

TABLE 2.5

STANDARDS FOR FOREIGN LANGUAGE LEARNING	TECHNOLOGY-BASED ACTIVITIES AND NETS•S
Participate in Multilingual Communities at Home and Around the World STANDARD 5.1: Students use the language both within and beyond the school setting. STANDARD 5.2: Students show evidence of becoming lifelong learners by using the language for personal enjoyment and enrichment.	• Videoconferencing allows teachers to connect with classrooms around the world and with individuals outside the traditional school classroom. Apple Computer's iSight and CUseeMe technologies have made it easy to communicate in ways only imagined just a few short years ago. NETS•S 2, 3, 4, 5 • Students now have access to both online and CD resources that allow them to continue their studies and learning outside the classroom. Many high-quality language learning resources are available to assist students in the continuation of studying and learning beyond the classroom. These tools, more dynamic than traditional print-based text systems, include video segments, audio files, and detailed images to assist in the learning process and let the students move at their own pace. Technology has made lifelong learning much easier to accomplish, because of the ease of access that we now enjoy. NETS•S 2, 3, 4, 5

Conclusion

While standards are powerful tools to direct student learning, the attitudes that we hold in regard to the standards are ultimately most critical. If we, as educators, see the value in the standards and integrate them into our individual education plans, we will incorporate them in a way that makes sense for us. The challenge is that standards are almost always externally created or dictated and easy integration is not the norm. Standards often mean change, and any amount of change takes time, effort, and dedication. As we look at the integration of technology standards, the process is further complicated by the level of comfort we ourselves have with using technology. Research has clearly shown that the best way to teach technology skills is through applying appropriate technology sources to accomplish tasks and solve problems. If we are not modeling the use of technology or if we do not include the use of technology in our lessons and activities, our students learn very quickly the lack of value we see in technology.

No other content area has shown a need for technology more than foreign languages. A variety of skills must be acquired in the foreign language classroom, each requiring continual practice with reading, writing, speaking, and listening, and there is no easy way to accomplish this daunting learning task without the use of technology. At the heart of the technology standards is the ideal that technology education is not about "learning how to use computers," but rather, how we can use technology in educational settings in a way that supports teachers in meeting their goals and assists students in accomplishing meaningful tasks. The challenge for true integration of technology continues to be how we view our classrooms. If we view our language classrooms as sealed containers where the teacher and textbook are all that are needed to teach, instruct, and lead the students, technology will be considered a hindrance to the goal of language acquisition and will be ignored. If, however, we view our classrooms as portals to the world and the languages that we teach, we will see technology as the only means possible to break out of the physical constraints of the classroom and the text, a way to encourage our students to communicate with others, connect with other disciplines, compare and contrast other cultures with their own, and reach into their communities in meaningful ways.

REFERENCES

American Council on the Teaching of Foreign Languages (ACTLF). (1999). *Standards for foreign language learning in the 21st century.* Yonkers, NY: Author.

International Society for Technology in Education (ISTE). (1998). *National educational technology standards for students.* Eugene, OR: Author. Also available online at http://cnets.iste.org/students/s_stands.html

chapter 3

RITA OLEKSAK AND KATHLEEN M. RIORDAN

Measuring What Matters

Performance Assessment and Technology

At this writing, we are in the midst of the Year of Languages, a campaign to promote the idea that people who can communicate in at least two languages are a great asset to the communities in which they live and work (Pufahl, Rhodes, & Christian, 2004/2005). The Department of Defense recently convened a national language conference to discuss how to make the U.S. a language-competent nation. Since the publication of Standards for Foreign Language Learning, classroom teachers have expanded the scope of language teaching to include culture, connections to other disciplines, comparisons among languages and cultures, and participation in multi-lingual communities.

All of these are indicative of a sea of change in the foreign language field. Language study used to be a credential of the properly educated, earned through disciplined memorization of vocabulary and grammar rules. Now, language learning develops the ability to truly communicate not just through linguistic mastery, but through a deeper understanding of how, when, and why to say what to whom (ACTLF, 1999). The success of this enterprise has profound implications for society, the economy, and the national defense. With the purpose of language education changing so signifi-cantly, it follows that the way we assess students must also change. Measuring student ability to conjugate verbs or memorize lists of words is no longer sufficient if we are to educate a generation of students to participate in the global economy and society.

In this chapter, we will discuss the use of technology to improve both our instruction and our assessment, and, as a result, to give our students the opportunity to become proficient in at least one language in addition to their first so that they become full citizens of the United States and of the world society. Using a positive and reflective approach, we will consider the importance of performance assessment, the use of technology to help educators organize and contextualize good performance assess-ments, and the relationship between performance assessment and online tests.

The Base of Assessment

The *ACTFL Proficiency Guidelines* (ACTFL, 1986) have influenced our profession for 20 years, first, in the area of assessment, and second, in the area of curriculum development. These guidelines describe language proficiency regardless of where and how it is acquired.

In 1993, foreign language education became the seventh subject area to receive federal funding to develop national K–12 standards. The task force faced the huge task of defining content standards—what students should know and be able to do. Three major organizing principles were used in developing the standards for foreign language learning.

The first includes the broad goals of language instruction, also known as the Five Cs—Communication, Cultures, Connections, Comparisons, and Communities (see chapter 2 for more on the Five Cs).

The second involves the curricular elements necessary for the attainment of the standards, which include a language system, cultural knowledge, communication strategies, critical thinking skills, learning strategies, other subject areas, and technology.

The third encompasses the framework of the communicative approach to language teaching, which places primary emphasis on the context and purpose of communication (Brecht & Walton, 1994). The three communicative modes are Interpersonal, Interpretive, and Presentational.

The *ACTFL Performance Guidelines for K–12 Learners* (ACTFL, 1998) expand on the above-mentioned guidelines by focusing on language use by students who participate in all levels of foreign language learning. Just as the Standards for Foreign Language Learning are content standards that define the "what" of foreign language learning, the performance guidelines are standards that define "how well."

The guidelines place a student's performance on a proficiency continuum.

Performance Assessment Fundamentals

Four basic principles should guide teachers in developing quality assessments:

1. Test what is taught.
2. Test the material in the way it was taught.
3. Focus on what students can do.
4. Capture creative language by learners.

Following these tenets, performance-based assessment is authentic and realistic and it incorporates real-world tasks. Performance assessment calls for the student to construct a response within a context (Lewin & Shoemaker, 1998). Performance assessments have two parts: a clearly defined task—called a product descriptor—and a list of explicit criteria for assessing students' performance or product—called a rubric (Blaz, 2001, p. 17). A performance-based format requires learners to demonstrate their level of competence and knowledge by creating a product as a response (Koda, 1998), hence the presentational piece.

A key aspect of performance assessment is that it not only measures student performance, but also helps develop it. Grant Wiggins (1998) proposes that the performance assessment be educative in two ways.

1. It should be designed to teach by improving the performance of both teacher and learner.

ACTFL Performance Guidelines
for K–12 Learners for Foreign Language Learning

NOVICE LOW
- Uses isolated words and a few high-frequency phrases to talk about very specific subjects, such as numbers, colors, and the names of common objects.

NOVICE MID
- Uses isolated words, memorized phrases, and occasional formulaic or stock phrases to talk about certain specific learned topics, such as weather, food, and names of family members.
- May contain long hesitations, silences, and/or repetitions and/or reversion to L1.
- May have poor pronunciation.

NOVICE HIGH
- Shows emerging ability to create with language by expanding on learned material.
- Relies on personalized recombinations of words, phrases, and stock phrases.
- Shows sporadic and inconsistent creation of sentences.
- Uses simple vocabulary to talk about personal and limited topics.
- May have long hesitations and/or repetitions and/or reversion to L1.
- May appear surprisingly fluent and accurate due to reliance on memorized utterances.

INTERMEDIATE LOW
- Shows ability to create with the language using basic novel sentences marked by frequent errors of word choice and verb formation.
- Uses limited, simple, basic vocabulary to talk about topics related to self, family, friends, and everyday life.
- Produces little variety of information.
- Shows emerging control of the present tense and near future.
- Response may be halting with frequent groping for words and occasional reversion to L1.
- May have poor pronunciation.

INTERMEDIATE MID
- Shows ability to create with the language using a variety of disconnected, discrete sentences with some errors in word choice and verb formation.
- May use few cohesive devices.
- Shows control of present tense and near future.
- Shows control of basic vocabulary and the ability to talk about topics related to self, family, home, school, daily activities, leisure activities, personal preferences, and interests.
- Produces some variety of information.
- Shows good fluency but speech still may contain frequent pauses, repetitions, and frequent groping for words.
- May show inaccurate pronunciation of words and a strong non-native accent.

INTERMEDIATE HIGH
- Shows evidence of connected discourse and emergence of organizational features.
- Produces longer sentences showing partial control of cohesive and subordinate devices.
- Shows control of present tense but uses the past tenses and the future inconsistently.
- Talks with ease about personal activities and immediate surroundings.
- Has only occasional pauses and groping for words.
- Is usually understood by native speakers unaccustomed to dealing with non-native speakers.

Reprinted with permission of the American Council on the Teaching of Foreign Languages.

2. It should evoke exemplary pedagogy. Educative assessment improves performance, not just audits it.

Curtain and Pesola (1994) in *Languages and Children: Making the Match* advocate that teachers assess their students' ability to put their language knowledge to use in authentic perfomance rather than simply testing that knowledge in a drill or multiple choice quiz. Thus we see that assessment can improve performance if students have access to:

1. the criteria and standards for the tasks they need to master;

2. feedback in the attempts to master these tasks; and

3. opportunities to use the feedback to revise the work and resubmit.

INTEGRATED PERFORMANCE ASSESSMENTS FROM ACTFL

The ACTFL Performance Assessment Units, now formally called Integrated Performance Assessments (IPAs), were designed to address a national need for measuring student progress toward the attainment of the goal areas and competencies described in the national standards and the ACTFL Performance Guidelines for K–12 Learners (ACTFL, 2003).

An IPA is a theme-based assessment in which the tasks revolve around an authentic story. The IPA features three tasks, each of which reflects one of the three modes of communication—Interpretive, Interpersonal, and Presentational. Each task provides the content and skills necessary for the next task, so that the tasks are interrelated and build on one another.

STUDENT FEEDBACK

If assessment is to improve performance, not just audit it, then assessment tasks need to be accompanied by quality feedback to students. Quality feedback needs to provide the student with information regarding his or her performance as compared to exemplars of model performance.

Students who participated in a pilot IPA program in Springfield, Massachusetts, commented that the assessment helped them to identify strengths in using the target language. They talked about increased fluency and the importance of having a broad vocabulary. Additionally, students acknowledged that access to Internet resources and references was invaluable. Students in Fairfax, Virginia, echoed these comments, talking about improved performances because strengths were identified as well as areas of needed improvement. Students felt they stretched to achieve higher expectations for performance and took greater risks with the language.

Teachers who participated in the Springfield pilot also noted that the opportunity to progress through the communication strands using authentic materials made the assessment much more realistic. Most important, this pilot afforded teachers the opportunity to reflect on their instruction and assessment and to see it as a cyclical process that spirals language learning.

TECHNOLOGY'S ROLE

A foreign language teacher might ask: How can the use of technology help to organize and contextualize good performance assessments? Technology allows us to access current real-life print, video, and audio, establishing a realistic context for the task. It offers the opportunity to compare and contrast issues in real time employing the different modes of communication: Interpretive, Interpersonal, and Presentational. Opportunities exist for feedback in an atmosphere that is more supportive and allows for growth. Access to technology opens the doors for presentational communication to be delivered in print, audio, or video though PowerPoint presentations, WebQuests, or authentic letters to the editor.

This is not only an efficient use of technology for language use but it is also an effective use of materials for an intended purpose. Access to information, and all the possibilities surrounding that information, necessitates professional development for foreign language teachers. To improve a program, investments in professional development have to be significant. Foreign language teachers and instructional technology specialists need to come together to reflect and brainstorm the possibilities for creative language use by teachers and students. Professional development needs to focus on technology to strengthen the regular curriculum.

Today's schools offer greater opportunities to use multimedia labs for random pairings, in which students can practice circumlocution and modeling of real-life situations, as well as questioning techniques. This use of technology enables students to become more independent learners who are willing to take risks and express themselves in a learned language using a broader range of contexts.

Case Study: Springfield Public Schools

The strands of assessment and technology come together in the story of the Foreign Language Department of Springfield Public Schools in Springfield, Massachusetts. In 1993, chapter authors Kathy Riordan (Springfield foreign language director) and Rita Oleksak (Springfield foreign language mentor teacher) joined with others teachers to begin an instruction and assessment journey that continues to this date.

Our story includes elements of professional development, school district commitment, teacher commitment, and a shared belief in the importance of foreign language learning as part of the general curriculum. The Springfield district has more than 26,000 students, as well as 46 school buildings and 125 foreign language teachers—not a narrow scope for the task at hand.

As a team, we developed and implemented a districtwide curriculum assessment program of the elementary, middle, and senior high foreign language program. The district supported this effort with funds for curriculum and professional development workshops on the Standards for Foreign Language Learning; the ACTFL K–12 Proficiency Guidelines; the development and implementation of large-scale assessments of speaking, listening comprehension, and writing; the evaluation of the assessments; and the use of the assessment data for the improvement of student learning and future professional development for teachers.

At the beginning, we thought that we understood the full magnitude of the task before us. At each step, however, we saw greater future possibilities in this work and the task grew even larger.

ELEMENTARY

At the elementary school level, teachers developed, implemented, and evaluated the results of a districtwide assessment of listening comprehension for students of Chinese, French, Russian, and Spanish. The listening comprehension assessment has been in use since 1993 and has been reviewed and improved annually. For two years teachers also implemented a speaking assessment. After the first two years, however, the speaking component became too burdensome given the large numbers of students and challenging testing conditions.

In recent years, the department added a reading assessment to the program as part of the district effort to focus on reading skills as mandated by the No Child Left Behind Act of 2001 and the state's high-stakes assessment program. This program is implemented by the foreign language teachers and uses a paper-and-pencil approach. The director shares results and recommendations for improvement with teachers, principals, and senior district-level administrators in an annual report. The elementary listening and reading assessment program is in place as of press time.

MIDDLE SCHOOL

At the middle school level, the assessment program evolved over time. At this level, language teachers developed and implemented an annual assessment of writing and speaking in all languages offered. All Grade 8 foreign language students submitted a writing sample in the language being studied. A randomly chosen sample of students also presented an audiotaped speech. The use of random sampling for the speaking component was necessary because of the limited access to technology for the administration of the assessment.

The teachers participated in professional development experiences to prepare them to evaluate the student samples. The classroom teacher ratings were used at the school level as part of the student grading process. All of the student writing and speaking samples were submitted to a districtwide team of experienced teachers and evaluators for review. These teachers reviewed samples of student work and shared their ratings with the appropriate teachers for their personal review. This process allowed all foreign language teachers to benefit from the thinking of other experienced colleagues. This is a form of teacher collaboration, although not face to face.

The middle school student data were reviewed and gathered with considerable time and effort. The data provided the material for the districtwide middle school report that included student results and recommendations for the improvement of instruction, professional development, and the program in general.

HIGH SCHOOL

At the high school level, the process mirrored the assessment program at the middle school—with one significant difference. All students were assessed in both speaking and writing. Most of the Springfield high schools have multimedia language centers that made possible the administration of the speaking assessment. At this level there was much more data to manage using a paper-and-pencil process. Because no data management system was available, there were limitations in our ability to aggregate and disaggregate the data. We knew we wanted to do more with the impressive amounts of data, but we lacked the technology to make this dream happen. We had to wait until our technology capacity matched our conceptual understanding of where we wanted to go.

This old-time approach to assessment produced wonderful results, but it was highly labor intensive at both the classroom teacher level and at the administrative level. In spite of the tremendous work effort, the department as a whole believed that the assessment was essential as we worked to monitor student progress and program improvement. We also believed that the foreign language department needed to have data and hard evidence about program results just as our colleagues in other subject areas have data from standardized tests and from the high-stakes state assessment program. Understanding the importance of data-driven instruction, the Springfield foreign language teachers took on another enormous task.

TECHNOLOGY TO THE RESCUE

Springfield Public Schools embarked on a massive school-building program in the early 1990s to replace and renovate schools that were outdated given new advances in technology. All new buildings included modern technology improvements in class-rooms and multimedia labs. All new middle and high schools included at least one foreign language multimedia center with the latest in technological advances. Older schools purchased wireless mobile units to address their needs. This technology upgrade paved the way for a significant leap forward in the use of technology in both the teaching and assessment of foreign languages.

The district continued to commit to teacher professional development as the new technology became available. We now had the technology and were acquiring the skills to make technology work for both instruction and assessment. The district now needed some outside support and expertise in both assessment and technology.

The expertise arrived in 2002 with the partnership of the Springfield Public Schools with Language Learning Solutions (LLS) in Eugene, Oregon. Foreign language professionals at the University of Oregon in Eugene worked with federal funds to develop a system of online foreign language assessments called the Standards-based Measurement of Proficiency (STAMP). Beginning in 2002 and continuing to this date, the language teachers in the Springfield Public Schools and their colleagues at LLS have worked together to develop and implement assessments of reading and writing for foreign language students in Grade 8 and in level two at the high school using an Internet-based software program. Other online assessments such as the Minnesota Language Proficiency Assessment (MLPA) and Pittsburgh Public Schools'

Online World Language Testing Software (OWLTS) were being developed at the time, but given the demographics of Springfield students and our need for immediate and detailed data reporting and analysis, STAMP was the best option for us. (For other assessment options, see the sidebar and comparison chart at the end of this chapter.)

STAMP is delivered entirely online. Reading, speaking, and writing sections are available in French, Spanish, Japanese, and Chinese. Listening assessments are being developed for Japanese, Spanish, and Chinese. Students begin with a computer-adaptive interpretive section (reading or listening). Based on those interpretive scores, students are given presentational speaking or writing prompts (Figure 3.1). Student writing or speaking samples are distributed to certified graders online. Interpretive results are available immediately and presentational results within a few weeks (Figure 3.2).

Figure 3.1 A STAMP reading question, above, and a writing question, below.

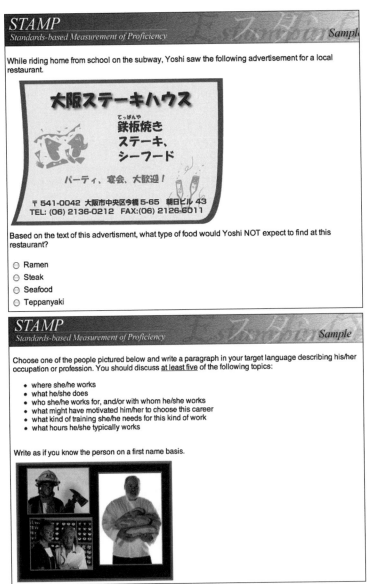

Reprinted with permission from the Center for Applied Second Language Studies/Language Learning Solutions.

Figure 3.2 An individual student report from STAMP breaks down topics for both interpretive and presentational skills.

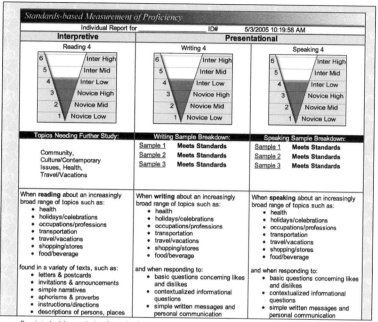

Reprinted with permission from the Center for Applied Second Language Studies/Language Learning Solutions.

The real power of STAMP is in the data reflected back to teachers and learners. Putting performance data in the hands of practitioners has the potential to change the way we think about teaching, professional development, and student performance. The advantage of the online assessment is the ability to aggregate and disaggregate the results in multiple ways to allow teachers, students, and administrators to draw conclusions about how individuals and classes of students perform on various item types (Falsgraf, 2005, p. 6). The breakdown on topics allows the teacher to adjust curriculum and improve instruction based on the data. The use of Classpak and Quizpak, language-specific instructional materials designed around the STAMP assessment, offers students multiple opportunities throughout the year to work on practice activities that are authentic and current (Falsgraf, 2005).

The STAMP assessments are administered in the multimedia centers or using the wireless mobile units. The reading and writing components of the assessment program use culturally appropriate sources for the materials. Students are interested in the content of the assessment because the materials are current. The students focus very intently on the assessment process. They are comfortable with the technology and the format of the assessment because they have used instructional materials similar to the assessment format. This classroom instruction component of the program reduces student anxiety.

This assessment program is computer adaptive to enable students to progress to their highest level of proficiency. The students begin with the reading component and with reading items until reaching their highest performance levels. Using the reading assessment results, the proficiency level for the writing assessment is set for each student. As a result, each student takes a personal and appropriate assessment in both reading and writing.

The LLS program allows the department to analyze the student result data in multiple ways: by class, by level, and by topic assessed. By merging the LLS data with the district student database, the department can look at student progress from grade to grade and school to school. The department can also view results using variables such as the grade level at which the student began language study, the student's first language, the student's ethnicity, and socioeconomic factors. This provides detailed information to identify targeted populations for which additional support is needed. This partnership has not only helped the department learn about the power of data but has also shed light on a previously untapped group of foreign language advocates—the targeted populations. In addition, the assessment data have become an essential component of the districtwide professional development program.

As is true in most districts, the assessment story in Springfield is a work in progress. The story began with a belief system that a strong assessment program is essential to the improvement of student learning. The story continues with the use of technology in foreign language instruction and in the administration and evaluation of assessments. But, most important, the partnership with LLS offers the foreign language teachers an effective method to analyze data to improve student learning in a way only imagined in 1993.

The foreign language teachers in Springfield are continuing on this challenging journey to use technology to improve foreign language instruction through performance-based assessments. These assessments are administered and evaluated using the power of technology and they provide the data needed to begin the dialogue to improve instruction. However, foreign language teachers should be mindful of the caution given by Jean W. LeLoup and Robert Ponteiro as stated in the *Center for Applied Linguistics Digest* (LeLoup, 2003).

> More important than the use of technology per se is the quality of what is done with this medium. A badly conceived interactive task or activity is poor whether it is done on a computer or face to face. Using technology is not enough. In order to promote successful learning, tasks must be meaningful, have a true interactional component, and have a comprehensible purpose for the language student (Chapelle, 1997; Liu et al., 2002; Warschauer & Healey, 1998). Future CALL research endeavors should begin with this premise.

One can only imagine future chapters in the Springfield story as foreign language teachers in Springfield and their partners at LLS in Oregon continue to collaborate with other colleagues around the country to realize the dream of data-driven foreign language instruction.

Conclusion

In this chapter we have discussed the use of technology to improve both instruction and assessment, and, as a result, to give students the opportunity to become proficient in at least one language in addition to their first so that they become full citizens of the United States and of the world society. We also shared the Springfield story, and considered the importance of performance assessment, the use of technology to help educators organize and contextualize good performance assessments, and the relationship between performance assessment and online tests.

Computerized Foreign Language Performance Assessment Options

While this chapter discusses the Standards-based Measurement of Proficiency (STAMP) in detail, other assessment options are available. Descriptions of some of these appear below along with Web addresses for more information. A comparison chart is on the next page.

COPI   Developed by the Center for Applied Linguistics, the COPI (for Computerized Oral Proficiency Instrument) is an oral performance assessment administered on a desktop computer. Examinees are presented a variety of picture-based, topic-based, and situation-based tasks requiring them to perform both basic and more advanced language functions, including asking questions, giving directions, narrating a sequence of events, apologizing, describing a process, and supporting an opinion. Examinees are scored as Intermediate, Advanced, or Superior, based on the ACTFL Proficiency Guidelines. Currently available in Arabic and Spanish, this computer-based assessment is being developed to replace the tape-based Simulated Oral Proficiency Interview (SOPI) that the center has administered since 1985. *www.cal.org/projects/copi/*

DIALANG   DIALANG is a European project for the development of diagnostic language tests in 14 European languages. Supported by the European Commission, these tests are computer-based and delivered on the Internet free of charge. Separate tests are available in reading, writing, listening, grammar, and vocabulary, covering all proficiency levels from beginning to advanced. Self-assessment is a key component of each test, and examinees' performance is scored based on the proficiency scales established in the Council of Europe's "Common European Framework of Reference." Instant, skill-specific feedback is provided to examinees, as well as advice on how to improve proficiency. *www.dialang.org/english/index.htm*

MLPA   Developed by the Center for Advanced Research on Language Acquisition at the University of Minnesota, the Minnesota Language Proficiency Assessments, or MLPA, are performance-based second language assessment tools for reading, writing, listening, and speaking. Currently offered in French, German, and Spanish, the MLPA are designed to measure second language proficiency levels from Intermediate Low to Intermediate High on the ACTFL Proficiency Guidelines scale. The assessments are offered in both computer-based and paper-and-pencil formats, and are equally suitable to large-group administrations or individualized testing. *www.carla.umn.edu/assessment/MLPA.html*

OWLTS   Originally developed by the Pittsburgh Public Schools District, OWLTS (for Online World Language Testing Software) is a Web-based application for authoring and administering oral proficiency examinations online. The OWLTS software allows language teachers to create their own performance-based assessments using images, audio, and video. Teachers can search for questions and tasks based on the ACTFL Proficiency Guidelines, and evaluate student performance using rubrics derived either from the ACTFL standards or from particular state or district foreign language standards. *www.owlts.com/owlts/*

WebCAPE — Developed by Brigham Young University as a placement exam for incoming college students, WebCAPE (Web-based Computer Adaptive Placement Exam) is an Internet-based foreign language reading assessment for French, German, Russian, and Spanish. It uses adaptive technology to adjust exam difficulty to the student's proficiency level, asking a more difficult question every time the student answers the previous item correctly, and an easier question when the student misses the previous item. In this way, an accurate assessment of the examinee's proficiency can be gauged and immediate feedback offered. *http://webcape.byuhtrsc.org/about-webcape.html*

Comparison Chart of Common Language Assessments

	AP	CLEP	DIALANG	IB Exam	MLPA	MultiCAT	OPI	OWLTS	SAT II	STAMP	WebCAPE
Available Nationally	■	■	■	■	■		■	■	■	■	■
Web-based			■							■	■
Computer Adaptive					■	■				■	■
Statistically Validated		■	■		■		■	■		■	■
Standards-based			■		■		■	■		■	
Proficiency-based, Culturally Authentic			■	■	■	■	■	■		■	
Reading Assessment	■	■	■	■	■	■			■		■
Writing Assessment	■		■	■	■					■	
Speaking Assessment	■			■	■		■	■		■	
Listening Assessment	■	■	■	■	■	■			■	■	
Externally Graded with Verified Inter-rater Reliability	■	■		■	■	■	■			■	
Staff Development Component	■			■	■					■	
Application(s)	CR, EP	CR, EP	EP, SA	CR, EP	EP, EX	EP	EP, EX	PE	EP	EP, EX, PE	EP

ASSESSMENTS KEY

AP: Advanced Placement Examination
CLEP: College Level Examination Program
IB Exam: International Baccalaureate Examination
MLPA: Minnesota Language Proficiency Assessments
MultiCAT: Multimedia Computer Adaptive Test
OPI: Includes OPI—Oral Proficiency Instrument;
    COPI—Computerized Oral Proficiency Instrument;
    SOPI—Simulated Oral Proficiency Instrument
OWLTS: Online World Language Testing Software
SAT II: Scholastic Aptitude Test II
STAMP: Standards-based Measurement of Proficiency
WebCAPE: Web-based Computer Adaptive Placement Exam

APPLICATIONS KEY

CR = credit granting
EP = entrance placement
EX = exit proficiency measurement
PE = program evaluation
SA = self-assessment

REFERENCES

American Council on the Teaching of Foreign Languages (ACTLF). (1986). *ACTFL proficiency guidelines.* Yonkers, NY: Author.

American Council on the Teaching of Foreign Languages (ACTLF). (1996). *Standards for foreign language learning: Preparing for the 21st century.* Yonkers, NY: Author.

American Council on the Teaching of Foreign Languages (ACTLF). (1998). *ACTFL performance guidelines for K–12 learners.* Yonkers, NY: Author.

American Council on the Teaching of Foreign Languages (ACTLF). (1999). *Standards for foreign language learning in the 21st century.* Yonkers, NY: Author.

American Council on the Teaching of Foreign Languages (ACTLF). (2003). *ACTFL integrated performance assessment.* Yonkers, NY: Author.

Blaz, D. (2001). *A collection of performance tasks and rubrics: Foreign languages.* Larchmont, NY: Eye on Education.

Brecht, R. D., & Walton, A. R. (1994). The future shape of language learning in the new world of global communication: Consequences for higher education and beyond. In R. Donato & R. M. Terry (Eds.), *Foreign language learning: The journey of a lifetime.* Lincolnwood, IL: National Textbook Co.

Curtain, H., & Pesola, C. (1994). *Languages and children: Making the match* (2nd ed.). New York: Longman.

Falsgraf, C. (2005). Reflective online assessment and empirical pedagogy. Proceedings of the 2005 Digital Stream Conference, California State University and Monterey Bay, CA.

Koda, J. (1998, June). *Authentic performance assessment. In CLASS (The Center on Learning, Assessment, & School Structure). Developing authentic performance assessments.* Presentation made to ACTFL, Beyond the OPI Assessment Group, Yonkers, NY.

LeLoup, J. W., & Ponteiro, R. (2003, December). Second language acquisition and technology: A review of the research. *CAL Digest* EDO-FL-03-11.

Lewin, L., & Shoemaker, B. (1998). *Great performances: Creating classroom-based assessment tasks.* Alexandria, VA: Association for Supervision and Curriculum Development.

Pufahl, I., Rhodes, N., & Christian, D. (2004/2005, December/January). Language learning: A worldwide perspective. *Educational Leadership, 62*(4), 24–30.

Wiggins, G. (1998). *Educative assessment: Designing assessments to inform and improve student performance.* San Francisco: Jossey-Bass.

ANN TOLLEFSON

Bringing the World to Students and Educators

Distance Learning Explored

Once, not so long ago, language teachers feverishly gathered *realia* from their trips abroad to help language and culture come alive in their classrooms. Today, the very nature of teaching and learning a language is changing as students are transported by technology almost literally into those cultures, enjoying opportunities to interact with the language and people who speak it, while never leaving their classrooms.

Educators can now reach colleagues around the globe to network and share experiences, ideas, and materials. They can also access and participate in professional development through technology, even if they live far from a major university or population center. Inarguably, the ever-evolving world of technology has enormous potential to leverage scarce human and material resources, providing equal access to information and experiences regardless of one's location.

In this chapter, we will examine a number of ways that technology can support language teaching and learning. Central to this discussion will be the premise that we should not use technology in our schools and classrooms simply because *it is there,* but rather when doing so will provide and enrich language learning.

This chapter is divided into the following sections:

- a brief definition of the technology-supported learning to be considered
- technology-supported instruction for language learners, including distance learning delivery methods and enrichment activities and experiences provided by distance learning
- technology-supported access for educators to information, professional development, and networks of colleagues

Distance and Distributed Learning Defined

While technology ranges in sophistication from a reel-to-reel tape recorder to interactive video equipment and beyond, this chapter will consider only technology-supported experiences that take the user into a new situation in which he or she can interact actively with information or people who are at a distance. As such, an important distinction is made between what are commonly known as *distributed learning* and *distance learning.*

Distributed learning refers to a large body of materials such as DVDs, computer programs, and videotapes used for classroom language instruction or enrichment but with which learners cannot interact for interpersonal communication. While these materials can certainly be valuable resources, the learner may not negotiate meaning or influence the direction of the learning through their use such as one might one find in a distance-learning situation. In some computer-based programs, for example, a learner may be able to answer a set of questions but cannot ask questions to clarify or change the direction of the interaction. A number of video programs are played in classrooms to provide instruction and enrichment, but no interaction is possible between the learner and the "instructor" on the video. As such, for the purposes of this chapter, technology-mediated learning that does not allow for negotiation of meaning or for changes in the direction of the learning is labeled as *distributed learning*.

By contrast, in distance learning, the student is able to communicate with, ask questions of, and actively negotiate meaning with a teacher or other learners who may be at a different location or who may participate at a different time. This means that discussions may be synchronous or asynchronous, taking place, for instance, in a teleconferencing call in real time or in a series of e-mails over several days. In some cases, distance learning might involve a satellite-delivered course that is backed up by ongoing teleconferencing among students and course facilitators. In others, it might be an online, project-based interaction with other students or teachers at a distance. It is the ability to negotiate meaning with those who may be at a different location or who may participate at a different time that distinguishes distance learning from distributed learning.

Because of its almost limitless potential to provide equal access to information for all, distance learning is the focus of the chapter.

Technology-Supported Instruction for Language Learners

There are essentially two foci of distance learning related to language learners:

- the delivery of courses
- the enhancement and enrichment of student learning inside and outside the language classroom

In both, technology is the great leveler, bringing equity of access to language learners regardless of where they live.

This is especially important for students in rural areas of the country, where speakers of other languages are typically in short supply and access to cultural and educational opportunities are limited. A class in New York City, for example, is able to visit the Museum of Modern Art to view an exhibition of contemporary European painting or Japanese woodblock prints. A class in Alaska, by contrast, must rely on technology to have similar opportunities. With the advent of the Internet, the Alaskan students may take a virtual field trip to the Louvre in Paris or the National Museum of Modern Art in Japan. In doing so, the students will be able to determine the direction of their exploration and learning rather than rely on a static body of materials. The playing field of learning has in many ways been leveled through technology.

Similarly, economies of scale, in this case relatively large numbers of students and teachers within a geographical area, make it much easier for large school districts to provide extended sequences of language study as well as a wide variety of situations and languages—from dual immersion to AP classes, from Chinese to Arabic programs. By contrast, limited enrollment in small schools presents great difficulties in hiring qualified teachers and implementing progressive programs.

Within the teaching profession there is wide acceptance of and excitement about the potential of technology to enhance and enrich language learning. Nevertheless, when it comes to the delivery of courses using technology there is considerable trepidation. Many fear that schools and districts will choose distance learning as a way to avoid hiring or replacing certified language teachers. To date, there is no evidence of this happening in any widespread manner around the country.

There is no argument that having a teacher working with students face-to-face is far preferable to the use of distance learning. Nevertheless, the reality of rural America does not always make this possible. Sometimes the use of technology is the only way to provide students access to language study. In very small schools, there may not be enough students or qualified teachers to provide traditional programs. Further, even in urban districts, programs in less commonly taught languages such as Arabic and Mandarin Chinese may well depend on technology to take full advantage of hard-to-find teachers or to reach small numbers of students scattered across a number of schools.

Technology is not a replacement for good instruction, but rather a delivery system that can leverage scarce resources by opening *access to good instruction* to more learners.

DISTANCE LEARNING DELIVERY METHODS

Delivery methods for distance learning include courses offered online, by satellite, and through interactive video. The choices for instruction within each of these methods are expanding each year, and it's worthwhile for educators to do some investigating to decide what's best for each classroom given the equipment available and individual student needs.

ONLINE COURSES

Many institutions and companies now offer online language courses for secondary and post-secondary students. With easier access to interactive computer-based technology such as CUseeMe and iCAM, the listening and speaking aspects of the Interpretive, Presentational, and Interpersonal modes of the Standards for Foreign Language Learning can be addressed in online courses.

Because the field of online courses is constantly shifting, with new opportunities opening all the time and others disappearing, we have made no attempt to provide an exhaustive catalog of online course. The following selection is a representative list.

- The West Virginia Virtual School Spanish program is offered by the West Virginia Department of Education to students throughout that state (http://wvde.state.wv.us/news/976/).

- The Kentucky Virtual High School offers four years of French, German, and Spanish, including AP courses. An online course in Chinese is currently in development. These courses are open to students nationwide (www.kvhs.org).

- The Georgia University System offers accredited university-level courses in Chinese, Japanese, and Russian. These courses are built on the WebCT program with regular interactive online sessions and are open to post-secondary students nationwide (www.usg.edu/oie/initiatives/forlangtech.phtml).

- The K–12 Distance Learning Academy at Oklahoma State University offers high school German and Spanish to secondary students nationwide (http://k12.okstate.edu).

SATELLITE COURSES

The satellite mode of delivery offers schools around the country relatively inexpensive access to language courses. The school must have a satellite dish and a telephone line, both common and inexpensive compared with some interactive video equipment. The satellite courses are enhanced through the use of teleconferencing, in which students interact by telephone with a speaker of the language, who reinforces and extends the learning delivered through satellite reception. Arguably, the best known of these courses are offered by Georgia Public Television (http://168.28.132.151/peachstar/workshop/aboutp/progorig.htm) and Kansas State University (www.k-state.edu/ecc/svs/index.html).

Georgia Public Television offers two types of Japanese courses via satellite. *Irasshai Explorer* is a Japanese exploratory program open to middle school students nationally. A two-year Japanese language and culture course, *Irasshai I and II,* is open for credit to secondary and post-secondary students nationally (http://168.28.132.151/peachstar/irasshai/).

Spanish Via Satellite (SVS) is offered to high school students nationwide by Kansas State University (www.ksu.edu/ecc/svs/).

INTERACTIVE VIDEO COURSES

Interactive video is a combination of video and computer technology in which the user's actions, choices, and decisions affect the way in which the program unfolds. By their very nature, language courses delivered through interactive video are rarely if ever offered to large numbers of students, especially when compared with courses delivered online or by satellite. In interactive video courses, the instructor must be able to see, hear, and communicate with all the students in the class *at the same time.* As a consequence, the number of students and the number of distance sites is limited.

In fact, those who teach through interactive video maintain that the class size should actually be *smaller* than one would find in a regular language classroom. Otherwise, the students at the remote sites have insufficient time to interact with the teacher and with the students at the other locations. And it is that very interaction that is the obvious advantage of this mode of technology-supported delivery over others. It adds significantly to the language learning experience of the students, coming as close as possible through technology-mediated instruction to that provided in a traditional classroom.

While examples of such courses can be found throughout the nation, two states have made interactive video the backbone of many of their course offerings in languages and in other specialized subjects: Alaska and Wyoming, where sparse populations spread across vast geographical areas have necessitated this use of technology.

The Wyoming Equality Network links interactive video sites in every high school in the state, providing free access to schools and teachers for the delivery of instruction. Community colleges, the University of Wyoming, and several comparatively large high schools offer live, interactive courses to small schools around the state. French, German, Spanish, and Russian are among the most popular high school courses shared among schools.

In Alaska, the Division of Teaching and Learning Support of the Alaska Department of Education (www.eed.state.ak.us/EdTech/distance.html) links schools in the larger cities with villages scattered throughout the state, ensuring that students in those isolated communities have equity of access to languages.

In other states, some districts link middle and high schools for the purpose of combining students into one class taught by one instructor. There still must be an adult in each classroom to monitor and support student learning, but the technology enables the schools to avoid having to move students physically to another site for instruction.

Although it rarely saves schools or districts money, an interactive video network is a prime example of how technology can leverage material and human resources to provide equity of access to high-quality instruction for all students.

ENRICHMENT PROVIDED BY DISTANCE LEARNING

In contrast to offering actual language courses, the most frequent use of technology in language learning is linking learners to information, activities, and other students around the world. It is of no import where a student lives; he or she can travel over the Internet to new places and experiences, meet others from around the world, and generally access the same information as his or her counterparts elsewhere.

RESEARCH   An Internet search will lead students and teachers to such wonders as the Louvre in Paris, where students can take a virtual tour of the exterior and many of the interior rooms of the museum; the Prado in Madrid, where students can choose an artist and research his or her paintings and life; the Bundestag, where students can take several different virtual tours of the new Berlin; the Palace Museum in Beijing's Forbidden City, where students can view, research, and download photos of many of the museum's exhibits; and the Winter Palace in St. Petersburg, Russia, where students can take a number of virtual tours of the palace and the Hermitage Museum (narrated in Russian or English), or even enroll in an Internet course on Ancient Rome that is taught using the museum's extensive collections of Roman art. At all of these sites, photographs and information are made available that might otherwise have been inaccessible to the students.

It goes without saying that teachers will want to provide preparatory experiences or materials to help students organize their interactions with these Internet resources, rather than just sending them out to surf the Web. Teachers should carefully define and direct online research assignments so that students can focus their research and choose more readily among the enormous number of options offered on the Internet.

KEYPALS Internet search will yield dozens of sites dedicated to linking students from around the world. Two examples of reputable sites that allow students to find pen pals in the country whose language they are studying are Intercultural Email Classroom Connections (www.iecc.org) and KeyPals Club from Teaching.com (www.teaching.com/keypals/).

You can find an excellent, standards-based unit that will help you establish and manage a keypal project in your classroom in ISTE's publication *National Educational Technology Standards for Students: Connecting Curriculum and Technology* (2000, pp. 86–89). This unit offers several ideas and strategies for integrating keypals into regular classroom instruction: creating class Web pages; exchanging photos and letters, digital sound and video clips, recipes and menus, and electronic holiday greeting cards; preparing and sharing multimedia presentations of keypal interactions; even arranging actual visits at the end of the year between the two classes involved. The author of the unit, a junior high school teacher in Wyoming, writes that this program has provided "a truly international educational experience" for both his students and the students in France with whom they correspond. He cautions, however, that to be successful, a keypals project requires active involvement on both sides:

> Teachers who have students who cannot visit foreign countries have found that the keypal experience is significantly enhanced when digital pictures are exchanged. Students enjoy finding out that a unique person really is on the other end of the exchange. Several Midwestern teachers have recounted that creating a calendar of activities, such as joint science projects, progressive stories, and simple tasks (e.g. movie reviews) kept the keypal relationship alive and thriving… [However,] both classes or groups must be committed to long-term, high-quality interaction, or the exercise develops no genuine meaning for students. (p. 89)

LANGUAGE EXPLORATORY COURSES Most of the Internet sites that offer basic language exploration are commercial sites. Many offer a few words and phrases as an introduction to a language. Perhaps the best site on which to explore other languages or to practice the basics in a language one is already learning is the BBC site www.bbc.co.uk/languages/. The BBC offers free, technology-supported language learning materials and exploratory courses for beginners in French, German, Spanish, Italian, Chinese, Greek, Portuguese, Gaelic, Welsh, Irish, and Japanese. Some languages have video clips. All have excellent pronunciation practice for beginning learners.

PROJECT-BASED LEARNING

While the Internet undoubtedly provides valuable support in accessing information, experiences, and people worldwide, it is arguably in project-based learning that its full potential is realized. Students in rural Idaho or Mississippi can link with students around the world, not simply to chat, but rather to work together, each learning from and contributing to the learning of others. This type of technology-mediated learning can be as modest as a project shared by two schools or as ambitious as a project shared by students in a number of countries.

Consider the examples shared by some individual teachers in Ohio.

- A teacher in Gahanna is working with a teacher in Africa. Her students are learning about the critical issues of disease and poverty.
- A teacher in Columbus has an active keypal program. She uses CUseeMe to enable students to talk together from their personal computers.
- A teacher in Akron engages her students in a real-time videoconference with their Japanese partner school during a FLES celebration. Students in both schools showcase their language learning in English and Japanese, play music for each other, and sing together.
- A teacher of Hebrew in Columbus makes it possible for her students to "visit" the Wailing Wall in Jerusalem with a group of Israeli students. They "participate" in tree planting and other cultural activities with their Israeli friends.

In addition to the efforts of individual teachers, consortia of schools around the country and world have joined together to create new experiences for their students. An excellent example is the SAXophone consortium (Students All Over the World Exchanging Over the Phone). Made up of schools in six states and five countries, SAXophone is housed at Nova Southeastern University (www.fgse.nova.edu/saxophone/). It is an international school project in which students from all over the planet come face to face with each other with the help of videoconferencing. Schools sign up for the discussion sessions that interest them, choosing from a variety of subjects. They can share lessons, take joint field trips, and hold concerts together. Any school with the proper equipment can sign up to participate in the SAXophone project. Other than the cost of the long distance call to the video bridge in Florida, participation is free. The project hopes to be able soon to connect schools with equipment as simple as an iCAM or CUseeMe software to the sessions.

The GLOBE Project (www.globe.gov), sponsored by NASA, the U.S. Department of State, and Colorado State University, links students around the world in hands-on science learning through the Internet. GLOBE offers a free way to deliver content-based instruction on science and world geography. The program can link students and classrooms in many countries, allowing them to work together on thematic projects and engage in authentic communication about science using the language they are studying. The GLOBE Web site states:

> Because GLOBE partners represent over half the countries in the world, with schools on every continent, in every time zone, and representing virtually every type of biome, the program naturally provides many resources for language teachers. Authentic materials ready for classroom implementation are available in all six United Nations' languages (Arabic, Chinese, English, French, Russian, and Spanish), and at least part, if not all, of the GLOBE Teacher's Guide is also available in Czech, Dutch, German, Greek, Hebrew, Japanese, Portuguese and Thai, with many other materials becoming available in other languages through GLOBE's 109 international partner countries.

Information about and examples of applications of this extraordinary program to the language classroom can be found at www.globe.gov/fsl/html/templ.cgi?actfl_2005&lang=en&nav=1.

The most extensive network to link students and schools around the globe in project-based learning, however, is iEARN, the International Education and Resource Network (www.iearn.org). iEARN is a nonprofit community of teachers and learners in over 20,000 schools in more than 110 countries. It is supported in large part by grant funds and is used in collaborative projects by government agencies such as the U.S. Department of State and the Peace Corps. iEARN provides a safe and structured environment in which youth around the world can communicate and work together on meaningful projects. It is indicative of the philosophy of the organization that teachers are asked before suggesting projects for the network to consider what good the project will do for the world and its people.

Schools or teachers may join existing online projects or work with colleagues from the U.S. or other countries to create and facilitate new projects that meet their own particular classroom and curriculum needs. Teachers and their classes also have the option to participate in what are called "learning circles" of eight or more schools around the world. Each circle chooses to develop a global project around a shared theme. Most last around 10 weeks and are especially well suited to a content-based teaching unit in which students practice communication and writing skills in the language they are studying.

All iEARN projects involve a final "product" or exhibition of the learning that has taken place as part of the collaboration. These have included magazines, creative writing anthologies, Web sites, letter-writing campaigns, reports to government officials, art exhibits, workshops, performances, and fundraising for causes that a learning circle has decided to support.

Consider just a few examples of the hundreds of online iEARN projects conducted during 2004–2005:

- *We Are Teenagers* (English, Russian, and Ukrainian): Students networked through this Web site to discuss the lives and challenges of youth in their various cultures. Hosted by a teacher in Ukraine.

- *Architecture and Living Spaces around the World* (French, German, English, and Norwegian): Students researched then shared with others the architecture and history of the buildings and monuments of their towns. Hosted by a class in the U.S.

- *My School, Your School* (Spanish and English): Students analyzed their school life and wrote comparisons of schools in different countries. Hosted by a teacher in Argentina.

- *Feeding Minds, Fighting Hunger* (French, Spanish, English, Chinese, Italian, Arabic, and Kiswahili): Students studied issues of hunger, malnutrition, and food security around the world. Hosted by teachers in Zimbabwe and the U.S.

- *Local History Project* (English, Russian, French, and German): Students researched the history of their own town or area and shared it in a Web page gallery. Correspondence and feedback among students was encouraged. Hosted by a teacher in Russia.

- *H20 Viva: El Aqua en Nuestras Vidas* (Spanish and English): Students tested and compared the water quality of their local rivers, streams, lakes, and ponds. They shared stories and practices managing water in local communities. The results of the testing and the students' findings and theories were posted on the project Web site. Hosted by teachers in Cameroon and the U.S.

WEBQUESTS Another excellent source of materials and engaging activities for the language classroom is San Diego State University's WebQuest site (http://webquest.org), which describes itself as the place to find "news and views about the WebQuest Model, a constructivist lesson format used widely around the world."

Since 1996, SDSU has maintained and continually updated a searchable database of sample WebQuests, with approximately 1,500 currently available in eight languages (Catalan, English, Dutch, French, German, Hebrew, Portuguese, and Spanish).

The site also offers information about and links to recently posted WebQuests, some of which are designed specifically for the language classroom. An example is a link to a WebQuest titled "Junge Mode," which engages German I students in teams as they design a German mail-order catalog.

Technology–Supported Access for Educators

No matter where they work, teachers now have access to a wide array of information and services through technology. In this chapter, we will divide the discussion into three components:

- teacher access to information
- teacher access to professional development opportunities
- teacher access to national and international networks of colleagues

ACCESS TO INFORMATION

A dizzying array of Internet sites provide information for today's language teachers. Listed in this chapter are but a few examples. They were included here because of the high-quality information they provide and, perhaps more important, their links to a wide variety of other sites and other types of valuable information.

American Council on the Teaching of Foreign Languages (ACTFL)
www.actfl.org
- a wide variety of resources, including the latest articles on languages and language education nationally and internationally
- information on the latest happenings in the profession
- links to state, regional, and national language organizations

Center for Advanced Research on Language Acquisition (CARLA)
www.carla.umn.edu
- many resources, including information on highly rated summer workshops for teachers
- many materials, some available for download (for example, *Proficiency-Based Instruction and Assessment: A Curriculum Handbook for Teachers*)

Center for Applied Linguistics (CAL)
www.cal.org
- a wide variety of resources from policy issues to international education
- links to information clearinghouses, online resources, and projects

Center for Applied Second Language Acquisition (CASLS)
www.casls.uoregon.edu
- many resources, with an emphasis on assessment
- free subscription available to InterCom, a service that sends automatic e-mail updates to subscribers on topics of their choice, such as curriculum, assessment, or funding

Multimedia Educational Resource for Learning and Online Teaching (MERLOT)
www.merlot.org
- selected, peer-reviewed materials
- multidisciplinary teaching materials for arts, education, humanities, science, technology, and social sciences
- links to online learning materials (for example, the BK Nelson site for Spanish grammar at Colby College: www.colby.edu/~bknelson/exercises/)

National Capitol Language Resource Center (NLRC):
www.nclrc.org
- information on a number of newsletters and guides to language-teaching methodology, most of which are free

National K–12 Foreign Language Resource Center
www.educ.iastate.edu/NFLRC/

- many resources, including publications and information on projects in progress

- information on a variety of highly rated summer institutes for K–12 language teachers

New Visions in Foreign Language Education
www.educ.iastate.edu/newvisions/

- information on the latest initiatives in the profession

- database of exemplary programs in teacher development; teacher recruitment and retention; and curriculum, instruction, articulation, and assessment

ACCESS TO PROFESSIONAL DEVELOPMENT

Teachers who live far from major universities and urban centers are often unable to find professional development opportunities in language acquisition and must enroll in generic education classes to maintain certification and to work for salary advances. With the advent of the Internet, however, an increasing number of opportunities have become available for instructors to access high-quality graduate courses that apply directly to the teaching and learning of languages.

The need to acquire professional development, however, is not limited to teachers in less populous areas of the nation. Their colleagues in urban areas share with them the difficulty of balancing work and family responsibilities while taking evening, weekend, and summer classes. For all teachers, the Internet has opened up opportunities to find professional development that they can pursue at the time and place of their choosing. It has also saved staff time and money for schools and districts that do not have to pay for teacher travel or for consultants to come to their districts.

Several state initiatives address professional development needs. The Kentucky Teacher Academies, for example, allow teachers to work collaboratively to better their skills while earning graduate credit. Recently, a group of Kentucky teachers worked with colleagues in Dijon, France. Beginning with closed chats, then videoconferences, then blogs, the partners have worked together to develop and share electronic field trips as models for future work.

In Wyoming, language teachers have access to a variety of courses offered through the Wyoming Equality Network. In addition to FLES methods training, the video network enables ongoing, just-in-time training and mentoring of native speakers working as classroom paraprofessionals in the state's elementary language program.

Further, several national initiatives offer professional development for language teachers. ACTFL has partnered with Weber State University in Ogden, Utah, to offer an online foreign language methods course. To see an outline and syllabus of this online course, go to http://wsuonline.weber.edu/flmethods.htm.

iEARN, the International Education and Resources Network, offers the Global Teacher's Professional Development Network, with courses designed to prepare teachers to lead their students in online, project-based learning experiences. Details of the courses may be found at www.iearn.org/professional.

ACCESS TO NETWORKING

A number of listservs enable networks of teachers to communicate and collaborate on professional issues. The best known and largest such listserv is the Foreign Language Teaching Forum (FLTEACH; www.cortland.edu/flteach/). FLTEACH is frequented by almost 5,000 language educators from around the world. Ideas are shared among colleagues regarding foreign language teaching materials and methods for all languages and all levels. The listserv is currently supported by the National Endowment for the Humanities through an Exemplary Education Project: Dissemination. The grant, entitled FLTEACH: A Model for Professional Development and Foreign Language Instruction, lasted through 2005. Any teacher could register to participate in the discussions and sharing of ideas.

An example of a language-specific listserv is the one hosted by the American Association of Teachers of German (AATG; www.aatg.org). AATG members who sign up for the listserv can participate in ongoing discussions of issues and ideas related to the teaching of the German language and culture. This sharing and mutual support is of special value to new teachers and to teachers who are far from their fellow teachers of German.

An example of a smaller, more focused listserv is operated by iEARN. Teachers easily network through iEARN, finding colleagues interested in similar topics, then linking their students together to consider those topics. A foreign language teacher in Algeria, Atmane Bedjou recently wrote, "As a teacher of English, I use iEARN especially in the written and reading topics. Our teaching programme consists of units that deal with different topics: mass media, pollution.… When we get to the written section, I just give the assignment to my students and tell them that I would get the best passages published on the net and probably in a book! Then I keep my promise!… You can also find a lot of reading material on the iEARN site that you can use and then ask your students to reply to some of the people who wrote passages."

Conclusion

In this chapter, we have considered projects and programs that utilize technology to expand and enhance language teaching and learning, both inside and outside the classroom. From providing actual language instruction through a variety of technologies to involving students and teachers actively in accessing and using information pertinent to language learning, technology is without question the gateway of today and tomorrow for education that is alive, always current, and ever evolving.

Reference

International Society for Technology in Education (ISTE). (2000). *National educational technology standards for students: Connecting curriculum and technology.* Eugene, OR: Author.

chapter 5

WALTER McKENZIE

Language Learners and Teachers Go Surfing

Successful Web Searching Strategies

ADAPTED FROM
Patricia J. Terry's "Successful
Searching in Social Studies,"
first published in the
2004 ISTE book *National
Educational Technology
Standards for Students: Social
Studies Units for Grades 9–12.*

Until recently, you could always identify foreign language teachers returning from overseas by their luggage. We were the ones with pamphlets, menus, newspapers, posters, parking tickets, electric bills, and any other piece of authentic material we could legally get our hands on. Now, all these things and more are available on the Internet, lightening our luggage and widening the world of authentic materials from what we could cram in our suitcases to whatever students can find on the Web. Finding the right materials on the Web, however, can be a proverbial needle-in-a-haystack challenge without the strategic use of search engines. This chapter is a quick introduction for those who still find themselves far out to sea when surfing the Web.

Search Tools

Search tools are utilities available on the Internet to help individuals locate information about specific topics. Many different search tools are available for student use. Some target specific types of documents or files. Others are designed for specific users, such as young children or business professionals. When students begin exploring the many tools available, they tend to use the same search tool for all their information needs. This may be due to their lack of exposure to other tools, and often results in identifying materials that do not adequately address the topic of the research. Search tools vary in their approach to recording Web sites in their databases, and update this information on varying schedules. Although many tools add new sites on a regular basis, few remove sites that are no longer available. As a result, using only one search tool can have a great effect on the results a student might obtain. Therefore, it is important to submit a search to several search sites to achieve the best results.

SEARCH ENGINES

Search engines are very popular and easy to use. They locate Internet resources by examining identified keywords in a document or the contents of each page, and organizing the words found. These sites are analyzed using technology to determine the placement of a specific resource within the engine's database. Each search engine establishes specific criteria for determining a target site's priority in the search engine's results. This may be based on frequency of words used, number of times a site is visited, or some other determining factor. Consequently, many searches by students result in thousands of potential resources. Popular search engines include Google, AltaVista, All the Web, and Teoma. *Metasearch engines* search several individual search engines and return the results in a compact format. Examples of metasearch engines include DogPile and iTools, which are well designed, easy to use, and return appropriate results quickly and efficiently.

Most search engines provide a basic search feature as well as an advanced search option. Although most research can be accomplished using the basic search strategy, students should be encouraged to review the process of conducting an advanced search when visiting a search engine. The directions provided allow students to become power searchers within minutes. Although the strategies employed for advanced searching are similar for each engine, they may not necessarily be exactly the same, so reviewing the procedures is necessary.

General searching can also be accessed through specific reference Web sites, which are designed to allow users to select from among the many resources and databases available on the Internet. Refdesk is one of the most popular sites in this category. It provides numerous links to tools targeted for specific information such as almanacs, dictionaries, encyclopedias, and other familiar reference materials. InfoPlease is similar to Refdesk and provides access to multiple search tools.

A recent development is the advent of "clustering" search engines, which categorize the results of a submitted search strategy. The user can quickly select from the appropriate categories, reducing the amount of time taken to verify unrelated links. Growing in popularity among professional educators and students is the search engine Vivisimo, which uses this clustering approach. This metasearch engine categorizes its findings and returns specialized results.

SUBJECT DIRECTORIES

Subject directories organize Internet resources into general categories and subcategories. The assignment of a Web resource to a specific category within a search directory's listing may be done through technology based on keywords in the title or description of the page, or by a person who scans the content and recommends a specific placement for that resource. Subject directories afford students the opportunity to scan through several levels within a topic to locate information. This is extremely helpful when students are not exactly sure what they want to find, and it exposes them to many possibilities for consideration in their research. It is an excellent tool to use for broad topic searches. Traditional search directories include Yahoo! and the Educator's Reference Desk.

SUBJECT GUIDES

Subject guides organize resources on the Internet by academic subject area and are likely to be juried by professionals who have analyzed page content for inclusion in the guide. These are wonderful resources for use in classroom activities and projects. Subject guides are available at Infomine, Librarian's Index to the Internet, and Academic Info.

SPECIALIZED DATABASES

Specialized databases are repositories of specific types of information. They may contain compilations of news articles, research reports, images, video segments, speeches, and primary source documents. The ERIC Database is an example of a specialized database.

The charts at the end of this chapter provide listings for foreign language search resources and general search tool resources.

Search Strategy Development

A critical skill for students, particularly at the secondary level, is the ability to define a search strategy. Teachers must provide opportunities for students to learn and strengthen their ability to construct efficient search strategies, because they will not inherently discover this skill on their own. Library and media specialists have always recognized the need for teaching students how to locate information and are generally willing to help teachers and students learn ways to access information on the Internet efficiently. Tap their knowledge and skill by having them plan instructional activities, supply resources, and provide support for students.

As students begin to learn how to construct a search strategy, they will need to understand several key concepts.

- Keywords are more specific than subjects.
- Boolean logic can refine a search.
- Synonyms are critical. Consider other options for word choice.
- Search tools are updated regularly.

KEYWORDS

A student searching for information about the Great Depression might begin by going to Google and simply entering the word "depression." The use of the generic term depression written with a lowercase "d" would include references to mental illness, as well as references to a technique used in the visual arts. Students could refine the search strategy for a more focused result by using the phrase "economic depression." In this case "economic depression" presents specific keywords for the search tool to use. This would limit the results to the desired information.

BOOLEAN LOGIC

By using Boolean operators (AND, NOT, OR), search results are further restricted, resulting in a list of resources that tends to be more focused on the topic. Although the words can be used within the search strategy, symbols present a shortcut to obtaining similar results. AND is represented by the plus sign (+), NOT is indicated by the minus sign (-), and OR is achieved by pressing the spacebar between two words that are not included inside a set of quotation marks. Using quotation marks around a phrase of any length causes the search engine to keep the phrase intact while looking for results. Not using quotation marks can result in a return of hits that are more indicative of having used Boolean logic, with the spaces between words acting as a hidden OR command.

The following examples illustrate two ways to use Boolean logic to limit search results:

+ "economic depression" + 1930

+ depression – illness – "art form"

SYNONYMS

A major challenge that students face when attempting to use search tools on the Internet is their limited vocabulary. This is particularly true for students whose primary language is not English and for young students. Once again, access to tools such as the thesaurus or assistance from a library or media specialist can provide students with techniques designed to increase the likelihood of a successful search.

Rather than searching for "economic depression," a student could try "Great Depression" or "economic crash" or "economic slump." By trying these various synonyms, new resources might be made available that would have been missed.

UPDATED TOOLS

Search tools are updated frequently. Using a variety of search tools and repeating searches after some time has passed may generate new, updated material for the researcher.

Multimedia Searches

Searching for specific forms of multimedia on the Internet is relatively easy. Many search engines provide links to video and audio files, as well as still images. For example, to locate a sound file for a poetry reading by Pablo Neruda, a student might go to any one of the search engines, click on the link to "audio," and enter the appropriate search criteria. Try the following exercise to see how this might work.

- Using the search engine All the Web, select the audio tab at the top of the screen.
- Type "Neruda" into the search window and click on search. The results will include any sound files that include the word Neruda. These will not be restricted to Pablo Neruda.
- Refine the strategy by adding quotation marks around the phrase: "Pablo Neruda."

These results will be much more specific. It may still, however, yield a sound file of Neruda giving a lecture or doing an interview. A revision to the strategy can be made to include the single word "poetry," and would more precisely target the results. This modified search strategy at All the Web, + "Pablo Neruda" + poetry, would result in sound files of Neruda reading his poetry. Changing the media type to video rather than audio would result in the actual video segment aired on television. Hearing Neruda reading his own poetry not only exposes the student to the sound of the poetry, but brings the material alive for media-saturated people of this generation in a way the printed word may not.

Evaluating the Quality of the Resource

Students should be encouraged to access more than one search tool, including a combination of search engines, directories, and specialized databases, to ensure access to quality materials and resources. Once a resource is located, students should take the time to evaluate the quality of the information before they use it in their work. Encourage students to check for the following:

Accuracy. How reliable and free from error is the information?

Authority. What are the qualifications of the author who wrote the information?

Objectivity. Is the information presented with a minimum of bias?

Currency. Is the information up to date? How can you tell?

Coverage. Is the topic explored in depth?

Foreign Language Search Resources

TABLE 5.1

BBC Languages	www.bbc.co.uk/languages/
CARLA (Center for Advanced Research on Language Acquisition)	www.carla.umn.edu/cobaltt/
Casa de Joanna	www.casadejoanna.com
CASLS (Center for Applied Second Language Study)	http://casls.uoregon.edu
iLove Languages	www.ilovelanguages.com
Jim Breen's Japanese Page	www.csse.monash.edu.au/~jwb/japanese.html
Language Links	www.langlink.net
Marjorie Chan's China Links	http://chinalinks.osu.edu
Professional Development	http://learner.org

Other Search Tools and Resources

TABLE 5.2

Able2Know	www.able2know.com
Academic Info	www.academicinfo.net
All the Web	www.alltheweb.com
AltaVista	www.altavista.com
Amazon.com	www.amazon.com
Census Information	www.census.gov
Direct Search Campaign	www.freepint.com/gary/campaign.htm
DogPile	www.dogpile.com
The Educator's Reference Desk	www.eduref.org
ERIC Database	www.eduref.org/Eric/
Federal Resources for Educational Excellence	http://wdcrobcolp01.ed.gov/cfapps/free/
Google	www.google.com
Infomine	http://infomine.ucr.edu
InfoPlease	www.infoplease.com
Internet Public Library	www.ipl.org
The Invisible Web	www.invisible-web.net
iTools	www.itools.com
Librarian's Index to the Internet	http://lii.org
National Archives and Records Administration	www.archives.gov/digital_classroom/index.html
Primary Sources on the Web	www.lib.berkeley.edu/TeachingLib/Guides/ PrimarySourcesOnTheWeb.html
Refdesk	www.refdesk.com
Teoma	www.teoma.com
Vivisimo	http://vivisimo.com
WorldAtlas.com (Maps)	http://worldatlas.com/webimage/testmaps/maps.htm
Yahoo!	www.yahoo.com

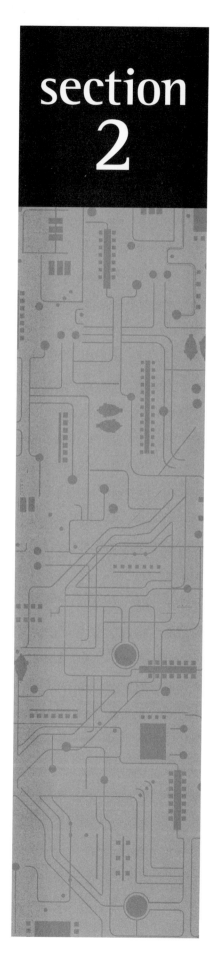

section 2

Resource Units

MOSAIC PROJECT ■ Content-Based Instruction in Spanish

MOSAIC PROJECT ■ Content-Based Instruction in Japanese

CoBaLTT PROJECT ■ Content-Based Language Teaching with Technology

IOWA STATE ■ National K–12 Foreign Language Resource Center

MOSAIC Project

Content-Based Instruction in Spanish

Introduction

ROBERT DAVIS

Language acquisition does not occur in a "content vacuum." Language is more than the words and rules that grammarians describe; it is used in social contexts in the real world, by real people talking, writing, reading, and listening to authentic sources, and communicating for authentic purposes about interesting ideas.

Recent research in second language acquisition argues strongly for content-based instruction, the practice of teaching new academic content in the second language. By exposing students to new concepts and real-world second language usage, we imbue the language acquisition process with additional meaning and give students authentic reasons to express themselves in the target language.

The Standards for Foreign Language Learning give a prominent place to connections to other content areas. Standard 3, Connections, encourages learners to "connect to other disciplines and acquire information." Its inclusion acknowledges the notion that "distinctive viewpoints . . . are only available through the foreign language and its cultures."

But what content should be taught in the level 2 classroom? The obvious answer is the content that second language teachers know how to teach. Most teacher training programs focus on the linguistic structure of the target language (such as phonetics and grammar), literature written in the language, and ancillary historical and cultural information from the target-language culture. These narrowly defined or superficial nonlinguistic content areas are increasingly out of step with student interests. Unless teachers have a double major in history, geography, art history, or some other academic discipline, students don't learn substantial content from these areas, and the methods and basic questions of the discipline are poorly understood.

By the same token, content-area teachers in geography and history may have a keen interest in other regions of the world, but they lack the second language ability that would allow them to access primary source materials in the target language or to communicate new perspectives on the target cultures to their students.

In response to this need, the Center for Applied Second Language Studies (CASLS) at the University of Oregon developed the MOSAIC project. (CASLS serves as the Northwest National Foreign Language Resource Center, accessible at http://casls.uoregon.edu/.) MOSAIC provides content-based units in Spanish and Japanese designed to provide teachers with the materials and methods to enrich their students' language learning experience. The units contain interesting academic content and promote continued development of language proficiency into the advanced levels.

The Spanish units in this section focus on physical, human, and cultural geography; the Japanese units in the next section teach history. These units are intended for use in high school and university language programs, but they could also be useful for immersion curricula or "language across the curriculum" contexts, in which a university-level geography class incorporates level 2 materials and discussion groups.

Geography is the perfect complement to the study of second languages. Geographers understand the relationships between human activities and physical environments, all of which are fodder for culturally relevant discussion in the second language context. On a superficial level, students learn to describe and compare the places and peoples of target-language regions, and these topics correlate perfectly to the second language standards that address the products and processes of other cultures. More important, acquiring proficiency in another language involves a process of personal transformation—a person figuratively leaves his or her own home and self to encounter other cultures and ways of thinking.

The name MOSAIC is appropriate for this project for a number of reasons. First, the content-language juxtapositions recall the mix and match of pieces in a mosaic, all of which come together to form a coherent visual whole. Also, teachers and scholars who compose the curriculum writing teams represent diverse backgrounds and expertise. Teams of four for each language consist of a university-level language teacher, a university-level content area scholar (for the Spanish team, geography), a high school language teacher, and a high school content teacher (geography/social studies). The content specialists identify relevant source materials and ensure that unit lessons include accurate and up-to-date content and methods of the discipline. The language specialists ensure the pedagogical and linguistic quality of the materials, keeping in mind the special challenges of learning new content in a second language.

The content and language educators are well versed in the national standards for both foreign languages and the content areas. Each activity identifies the second language and geography or history standards addressed. Thus, students completing the units make progress toward meeting standards in multiple areas.

The project design hinges crucially on technology. Activities are presented as Dynamic Activity Templates, a format developed independently by the Center for Applied Second Language Studies. Copious visual and textual resources are provided for each activity, such as readings, maps, and tables with demographic data, so that teachers won't have to research the topics or create new materials. All of the MOSAIC activities in this book can be printed out from the supplemental CD and used as is. But the activities are also dynamic—you can download them from the MOSAIC Web site, and modify them to suit your instructional context. The database at http://casls.uoregon.edu/mosaic/index.php also provides units not in this book.

The following units are an exciting integration of geography and Spanish language studies that address a topic of critical national and local importance around the globe: immigration. Using case studies from Oregon, a state with a substantial Spanish-speaking population and vibrant immigrant communities, students will

Follow Your Immigration Patterns

These units are built on geography content and revolve around the theme of immigration. Some of the activities depend on authentic materials specific to Oregon, where the authors reside. Every state in the U.S., of course, has its own immigrant populations and stories, and the activities described in these units can be modified to fit your local context. Simply replace the demographic data for Oregon with similar data from your own state and you can customize these units for your students without recreating the entire unit.

These units can also be adapted for languages other than Spanish, since immigration is not exclusively a Hispanic phenomenon. The same basic activities can be used to explore immigrant Chinese, French, German, Italian, and Japanese populations throughout North America.

Demographic and geographic information is generally available from state or local government Web sites. If you don't know where to find this information, this may be a wonderful opportunity to approach geographers or historians at your school and connect with teachers of other disciplines.

learn the fundamentals of geographical analysis as they plot the growth and settlement patterns of Hispanic populations across the state. Students will explore these key important geographical questions:

- What compels people to uproot themselves from their home culture and reestablish their lives somewhere else?
- What is the effect of immigration on the places that receive immigrant populations?
- What is the life of an immigrant like?

Each of these questions draws students deeper into the issues surrounding immigration. The customizable activities allow teachers to personalize the topics for their students by examining their own local communities (see the sidebar "Follow Your Immigration Patterns").

At the same time, students are receiving linguistic input and producing work that demonstrates crucial advanced-level language functions such as detailed descriptions, comparisons, and past narration.

Unit 1

Being literate in geography is essential if students are to leave school equipped to earn a decent living, enjoy the richness of life, and participate responsibly in local, national, and international affairs.

—Richard Boehm and Sarah Bednarz,
Geography for Life: National Geography Standards

Introduction to Immigration: Basic Human Geography

OVERVIEW

Target Age: High school

Language: Spanish

ACTFL Proficiency Level: Intermediate Mid

Primary Content Area: Physical, human, and cultural geography

Connections to Other Disciplines: Math, history

Time Frame: 7 class days, plus assessment time

OBJECTIVES

Students will be able to:

- Describe the physical and human characteristics of cities and geographic features.
- Identify economic activity in the state.
- Describe relative and absolute location, as well as weather conditions.
- Compare urban and rural landscapes.

DESCRIPTION

This unit is designed for a second- or third-year high school (or second-year university level) Spanish class, and introduces basic human, cultural, and physical geography, with a focus on topics that will prepare students specifically to study issues in immigration. It is assumed that students who study this unit will have had some exposure to geography and social studies in their first language; these lessons serve as a review of basic concepts and an overlay of new second-language vocabulary.

Geography as a discipline is characterized by a spatial approach to description and problem solving, with a crucial emphasis on the notion of mapping, or representing data in graphical or other nonlinguistic formats. In this unit, students will engage in activities that require them to "translate" personal and new content information expressed in Spanish to maps and diagrams, and vice versa, consolidating their

Standards Addressed

NETS•S 3, 4, 5

STANDARDS
FOR FOREIGN
LANGUAGE
LEARNING

Communication Standards 1.1, 1.2, 1.3
Cultures Standard 2.1
Connections Standard 3.1
Comparisons Standard 4.2
Communities Standard 5.1

NATIONAL
GEOGRAPHY
STANDARDS

© National Geographic Society

The World in Spatial Terms
   1. How to use maps and other geographic representations, tools, and technologies to acquire, process, and report information.
   2. How to use mental maps to organize information about people, places, and environments.
   3. How to analyze the spatial organization of people, places, and environments on Earth's surface.

Places and Regions
   4. The physical and human characteristics of places.
   5. That people create regions to interpret Earth's complexity.
   6. How culture and experience influence people's perceptions of places and regions.

Human Systems
   9. The characteristics, distribution, and migration of human populations on Earth's surface.
   10. The characteristics, distributions, and complexity of Earth's cultural mosaics.
   11. The patterns and networks of economic interdependence on Earth's surface.
   12. The process, patterns, and functions of human settlement.

Environment and Society
   15. How physical systems affect human systems.

language proficiency and building their understanding of how information is represented and presented. Specifically, the lessons lead students to answer the following key questions:

- What is our basic environment like: its climate, geography, and population?
- What connections are there between the physical environment and the economic activity in a region?
- How do urban and rural lifestyles differ?

By answering these questions, students will learn to describe a variety of contexts in which humans live, both physically (terrain, weather, etc.) and in terms of social organization and economic activity (urban versus rural settings). In each case, students are encouraged to personalize the information, either by expressing their own reality or by viewing another's reality through a character's perspective. This approach should make the new information more engaging for students at all levels.

The specific examples used in the activities are based on the U.S. state of Oregon, but maps and demographic information for other states are available on the Internet or in libraries. Teachers should be able to use these activities as templates for personalizing materials for their students' own context.

CONNECTIONS TO OTHER DISCIPLINES

As mentioned in the introduction to these Spanish units, content-based instruction, by definition, includes intellectual content other than the study of language for its own sake. It is the new academic content that gives meaning to the language forms and social contexts for language use presented in these lessons. *Physical, human,* and *cultural geography* are the core content areas addressed in this unit.

The work of geographers also involves the manipulation and mapping of information. Students are required to use fundamentals of *math* to study demographic trends and perform calculations of percentages, and to represent information graphically on maps and in charts.

A background in *history* is crucial to understanding the context of immigration in Oregon. In terms of language development, activities that require students to recount family histories promote the advanced-level language functions of narration in the past time frame.

SPOTLIGHT ON TECHNOLOGY

Word Processing: Student assessments and creative projects require the production of authentic documents (e.g., letters, brochures) that include text and graphics. Academic writing involves reading and producing tables and graphs to organize information logically.

Data Management and Mapping: Students can use Excel spreadsheets and the program's chart-making functions to produce climographs and other visual representations of data.

Internet Research: While most resources are provided within the unit, students will need to find additional information on the Internet. As mentioned above, these units can act as templates for lessons on immigration into any area, not just Oregon. To contextualize the topic for a different locale, students can do extensive research on government sites for demographic information and on the Web in general for historical and cultural information relevant to their area.

Graphics: Students have the option of taking photos with a digital camera to use in a PowerPoint presentation on their family tree.

The NETS include technology standards for teachers as well as for students. Many resources used in this unit are available on the Web, requiring teachers to access text and graphics online and prepare them for use in their local context.

TECHNOLOGY
RESOURCES NEEDED

Hardware
computers with Internet access
digital cameras (optional)

Software
word processing software
spreadsheet software with graphic features such as Excel
photograph manipulation software
presentation software such as PowerPoint

SUPPLEMENTARY
RESOURCES

Web Resources

Map Resources
Mexico Maps: www.lib.utexas.edu/maps/mexico.html
World Atlas.com: http://worldatlas.com/webimage/testmaps/maps.htm

Migration Basics
Migration: www.scalloway.org.uk/popu14.htm

Country Profiles
BBC News Country Profiles: http://news.bbc.co.uk/2/hi/country_profiles/

Online Dictionary
diccionarios.com: www.diccionarios.com

Demographic Information
Federation for American Immigration Reform: www.fairus.org
Historical Census Browser: http://fisher.lib.virginia.edu/collections/stats/histcensus/
Sources of Demographic Data on the Web:
www3.uakron.edu/ul/subjects/demographics.html
U.S. Census Bureau: www.census.gov/, http://factfinder.census.gov

Climate Information
CNN en Español: www.cnn.com/espanol/
Current weather in Mexico: www.mexonline.com/weather.htm
Mexico's Climate: www.surf-mexico.com/weather/index.html
Model climograph: http://maps.esri.com/climo/help.html,
http://maps.esri.com/climo/climograph.html
Producing a climograph using Microsoft Excel (see page 26):
http://edmall.gsfc.nasa.gov/aacps/unit/unit5.pdf

Literature Resources
Boehm, R., & Bednarz, S. (1994). *Geography for life: National geography standards.*
Washington, DC: National Council for Geographic Education.
Loy, W. G., & Allan, S. (2001). *Atlas of Oregon* (2nd ed.). Eugene, OR:
University of Oregon Press.

teaching
the unit

Introduction to Immigration: Basic Human Geography

The following unit outline provides a summary of activities, with mention of the content (geography) and language objectives covered. Each activity is identified by title (e.g., **¿Qué lugar es?**) and number (e.g., Activity 1, Day 1).

ACTIVITY 1 (DAY 1)

¿Qué lugar es?

In this activity, students describe physical and human characteristics of cities and geographic features of the different regions of the state. They produce simple descriptions of places and weather conditions, as well as express relative and absolute locations of the main cities, locating them on a blank map.

PREVIEW

Before beginning this activity, review or preteach geography vocabulary with students using maps of your state.

FOCUSED LEARNING

Step 1. Before class, prepare the student activity sheet (Handout 1) and the transparencies (resources included on CD).

Step 2. Using the list of geographical terms provided, review vocabulary with the class.

Step 3. Place students into groups of two and distribute the handout to each pair. Read the directions with the class.

Step 4. Place one of the provided transparency maps (Figure 1) onto the overhead and allow Student A to guess the different locations that are being described by Student B.

Step 5. Repeat this process reversing the roles of Students A and B. Rotate the transparencies to add variety.

EXPANSION

For additional listening practice, read more short geographic descriptions of places and have students guess the place being described.

TEACHING TIPS

While Spanish vocabulary words (from the CD's vocabulary list) are being read aloud, have students label blank maps of the state (printed on transparencies) with geographical features. Sentences should be modeled by using *está/están* plus prepositions.

This activity could also be expanded to include use of *hay*. Provide models, such as *Hay un río que pasa por la ciudad de Portland*. Change the place names to reflect your region.

Figure 1.1 Geographical map of Oregon.

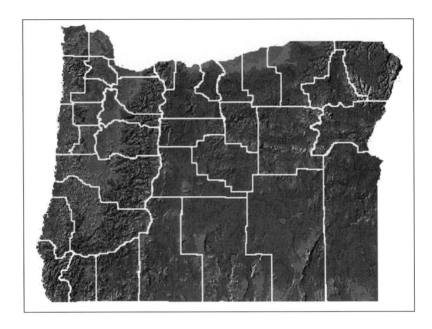

ACTIVITY 2 (DAY 2)

Los mapas cloropleth

This activity teaches students how to make cloropleth maps, a common tool in analyzing demographic data that represents numerical information in a visual, color-coded format on a physical or political map. This type of map allows students to see easily the relationships between different geographical areas by any type of category (e.g., ethnic population, economic activity, or distribution of natural resources). It is a crucial tool in studying any topic in human geography and will be used throughout this and other units.

PREVIEW

Using a map or a globe, review basic vocabulary for describing maps (*frontera, país, condado, norte, sur, este, oeste,* etc.).

FOCUSED LEARNING

Step 1. Before class, prepare the handout and transparency.

Step 2. Use the example map provided (Figure 1.2) to introduce the concept of cloropleth maps. Point out to students the color gradations, light to dark, and how they correlate to the figures in the map legend.

Step 3. Distribute Handout 1. Have students read the introductory explanation of cloropleth maps in Spanish. Ask a few questions to confirm comprehension.

Step 4. Put transparency 1 on the overhead. Have students follow the instructions, Pasos 1–8, on the activity handout to complete their own maps.

Figure 1.2 Cloropleth map of the United States.

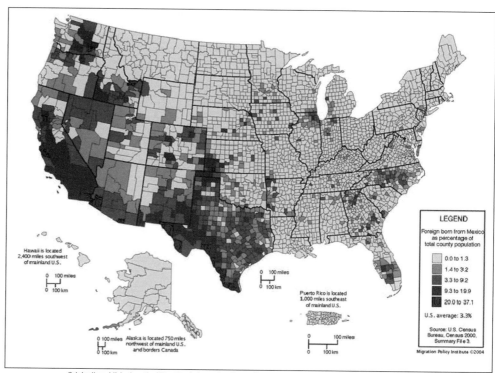

Originally published on the Migration Information Source (www.migrationinformation.org), a project of the Migrtaion Policy Insitute.

EXPANSION

Have students make additional cloropleth maps using data that they collect from the Internet or their own research (local ethnic population, school demographics, etc.).

ACTIVITY 3 (DAY 3)

¿En qué trabajamos?

After reviewing basic vocabulary for professions and learning new items, students use demographic information to identify economic activity in the different regions of the state. They express detailed comparisons between regions and the types of jobs people hold. A follow-up activity has them connect these generalized comparisons to their personal experience: professions and relocations of family members or the economic history of their own community.

PREVIEW

Review basic Spanish vocabulary for the most common professions and jobs in your region (see vocabulary list on CD).

FOCUSED LEARNING

Step 1. Before class, prepare the handout and transparencies (Transparency 3 appears in Figure 1.3.)

Step 2. Place students into groups of three and distribute the handout and two blank sheets of paper to each group.

Step 3. Have students complete Paso 1 of the handout: Working in groups of three, students pick two counties from the map that vary in socioeconomic level or economic activity. Have them write sentences in Spanish that compare the two counties.

Step 4. Have students draw the two counties on the blank sheets of paper and complete Paso 2.

Step 5. Have students present their findings to the class (Paso 3).

Figure 1.3 Employment map of Oregon.

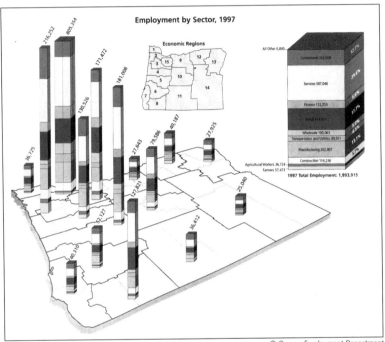

© Oregon Employment Department

EXPANSION

Have students describe in Spanish the county in which their school is located (Lane, for example). Report the Lane County information to the class on a transparency. Have groups of three or four students then come up with specific examples from their personal experience that illustrate the statistics they have just learned about their county—for example, local industries that make certain products (agricultural, industrial, or commercial), or visible examples of the presence of certain ethnic populations (markets, restaurants, cultural events).

TEACHING TIPS

You can do this activity using regions of the state, rather than counties (e.g., for Oregon, the Willamette Valley, coastal Oregon, high desert, or Columbia Valley).

Students may need examples in Paso 2 to help them represent the data graphically. For example, for economic sectors, they could draw small pictures or use magazine cutouts of computers, trees in a forest, or farm products and equipment. See also Unit 1, Activity 2, **Los mapas cloropleth**.

The vocabulary list on the CD is extensive; review or preteach only the vocabulary for jobs, industries, or sectors that are appropriate to the regions being discussed. Be sure to provide any additional items that are of interest to students. To integrate this vocabulary, have students do circumlocution activities; for example, ask students to write definitions of what each profession does, and then read their definitions to a partner, who tries to guess the profession.

ACTIVITY 4 (DAY 4)

¿Quién vive en esta región?

Using demographic information from the U.S. Census Bureau and other sources, students describe and compare the ethnic composition of different counties or regions of the state. As a follow-up to Day 3 content, this activity previews the topic of immigration by having students investigate the possible connections between the settlement of ethnic groups in the state and sites of economic activity.

PREVIEW

Preteach or review vocabulary for ethnic groups, using the list provided on the CD. Add any terms that are useful for describing the ethnic composition of your state.

FOCUSED LEARNING

Step 1. Before class, prepare the handout and transparencies.

Step 2. Distribute the handout to the class and review the directions, using the map transparencies to point out the various counties and regions.

Step 3. Working in groups of three, students should pick two counties or regions from the map that vary in their ethnic composition. Each group should write sentences in Spanish that describe and compare the ethnic composition of the two areas (Paso 1).

Examples

En la región de Portland, hay más rusos que en el condado de Lane.

El condado de Marion tiene más personas de origen mexicano que el condado de Sherman.

Step 4. Have students use a map of the two counties or regions to complete Paso 2, indicating visually the difference in the statistics they described in Paso 1.

Step 5. Each group should present its information to the class (Paso 3). They should include a description of the geographical location and place their map in its correct position relative to the other groups' maps on a bulletin board or wall.

EXPANSION

Have students discuss why the immigrant population is distributed the way it is. If you have done Unit 1/Activity 3, **¿En qué trabajamos?**, have students combine the data from the maps in the two activities. Then they can try to make more complicated comparisons in Spanish, relating ethnic composition and economic activity.

Example

En el valle del Willamette, la mayoría de los inmigrantes mexicanos trabajan en la agricultura, no en la selvicultura.

Also, have student find symbols of ethnic identity associated with different immigrant groups in the state and do a "show and tell" presentation in class, describing what they have found.

Examples

Los rusos en Oregon son cristianos ortodoxos. Sus iglesias suelen tener una forma especial, con techos en forma de cebollas.

Los mexicanos tienen muchas panaderías y mercados en el estado. Aquí hay una foto del Mercado Latino de Eugene.

TEACHING TIPS

You can do this activity using regions of the state, rather than counties (e.g., for Oregon, the Willamette Valley, coastal Oregon, high desert, or Columbia Valley).

Students may need some examples in Paso 2 of the handout to help them represent the data graphically. For example, to represent relative populations, they could use stickers of smiley faces or cutouts of stick figures, each of which could represent 1,000 inhabitants.

ACTIVITY 5 (DAY 5)

¿Qué tiempo hace?

Students differentiate the weather conditions in regions of the state and relate weather to the physical geography. They learn to prepare climographs of different cities around the state, mapping numerical information in tables onto charts. (A Web site with instructions for using Microsoft Excel chart features is listed in Web Resources and on the CD.) Students also preview the topic of immigration by comparing climographs for one city in the state and one city in Mexico.

PREVIEW

Review basic weather vocabulary in Spanish (see the list on the CD). Personalize the topic by asking students about the typical weather in their region.

FOCUSED LEARNING

Step 1. Before class, prepare the handout and transparencies. Using the map provided, prepare two different transparency weather maps of the state that will be projected onto the overhead, one for Student A and the other for Student B (see Paso 1 of the handout). Each map should include weather icons (which are provided on the CD) and the temperatures of cities in the different geographical regions of the state.

Figure 1.4 Climograph.

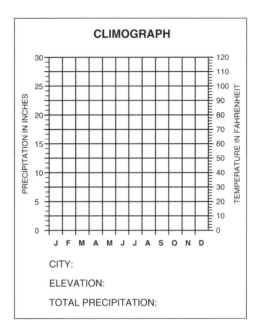

Step 2. Distribute a blank map of the state to each student. Place students into pairs and distribute one copy of the activity to each group.

Step 3. Place a transparency map onto the overhead and allow one student from each group to be interviewed about the state's weather. As the students listen to their partners describe the weather, have them record the information on their own map.

Step 4. Allow students to switch roles by repeating Step 3 and using the second transparency of the state's weather.

Step 5. Once each student has recorded information about the state's weather, distribute a climograph to each student (Figure 1.4). Place the provided information about the state's and Mexico's weather onto the overhead, and then allow students to graph and compare the weather from one city in the state and one city in Mexico. You may want to use Microsoft Excel for this portion of the activity (see CD).

Step 6. Have students share their climographs with the class.

EXPANSION

Ask students to role-play meteorologists, describing current weather conditions in a specific region of the state or Mexico. Students should work in groups of three, creating a weather report and map. One of the group members is "on location," and is interviewed by the reporter. This activity can be expanded to include additional vocabulary, such as sports and headline news, celebrations happening in the same location, and narrating in the past tense.

Other expansion ideas are provided on the CD.

ACTIVITY 6 (DAY 6)

La ciudad y el campo

In this activity, students learn to explain connections between humans and their environment by comparing messages in an e-mail exchange between two fictional characters: Kate, an American teenager from Portland, Oregon, and Pedro, a Mexican from Morelia, Michoacán. By extracting details from the two messages, students infer comparisons of urban and rural landscapes and lifestyles. Students are also introduced to the concepts of push and pull factors in migration.

PREVIEW

Review the vocabulary and conventions associated with meeting a person for the first time, especially through an e-mail exchange.

FOCUSED LEARNING

Step 1. Before class, prepare the handout.

Step 2. Distribute the activity to each student and read the instuctions with the class.

Step 3. Have students complete Paso 1 of the handout. They should read the e-mail exchange between Kate, an American from Portland, Oregon, and Pedro, a Mexican from Morelia, Michoacán. As they read, they should take notes using the categories in the Handout 1 graphic organizer provided (Figure 1.5).

Figure 1.5 Kate and Pedro correspond by e-mail. Excerpt from the student activity handout.

	KATE	PEDRO
¿Dónde vive?		
¿Cómo es el lugar?		
¿Cómo es el clima?		
¿Qué actividades le gusta hacer?		
¿Cuáles son las comidas típicas / favoritas?		
¿Cuál es su origen? (¿De dónde son los antepasados?)		
¿Qué trabajos se mencionan?		

Step 4. Students should choose a partner and answer comprehension questions based on the messages (Paso 2).

Step 5. Have students complete Paso 3 of the handout. They should read the description of factors that encourage people to move from the country to the city at www.scalloway.org.uk/popu14.htm. Have students identify these factors in the messages from Kate and Pedro, listing specific details from each person's letter that correspond to these factors. If no aspects are mentioned for a category, they should write "no hay información."

EXPANSION

Have students devise questions for Pedro and Kate about other aspects of their surroundings or other things that interest them.

Have students rewrite the sentences in Pedro's section with their own personal information, in Spanish. Review the necessary vocabulary before they begin.

ACTIVITY 7 (DAY 7)

La historia de mi familia

The U.S. is predominantly a country of immigrants, and every student has a family history that includes immigration at some point. This activity reviews basic family vocabulary, adds terms for extended family, and then connects students' own family history to the topic of immigration. Students create a family tree and either report the actual reasons or speculate on possible motivations for why their ancestors came to the U.S. The activity practices narration in the past tense and recycles geographical content on the push and pull factors for immigration.

PREVIEW

Review the vocabulary for the topic of family, using the list provided on the CD.

FOCUSED LEARNING

Step 1. Before class, prepare the handout.

Step 2. Distribute the handout. Have students interview relatives using the cues provided.

Step 3. Students should use the information from their interviews to draw their family tree. In Step 4, they will present the tree to the class as they narrate and describe their family, so encourage an appealing visual format (posters with photos, drawings, and so forth, or a PowerPoint slideshow with digital photos).

Step 4. Have students use their visuals to present their family to the class. They should not read from notes; their only cues should come from the visuals.

Examples

Mi familia somos originalmente de Inglaterra. Llevamos cuatro generaciones aquí en Estados Unidos. Los primeros Smith llegaron a Massachussetts en el siglo XIX. Éste es mi tatarabuelo materno, James Smith, nació en Inglaterra en 1823 y llegó a América en 1840. Se casó con...

Mi familia es griega. Llevamos dos generaciones en Estados Unidos. Mi abuelo, Kostas Petrakis, llegó a San Francisco en 1948...

EXPANSION

Have students take notes while their classmates present their family trees. When all the presentations are finished, students can vote on the "Guinness Book of Records" for family history: *el pariente más interesante, la familia más arraigada en la región, la familia más grande,* and so on.

TEACHING TIPS   Students can produce the graphics for their family trees on a large poster board (using photos or hand-drawn figures, or a combination of the two), or by using a graphics program or PowerPoint.

A vocabulary list is provided on the CD. To help students tell why their ancestors came to the U.S., review the uses of *por* and *para*.

por is for *preexisting* conditions (past reasons)	Mis abuelos vinieron **por** razones políticas; no podían vivir en Alemania.
para is for *future* goals	Mis abuelos vinieron **para** tener una vida mejor para sus hijos.

Assessments

ASSESSMENT 1   **Una carta a un amigo:** Tell students to imagine they are on a visit to a friend in Mexico, and are writing back to their Spanish classmates in Oregon, describing what they have experienced on the trip. In their letter, they should include the following:

- A description of Pedro and his house.
- A description of where he lives (general region, climate, etc.), including a map.
- A comparison of the weather in your city versus that of Pedro's hometown, using the blank climograph form to create climographs of your region and Pedro's region in Mexico.
- A description of Pedro's family life (work, chores, free time, food, etc.).

See the CD for more information on Assessment 1.

ASSESSMENT 2   **¡Bienvenidos a Oregon!:** Ask students to prepare a presentation on their state or region for a professional delegation of visitors from Mexico (artists, business people, doctors, factory workers, farmers, and teachers). They should synthesize the demographic, economic, and physical geographical features studied in the unit in detailed descriptions and identify one region of the state that each group in the delegation might find interesting.

See the CD for more information on Assessment 2.

ASSESSMENT CRITERIA   A rubric for this unit is provided in appendix A. Not all the activities in this unit will elicit all the criteria listed in the rubric. Teachers should consider the nature of the task and choose the appropriate items from the rubric to evaluate. The target level of performance for these units ("meets standard") corresponds to Benchmark 5, or ACTFL Proficiency Level Intermediate Mid. Student production at a higher level exceeds the standard.

Unit 2

Basques dominated the sheep industry in the U.S. for almost exactly 100 years beginning with the establishment of the Altube brothers' Spanish Ranch in Nevada in 1873. By the 1970s, most of the second- and third-generation Basques had [left] behind agricultural labor. However, Basque ethnic identity in the United States remains tied to the collective past they share of sheepherding.

—Gloria Totoricagüena Egurrola,
Ethnic Industries for Migrants: Basque Sheepherding in the American West

Basque Immigration to Oregon

OVERVIEW

Target Age: High school

Language: Spanish

ACTFL Proficiency Level: Intermediate Mid

Primary Content Area: Physical, human, and cultural geography

Connections to Other Disciplines: Math, history

Time Frame: 8 class days, plus assessment time

OBJECTIVES

Students will be able to:

- Describe the physical and human characteristics of cities and geographic features.
- Explain the push and pull factors that motivate immigration.
- Identify economic activity in the state.
- Describe relative and absolute location, as well as weather conditions.
- Compare urban and rural landscapes.

DESCRIPTION

The movement of peoples has been a feature of human existence for millennia and continues to shape modern societies. This unit, designed for a second- or third-year high school (or second-year university level) Spanish class, examines an interesting and little-studied wave of immigration to Oregon: Basques from northern Spain came to the western U.S. in the late 19th and early 20th centuries and established stable communities that are still in existence today. The examination of this group serves as a "case study," introducing students to the general phenomena that characterize human migration. Students learn about the basic "push" and "pull" factors that motivate migration and study details of the consequences of displacement on peoples and their communities. Changes in demographics have an effect on every aspect of human activity, language, and culture.

Standards Addressed

NETS•S 3, 4, 5

STANDARDS
FOR FOREIGN
LANGUAGE
LEARNING
Communication Standards 1.1, 1.2, 1.3
Cultures Standards 2.1, 2.2
Connections Standards 3.1, 3.2
Comparisons Standard 4.2

NATIONAL
GEOGRAPHY
STANDARDS

© National Geographic Society

The World in Spatial Terms

1. How to use maps and other geographic representations, tools, and technologies to acquire, process, and report information.

2. How to use mental maps to organize information about people, places, and environments.

3. How to analyze the spatial organization of people, places, and environments on Earth's surface.

Places and Regions

4. The physical and human characteristics of places.

6. How culture and experience influence people's perceptions of places and regions.

Physical Systems

8. The characteristics and spatial distribution of ecosystems on Earth's surface.

Human Systems

9. The characteristics, distribution, and migration of human populations on Earth's surface.

10. The characteristics, distributions, and complexity of Earth's cultural mosaics.

12. The process, patterns, and functions of human settlement.

Environment and Society

15. How physical systems affect human systems.

The unit is designed to lead students to explore the following key questions:

- Who are the Basques and why are they unique? How do they differ from other Spaniards and Spanish-speakers from other regions?

- Why and how did they come to settle in the western United States?

- Where in Oregon have the Basques settled, and what factors influenced their final destination?

- What are the cultural footprints that Basque immigrants have left (or are now leaving) on the state?

The history, and the very existence, of the Basques in the western U.S. is known to very few, even to residents of the states of Oregon, Idaho, Nevada, and California, where most of the century-old Basque communities continue to thrive. Basques are typically bilingual in Basque (a non-Romance language) and Spanish, and their culture is an interesting combination of indigenous and Catholic peninsular traditions and customs. By studying this group, students will gain a unique historical perspective on the persistent presence of Spanish speakers in the northwestern U.S. In unit 3, comparison of Basque immigration with later waves of other Spanish-speaking groups (predominantly Mexicans) should serve to illuminate changing attitudes toward immigration in different periods.

CONNECTIONS TO OTHER DISCIPLINES

As mentioned in the introduction to these Spanish units, content-based instruction, by definition, includes intellectual content other than the study of language for its own sake. It is the new academic content that gives meaning to the language forms and social contexts for language use presented in these lessons. *Physical, human,* and *cultural geography* are the core content areas addressed in this unit.

The work of geographers also involves the manipulation and mapping of information. Students are required to use fundamentals of *math* to study demographic trends and perform calculations of percentages, and to represent information graphically on maps and in charts.

A background in *history* is crucial to understanding the context of immigration in Oregon. In terms of language development, activities that require students to recount family histories promote the advanced-level language functions of narration in the past time frame.

SPOTLIGHT ON TECHNOLOGY

Word Processing: Student assessments and creative projects require the production of authentic documents (e.g., letters, brochures) that include text and graphics. Academic writing involves reading and producing tables and graphs to organize information logically.

Internet Research: While most resources are provided within the unit, students will need to find additional information on the Internet. As mentioned previously, these units can act as templates for lessons on immigration into any area, not just Oregon. To contextualize the topic for a different locale, students can do extensive research on government sites for demographic information and on the Web in general for historical and cultural information relevant to their area.

The NETS include technology standards for teachers as well as for students. Many resources used in this unit are available on the Web, requiring teachers to access text and graphics online and prepare them for use in their local context.

TECHNOLOGY RESOURCES NEEDED

Hardware
  computers with Internet access

Software
  word processing software

Web Resources

Map Resources
Basque Country maps: www.map-of-spain.co.uk/
World Atlas.com: http://worldatlas.com/webimage/testmaps/maps.htm

Migration Basics
Immigration Background Reading (in Spanish):
  http://home.nethere.net/salatorre/historia/historia.html#Inmigrantes
Migration: www.scalloway.org.uk/popu14.htm

Country Profiles
BBC News Country Profiles:
  http://news.bbc.co.uk/2/hi/country_profiles/default.stm

Online Dictionary
diccionarios.com: www.diccionarios.com

Demographic Information
Federation for American Immigration Reform: www.fairus.org
Historical Census Browser:
  http://fisher.lib.virginia.edu/collections/stats/histcensus/
Migration Information Source: www.migrationinformation.org
Sources of Demographic Data on the Web:
  www3.uakron.edu/ul/subjects/demographics.html
U.S. Census Bureau: www.census.gov

History of Basques in America
Basque Museum and Cultural Center (oral interview transcriptions in English):
  www.basquemuseum.com/oralhistory/
Center for Basque Studies: http://basque.unr.edu

Basque Country Information
Tourist information Web sites:
  www.paisvascoturismo.net
  www.red2000.com/spain/region/1r-vasc.html

Literature Resources
Egurrola, G. H. (2003, May). Ethnic industries for migrants: Basque sheepherding in the American West. *Euskonews, 212.* Available online at www.euskonews.com/0212zbk/kosmo21201.html
Loy, W. G., & Allan, S. (2001). *Atlas of Oregon* (2nd ed.). Eugene, OR: University of Oregon Press.

Basque Immigration to Oregon

The idea behind this case study is to have the students start in present-day Spain to develop an understanding of the geography and cultural identity of the Basque region. After comparing the Basque Country with Oregon, students will examine the reasons behind the migration of the Basques from Spain to Oregon in the 19th and 20th centuries. Students will trace the route to Oregon and study the Basque culture as it developed in Oregon.

The following unit outline provides a summary of activities, with mention of the content (geography) and language objectives covered. Each activity is identified by title (e.g., **¿Dónde se encuentra?**) and number (e.g., Activity 1, Day 1).

ACTIVITY 1 (DAY 1)

¿Dónde se encuentra?

In this activity, students review basic geographic terminology and identify major place names and geographical features of the Iberian peninsula. They review the language necessary for describing relative and absolute location and locate geographical features, regions, and cities on maps of Spain.

PREVIEW

Preteach or review the main geographical features, regions, and cities of Spain using the transparencies provided.

FOCUSED LEARNING

Step 1. Before class, prepare the handout, maps, and transparencies.

Figure 2.1 The 17 autonomous regions of Spain.

Step 2. Place students into groups of two. Distribute the activity sheets and two blank maps to each pairing. Working with a partner, students will label the two maps of Spain. One map will include major geographical features of the country; the other map will include Spain's cities and 17 autonomous regions (Figure 2.1).

Step 3. Working with a different partner, students will describe the location of geographical features and cities in Spain. The partner will try to guess the name of each place.

Example	[Córdoba] Esta ciudad está en el sur de España en la autonomía de Andalucía. Está lejos de Barcelona y San Sebastián pero cerca de Sevilla. El río Guadalquivir pasa por la ciudad. ¿Qué ciudad es?

ACTIVITY 2 (DAY 2)

Comparación y contraste: España y Oregon

Students begin to connect the physical and human geography of Spain and Oregon (or a different state) by comparing and contrasting the two places. They preview the topic of Basque immigration to the U.S. by establishing the connections between physical geography and economic activity in Spain and the western U.S., thus setting the stage for studying logical push and pull factors that motivated migration.

PREVIEW

Review the map of Spain from the previous activity and tell students that they will compare and contrast Spain and Oregon (or a state of your choosing). Have them brainstorm some possible similarities and differences based on what they know so far.

FOCUSED LEARNING

Step 1. Before class, prepare the handout.

Step 2. Distribute the handout and read the directions with the class.

Step 3. In pairs, students should complete the sentences of Paso 1 using two maps (one of the state and one of Spain), drawing on the geographical vocabulary from the previous activity.

Step 4. Using what they know about the state and geography in general, students should make educated guesses with a partner about where one might find the following areas in Spain (Paso 2).

    1. áreas de agricultura

    2. áreas de industria

    3. áreas de pesca

    4. áreas de turismo

5. bosques

6. desiertos

Step 5. Students should compare their guesses with those of a partner or the entire class (Paso 3).

EXPANSION

For a higher-level group, you could extend this activity to integrate practice with the present subjunctive. Review the appropriate structures (impersonal expressions, *querer que, insistir que, dudar que,* etc.). Then have students conjugate the verbs before they complete their sentences.

Examples	Es posible que los áreas de agricultura estén (estar) en _____ porque _____.
	Nosotros dudamos que España tenga (tener) tantos bosques como Oregon, porque _____.

ACTIVITY 3
(DAYS 3–4)

El País Vasco/Euskal Herria

In this activity, students identify the major cultural traits of the Basque people—unique physiology, linguistic stock, unique customs, and so forth—and describe the geographical features of the Basque region. The information learned is personalized by having students plan and present a travel itinerary through the Basque Country. This format also integrates and recycles the basic proficiency topics of travel and leisure activities.

PREVIEW

Have students brainstorm the basic vocabulary needed to talk about a trip itinerary: Where do travelers typically stay? What do travelers typically do while on a trip? Preteach any gaps in their target-language vocabulary.

Review the future tense and its two main uses: (1) narrating events in future time and (2) expressing probability in the present time frame.

FOCUSED LEARNING

Step 1. Before class, prepare the handout, maps, and transparencies.

Step 2. Give students random names of different locations around the U.S. or Spain (or the places indicated in the list on the CD) and ask them to guess the appearance of the region's physical environment. For example, you might ask: If you were standing in each of these places, what might you see? What might the weather be like? Use the "future of probability" in your questions (e.g., *Este lugar tendrá . . .*), and elicit this form in their responses.

Step 3. Place students into pairs and distribute the handout to each pair, along with maps of the Basque Country.

Step 4. Set up the following situation for students from the activity sheet: You and a friend are planning a backpacking trip through Spain this summer. You have decided to spend five days in the Basque Country of Spain. Discuss with your friend the details of your trip to *el País Vasco,* focusing on the following two areas:

- Identify the items you will need to pack. Think about what the weather might be like, given the geography and climate of the region.
- Plan your itinerary for the five days in the region. Describe each place you will visit and the activities you plan to do in each location. Indicate each day and the activities on a map of the Basque Country.

The five-day itinerary can be an oral presentation or a written report.

EXPANSION

Supply students with blank postcards on which they can write to a friend back home and describe their trip through the Basque Country. Students can also illustrate the postcard with images of the region that they find on the Internet.

ACTIVITY 4 (DAY 5)

Comparación y contraste: El País Vasco y Oregon

Once students have compiled their information on the Basque Country (Activity 3), have them contrast this region with Oregon (or a state of your choice). The format, vocabulary, and language functions are similar to those of Activity 2. Student descriptions and comparisons should become increasingly more detailed as they recycle language and content material.

PREVIEW

Review the maps of the Basque Country from the previous activity and tell students that they will compare and contrast the Basque Country and Oregon (or a state of your choice). Have them brainstorm some possible similarities and differences based on what they know so far.

FOCUSED LEARNING

Step 1. Before class, prepare the handout.

Step 2. Distribute the handout and read the directions with the class.

Step 3. Have students complete the sentences of Paso 1 in pairs, using two maps (one of the state and one of the Basque Country) and the geographical vocabulary from the previous activities.

Step 4. Using what they know about the state and geography in general, students should work with their partner to make educated guesses about where one might find the following areas in the Basque Country (Paso 2).

1. áreas de agricultura
2. áreas de industria
3. áreas de pesca

4. áreas de turismo

5. bosques

6. desiertos

Step 5. Student pairs should compare their guesses with those of other pairs or the entire class (Paso 3).

EXPANSION

For a higher-level group, you could also use this activity to integrate practice with the present subjunctive. Review the appropriate structures (impersonal expressions, *querer que, insistir que, dudar que,* etc.) and have students conjugate the verbs before they complete their sentences.

Examples

Es posible que los áreas de agricultura estén (estar) en_____ porque_____.

Dudamos que el País Vasco tenga (tener) tantos desiertos como nuestro estado, porque_____.

ACTIVITY 5 (DAY 6)

Lectura: Los vascos en Oregon

This reading activity presents a basic history of Basque immigration to the U.S. A series of guiding questions serve to confirm student comprehension of the text, and they must extract detailed descriptions of the places and communities involved. A follow-up activity asks students to personalize this historical information by creating a description of the daily life of a recent Basque immigrant. This historical reading gives students a context for later discussion of other waves of immigration of Spanish speakers to the state.

PREVIEW

Ask students to share what they know of late 19th-century immigration in general: What groups arrived in the U.S.? Why did they come? Where did the various groups tend to settle? If necessary, use additional readings (such as those available at http://home.nethere.net/salatorre/historia/historia.html#Inmigrantes/) to provide contextual background knowledge.

FOCUSED LEARNING

Step 1. Before class, prepare the handout.

Step 2. Distribute the handout. Before students read the text for Paso 1, have them look over the comprehension questions that follow it. Clarify any vocabulary concerns they may have about the questions, and then have them search for the answers as they read the text. (A list of vocabulary is available on the CD.)

Step 3. Using the *Atlas of Oregon* or other sources, have students research information about Malheur County, Oregon, in order to compare it with the Basque Country in Spain (Paso 2). Suggested topics include economic activity, population, and geographical land features of the two regions. Have them fill in a graphic organizer with the information they find.

EXPANSION

Have students write a "Day in the life of…" account of a Basque shepherd in eastern Oregon in the late 19th century. If past description is beyond their level, they could frame the composition as a letter, in the present tense, to their family back home in Spain.

The Basque Museum in Boise, Idaho, has a wealth of oral interview transcriptions (in English) in which Basques tell of their lives in the Northwest (www.basquemuseum.com/oralhistory/). Students could mine these interviews for detailed information about life during the period in question.

TEACHING TIPS

Another way to use this reading is to do a jigsaw activity. Divide the reading into its five paragraphs, and copy each paragraph onto a different colored paper so that all copies of paragraph 1 are pink, all copies of paragraph 2 are blue, and so on. Divide the class into five groups. Give each group *one* paragraph of the reading. Tell students to learn the information in their section well enough to present it to the group and answer questions about it. You may want students to prepare this outside of class, as homework. When all groups are ready (or the time limit you set runs out), have one student from each group come together to form a new group; this new jigsaw group should have each of the colored paragraphs represented, since each new group will contain one person from each of the original groups. In this new group, students should try to reconstruct the original text. Each student should present the information from his paragraph to his group members, who take notes.

In Paso 2, students could use a two-circle Venn diagram to organize their information: one circle could contain information on the Basque Country, the other on Oregon, and the characteristics that the two regions share could be written in the intersection of the circles.

ACTIVITY 6
(DAYS 7-8)

Preparamos nuestro juego: ¡PELIGRO!

In this activity, students first consolidate their understanding of the history of Basque immigration and Basque culture in the U.S. by researching trivia questions for a Jeopardy-type game. They identify geographic and demographic facts and provide detailed descriptions. When they play the game with classmates, they practice the important linguistic function of asking information questions.

PREVIEW

Have students brainstorm all the categories of information they have studied about the Basques. Prompt them to include at least the following:

- La geografía de España
- La geografía del País Vasco
- La cultura vasca
- El viaje del País Vasco a Oregon
- La comunidad vasca en Oregon
- Motivos por la decisión de ir a Oregon (push-pull factors)

FOCUSED LEARNING

Step 1. Before class, prepare the handout.

Step 2. Place students into groups of four, and assign each group a category or categories.

Step 3. Working in their groups, students should review the information from each of the categories assigned by the teacher. Students should write four answers for each category, and then write questions corresponding to each answer. Remind students that, as in the game of Jeopardy, they will see the answer first and then have to ask the question to win points.

Example	CATEGORIA:	Geografía de España
	RESPUESTA:	Esta ciudad es la capital de España.
	PREGUNTA:	¿Que es Madrid?

Step 4. Play Jeopardy.

TEACHING TIPS

Review the process for creating questions and write a couple of questions together as a class before sending the groups off to write their own questions.

Teachers can add categories with target vocabulary or verbs, and organize the categories by degree of difficulty.

Unit Extension Activities

Many of the individual activities have follow-up suggestions to expand on unit themes.

The unit as a whole is a case study; students will gain the tools necessary to approach the study of immigration in another region of the U.S. or involving other immigrant groups.

After completing this unit, students would also be prepared to investigate the history of migration in Spain. In a very short time, Spanish society has undergone a transformation from a culture of emigration to one of immigration. Large numbers of Spaniards emigrated to other European countries and to the Americas in the early- to mid-20th century. Now in the 21st century, Spain has received thousands of immigrants from Africa, Latin America, and Eastern Europe.

Assessment

Un hogar nuevo: This culminating activity asks students to integrate all their new information about Basque immigration into the personalized format of a letter from a recent immigrant to a friend back in the Basque Country. Guiding questions cover all aspects of the Basque experience: push and pull factors, the logistics of travel to Oregon, descriptions of the physical geography of the new home and comparison to what the immigrant left behind, economic opportunities, and future plans.

ASSESSMENT CRITERIA

A rubric for this unit is provided in appendix A. Not all the activities in this unit will elicit all the criteria listed in the rubric. Teachers should consider the nature of the task and choose the appropriate items from the rubric to evaluate. The target level of performance for these units ("meets standard") corresponds to Benchmark 5, or ACTFL Proficiency Level Intermediate Mid. Student production at a higher level exceeds the standard.

Unit 3

The lasting effect of the Bracero Program has been that it spawned and in-stitutionalized networks and labor market relationships between Mexico and the United States. These ties continued and became the foundation for today's illegal migration from Mexico. Thus, ending the agreement as a legal matter did not alter the migration behavior that had been established over the course of more than 20 years; the migrant flows simply adapted to new conditions.

—Doris Meissner, *U.S. Temporary Worker Programs: Lessons Learned*

Waves of Mexican Immigration

OVERVIEW

Target Age: High school

Language: Spanish

ACTFL Proficiency Level: Intermediate Mid

Primary Content Area: Physical, human, and cultural geography

Connections to Other Disciplines: Math, history

Time Frame: 7 class days, plus assessment time

OBJECTIVES

Students will be able to:

- Describe the physical and human characteristics of cities and geographic features.
- Explain the push and pull factors that motivate immigration.
- Identify economic activity in the state.
- Describe relative and absolute location, as well as weather conditions.
- Compare urban and rural landscapes.

DESCRIPTION

The movement of peoples has been a feature of human existence for millennia and continues to shape modern societies. This unit, designed for a second- or third-year high school (or second-year university level) Spanish class, examines two waves of immigration from Mexico to Oregon. The first group arrived in the years following World War II under the Bracero Program. The second group began arriving in the 1980s and continues to the present day. These activities allow students to gain a historical perspective through chronological ordering. Also, they investigate the specific demographic differences between the groups, in terms of occupations held, settlement patterns, and cultural effects on the state.

This history also serves as a "case study" that introduces students to the general phenomena that characterize human migration. Students learn about the basic push and pull factors that motivate migration and study details of the consequences of

Standards Addressed

NETS•S 3, 4, 5

STANDARDS
FOR FOREIGN
LANGUAGE
LEARNING

Communication Standards 1.1, 1.2, 1.3
Cultures Standards 2.1, 2.2
Connections Standards 3.1, 3.2
Comparisons Standard 4.2

NATIONAL
GEOGRAPHY
STANDARDS

© National Geographic Society

The World in Spatial Terms

1. How to use maps and other geographic representations, tools, and technologies to acquire, process, and report information.

2. How to use mental maps to organize information about people, places, and environments.

3. How to analyze the spatial organization of people, places, and environments on Earth's surface.

Places and Regions

4. The physical and human characteristics of places.

6. How culture and experience influence people's perceptions of places and regions.

Human Systems

9. The characteristics, distribution, and migration of human populations on Earth's surface.

10. The characteristics, distributions, and complexity of Earth's cultural mosaics.

12. The process, patterns, and functions of human settlement.

The Uses of Geography

17. How to apply geography to interpret the past.

---

displacement on peoples and their communities. Changes in demographics have an effect on every aspect of human activity, language, and culture. Specifically, this unit is designed to lead students to explore the following key questions:

- When did immigrants from Mexico first come to Oregon? What motivated them to leave their home communities?

- Where in the state have Spanish-speaking immigrants settled, and what factors influenced their final destination?

- How have successive waves of immigration from Mexico changed over the past half century? What factors influence their continued arrival and movement?

- What are the cultural footprints that Spanish-speaking immigrants have left (or are now leaving) on the state?

This historical perspective highlights the persistent presence of Spanish speakers in the northwestern U.S. Studying the circumstances of each wave of migration should serve to illuminate changing attitudes toward immigration in the different periods.

CONNECTIONS TO OTHER DISCIPLINES

As mentioned in the introduction to these Spanish units, content-based instruction, by definition, includes intellectual content other than the study of language for its own sake. It is the new academic content that gives meaning to the language forms and social contexts for language use presented in these lessons. *Physical, human*, and *cultural geography* are the core content areas addressed in this unit.

The work of geographers also involves the manipulation and mapping of information. Students are required to use fundamentals of *math* to study demographic trends and perform calculations of percentages, and to represent information graphically on maps and in charts.

A background in *history* is crucial to understanding the context of immigration in Oregon. In terms of language development, activities that require students to recount family histories promote the advanced-level language functions of narration in the past time frame.

SPOTLIGHT ON TECHNOLOGY

Word Processing: Student assessments and creative projects require the production of authentic documents (e.g., letters, brochures) that include text and graphics. Academic writing involves reading and producing tables and graphs to organize information logically.

Internet Research: While most resources are provided within the unit, students will need to find additional information on the Internet. As mentioned previously, these units can act as templates for lessons on immigration into any area, not just Oregon. To contextualize the topic for a different locale, students can do extensive research on government sites for demographic information and on the Web in general for historical and cultural information relevant to their area.

Graphics: Students have the option of taking photos with a digital camera to use in a PowerPoint presentation showing a genealogical tree of a Mexican family.

The NETS include technology standards for teachers as well as for students. Many resources used in this unit are available on the Web, requiring teachers to access text and graphics online and prepare them for use in their local context.

TECHNOLOGY RESOURCES NEEDED

Hardware
  computers with Internet access
  digital cameras (optional)

Software
  word processing software
  photograph manipulation software
  presentation software such as PowerPoint

Web Resources

Map Resources
World Atlas.com: http://worldatlas.com/webimage/testmaps/maps.htm

Migration Basics
Migration: www.scalloway.org.uk/popu14.htm

Country Profiles
BBC News Country Profiles:
http://news.bbc.co.uk/2/hi/country_profiles/default.stm

Online Dictionary
diccionarios.com: www.diccionarios.com

Demographic Information
Federation for American Immigration Reform: www.fairus.org
Historical Census Browser:
http://fisher.lib.virginia.edu/collections/stats/histcensus/
Migration Information Source: www.migrationinformation.org
Sources of Demographic Data on the Web:
www3.uakron.edu/ul/subjects/demographics.html
U.S. Census Bureau: www.census.gov

Literature Resources

General History
Meissner, D. (2004). *U.S. Temporary worker programs: Lessons learned.*
Washington, DC: Migration Policy Institute. Available online at
www.migrationinformation.org/Feature/display.cfm?ID=205/
Stavans, I. (2000). *Latino USA: A cartoon history.* New York: Basic Books.

Sources on Pre-1980s Mexicans in Oregon
Cook, W. L. (1973). *Floodtide of empire: Spanish and the Pacific Northwest,
1543–1819.* New Haven: Yale University Press.
Durand, J., Massey, D. S., & Charvet, F. (2000). The changing geography of
Mexican immigration to the United States, 1910–1996. *Social Science Quarterly
81,* 1–15.
Gamboa, E. (1990). *Mexican labor and World War II: Braceros in the Pacific
Northwest, 1942–1947.* Austin, TX: University of Texas Press.
Gamboa, E., & Baun, C. M. (Eds.). (1995). *Nosotros: The Hispanic people of Oregon.*
Portland, OR: Oregon Council for the Humanities.

Sources on Mexican Migration to Oregon
Dash, R. C. (1996). Mexican labor and Oregon agriculture: The changing terrain of
conflict. *Agriculture and Human Values 13,* 10–19.
McGlade, M. S. (2002). Mexican farm labor networks and population increase in
the Pacific Northwest. *Yearbook of the Association of Pacific Coast Geographers
64,* 28–54.
Saenz, R. (1991). Interregional migration patterns of Chicanos: The core, periphery,
and frontier. *Social Science Quarterly 72,* 135–148.
Valle, I. (1994). *Fields of toil: A migrant family's journey.* Pullman, WA: Washington
State University Press.

teaching
the unit

Waves of Mexican Immigration

The following unit outline provides a summary of activities, with mention of the content (geography) and language objectives covered. Each activity is identified by title (e.g., **La línea cronológica**) and number (e.g., Activity 1, Days 1–2).

ACTIVITY 1
(DAYS 1-2)

La línea cronológica

This activity uses excerpts from a unique publication, *Latino USA: A Cartoon History* (by I. Stavans), to initiate students into the major events of Mexican and Mexican-American history. Students can read the selections in the original version (mostly English, some Spanish) or in the Spanish translations provided with the activity. The cartoon format makes the reading more accessible to students. Their task is to discern the chronological ordering of the events that are crucial to understanding the long history of Mexicans in what is now the western U.S.

PREVIEW

Elicit students' previous knowledge about the events that appear in this timeline with a trivia quiz, using the following cues:

- Cristóbal Colón
- Ponce de León
- La Virgen de Guadalupe
- Santa Fe
- Miguel Hidalgo

FOCUSED LEARNING

Step 1. Before class, prepare the handouts and transparencies. Make copies of the instructions (Handout 1) and timeline (Handout 2) for each student. Make copies of the historical events (Handout 3), cut them into strips, and place each set in its own envelope.

Step 2. Pass out the timelines to students. The timelines include 12 important dates in Mexican and Mexican-American history. Next, pass out the envelopes containing the slips with the historical events.

Step 3. Tell students to work individually (or with partners) to match the events to the dates, making the best guesses possible. Monitor the activity and give hints when appropriate. Students will be able to verify their answers once they start the reading assignment.

Step 4. Pass out the reading materials (Handout 4) and give the students time to read the excerpts. Teach or review vocabulary as necessary, using Handout 1 as a guide.

Step 5. After reading the excerpts, students can check their timelines with the information given in the cartoons. At this point, students can glue the descriptions in place with the correct dates and add extra details (one or two sentences) for each event from the reading. Use Transparencies 1 and 2 to guide students in this activity.

EXPANSION

Have students research other important events in Mexican history to add to this timeline. Then, have them create a large butcher-paper version that wraps around the classroom, illustrating events with images they cut out of magazines, print out from Web pages, or draw themselves. They can also include appropriate texts that they find on the Internet (historical summaries, lyrics to *corridos*, etc.).

TEACHING TIPS

Review the higher numbers used for dates before beginning the activity: *mil*, 200–900, and tens-and-ones combinations (*sesenta y cinco, veintiuno*, etc.).

Do a quick dictation in which you read out the following years, and have students write the corresponding dates. Or give students these dates on flashcards and have them read the dates to a partner, who then writes down the numbers.

1492, 1513, 1910, 1565, 1848, 1531, 1836, 1781, 1810, 1610, 1821, 1847

Review preterit tense with students before they write their timelines. Have each student scan the selections from *Latino USA* and write on an index card the infinitive form of any five verbs found in the text. Check to make sure they have a variety of regular and irregular verbs. Write a verb person on the board (e.g., *ellos*). Students, armed with their cards, should circulate around the room and give a quick oral quiz to classmates on the preterit form you have chosen. After two minutes, change the form on the board to, say, *nosotros,* and have students continue the quizzes with that person. Continue until at least four persons have been quizzed.

ACTIVITY 2
(DAYS 3–4)

La población mexicana en Oregón: Un vistazo histórico

Students complement the historical information derived from reading in the previous activity with demographic data on Mexican immigration to the U.S. They are provided with the number of Mexican immigrants in each Oregon county and the total population of each county for the years 1950, 1970, 1990, and 2000. They are given similar census data for several Oregon cities as well and are asked to calculate percentages of Mexican population for selected cities in different regions of the state for the indicated years. In follow-up activities, they construct a cloropleth map for each of the time periods and compare how concentrations of immigrants have changed over the past half century. Then they consider the connection between economic activity in the state and settlement patterns of immigrants at different points in history.

PREVIEW

Review numbers with students by calling out numbers and having them write down what they hear. Spot check their answers as students hold them up (on dry-erase boards or scratch paper). Review and explain numbers as necessary. Focus first on two-digit numbers (10–99) and gradually progress to three-, four-, five-, six-, and seven-digit numbers as students are ready.

Continue the review session by having students create numbers to read to their partners so they can write them down. For a follow-up, call on two to three students to share their numbers with the entire class.

As a final review of numbers before moving on to the raw data in this activity, read math problems to the students and have them write the answers: *150 y 350 son _____; 400 dividido por 4 son _____;* and so on. At this point, review converting fractions into percentages with students to get them ready for the final section of the activity. (Use ratios relevant to the class, e.g., the percentage of girls and boys in the class or in the school, or the number of each letter grade on the last test.)

FOCUSED LEARNING

Step 1. Before class, prepare the handouts and transparencies.

Step 2. Pass out whiteboards and dry-erase markers to students.

Step 3. Give students the handouts with the two different tables of census data (Handouts 1 and 2). Randomly read numbers from each decade and have students name which city or county you are describing (listening comprehension), then ask students to read the populations for cities or counties you name (production). See Figure 3.1.

Step 4. Have students choose three cities and read the populations to their partner. The partner should guess the correct city. Make sure the student reading the numbers identifies the corresponding decade for each city to simplify the guessing. *(En 1950, la población de esta ciudad fue de _____ habitantes. ¿Qué ciudad es?)*

Figure 3.1 Oregon residents born in Mexico, listed by city.

Los residentes de ciudades de Oregon nacidos en México
1950, 1970, 1990, 2000

Ciudad	1950			1970			1990			2000		
	población mexicana	población total	%	población mexicana	población total	%	población mexicana	población total	%	población mexicana	población total	%
Albany	13	10115	0.13%	38	18181	0.21%	683	29950	2.28%	1898	40852	4.65%
Ashland	4	7739	0.05%	74	12342	0.60%	216	16252	1.33%	1018	19522	5.21%
Astoria	1	7739	0.01%	56	12342	0.45%	175	10069	1.74%	448	9813	4.57%
Beaverton	2	2512	0.08%	7	18577	0.04%	1044	53307	1.96%	6184	76129	8.12%
Bend	2	11409	0.02%	57	13710	0.42%	1044	20449	5.11%	6184	76129	8.12%
City of the Dalles	3	7676	0.04%	295	10423	2.83%	592	11021	5.37%	1081	12156	8.89%
Coos Bay	3	6223	0.05%	29	13466	0.22%	592	15076	3.93%	1081	15374	7.03%
Corvallis	1	16207	0.01%	84	35056	0.24%	1672	44757	3.74%	1949	49322	3.95%
Eugene	7	35879	0.02%	128	79028	0.16%	1822	112753	1.62%	4712	137893	3.42%
Grants Pass	2	8116	0.02%	32	12455	0.26%	363	17503	2.07%	923	23003	4.01%
Hillsboro	2	5142	0.04%	240	14675	1.64%	3702	37598	9.85%	10924	70186	15.56%
Hood River	0	3701	0.00%	0	3991	0.00%	396	4632	8.55%	1135	5831	19.46%
Klamath Falls	33	15875	0.21%	126	15775	0.80%	873	17737	4.92%	1469	19462	7.55%
Lake Oswego	0	8906	0.00%	13	14615	0.09%	220	30576	0.72%	435	35278	1.23%
McMinnville	1	6635	0.02%	129	10125	1.27%	1213	17894	6.78%	3156	26499	11.91%
Medford	5	17305	0.03%	73	28454	0.26%	1891	47021	4.02%	4715	63154	7.47%
Milwaukie	1	5253	0.02%	18	16444	0.11%	248	18670	1.33%	526	20490	2.57%
Pendleton	10	11774	0.08%	7	13197	0.05%	550	15142	3.63%	763	16354	4.67%
Portland	135	373628	0.04%	458	379967	0.12%	8631	438802	1.97%	25136	529121	4.75%
Roseburg	2	8390	0.02%	5	14451	0.03%	323	17069	1.89%	524	20072	2.61%
Salem	12	43140	0.03%	557	68725	0.81%	5348	107793	4.96%	16636	136924	12.15%
Springfield	0	10807	0.00%	15	26874	0.06%	898	44664	2.01%	2853	52864	5.40%

© U.S. Census Bureau

Step 5. Choose your hometown or a nearby city and practice together as a class figuring out the percentage of Mexican-born residents in the last four census years. Students can use calculators or do the math on paper. Have students practice reading the percentages, and remind them to use the definite article (e.g., *El 23 por ciento de los habitantes son de origen mexicano.*).

Step 6. Pass out Handout 3 to the students and go over the instructions. Students should first work individually to calculate the percentages for their assigned cities. Then, have them interview one another to fill out their tables with the missing data. Use Transparency 1 to guide students in this activity.

EXPANSION

Have students use their percentages from the county information to create a cloro-pleth map. Students could also make a series of maps, one for each year represented in the graph, illustrating the growth in residential numbers for each county.

Have students make predictions to explain why the numbers change as they do. Offer guiding questions, such as: *¿Qué ciudades han visto los cambios más grandes en su población de origen mexicano? ¿Dónde están estas ciudades? (¿En qué región del estado?) ¿Qué actividades económicas son importantes en esta región?* Review the push-pull factors of immigration (www.scalloway.org.uk/popu14.htm). Have students guess which factors may help explain these demographic changes.

ACTIVITY 3 (DAY 5)

Lectura: Los primeros mexicanos en Oregon

The reading in the handout allows students to confirm or revise the predictions they made in the previous activity about historical settlement patterns and economic activity. A follow-up activity has students view early Mexican immigration to Oregon from the other side of the border. They research and report on the political and economic conditions in Mexico that would have impelled Mexicans to leave their country, reviewing the notion of push-pull factors.

PREVIEW

Review the concepts of push and pull as they relate to immigration. Have students summarize the push-pull factors for the Basques, and then speculate on how the Mexicans in 1940–1970 might be different.

FOCUSED LEARNING

Step 1. Before class, prepare the handout.

Step 2. Distribute the handout to students. Have students first read the comprehension questions and then read the text, taking notes on the answers to the questions.

Step 3. In pairs or as a whole class, have students review the answers to the comprehension questions.

Step 4. In pairs or small groups, have students discuss Paso 2 of the handout (Figure 3.2) and report their responses back to the class.

Figure 3.2 The first wave of Mexican immigration to Oregon. Excerpt from the student activity handout.

1. Considera el tipo de trabajo que hacían los mexicanos en los décadas de 1940 a 1980. ¿Dónde vivían principalmente—cerca o lejos de los centros de población anglo? ¿Los inmigrantes tendrían mucho contacto con las poblaciones establecidas? ¿Qué impacto tendría esta distribución de población en las actitudes de las personas: favorece el sentimiento anti-inmigrante o la tolerancia?

2. La lectura dice que muchos mexicanos se quedaron un rato en California o Tejas antes de llegar a Oregon. ¿Qué impacto tendría este contacto en la vida o cultura de estos grupos? Considera los siguientes aspectos:

   - lengua
   - comida
   - comportamiento social
   - vestimenta (ropa)

EXPANSION

The reading mentions "las malas condiciones económicas" and "un sistema político opresivo" in Mexico during the 1940s and 1950s. Have students research what was going on in Mexico during this period, using the following guiding questions:

1. ¿Qué gobierno tenía México durante los 1940 y los 1950? ¿Qué impacto tenían este gobierno en la vida cotidiana de los ciudadanos?

2. ¿En qué trabajaban los mexicanos de esta época en su país? ¿Qué sueldo ganaban? ¿Cuál era la cifra de paro (unemployment) en la época?

TEACHING TIPS

This reading activity could also be done as a jigsaw activity (see Teaching Tips in Unit 2, Activity 5, or the CD file for instructions).

ACTIVITY 4 (DAY 6)

Lectura: Llegadas más recientes

Another text-based activity, this reading provides information on the most recent waves of Mexican immigration to Oregon. With this information, students will now be able to compare and contrast in detail the two principal historical waves of immigration. By studying settlement patterns and learning the thoughts of majority groups in Oregon, students will be able to explain shifts in attitudes toward immigrants in the state. Finally, students personalize the content of the reading by writing a letter in which they respond to a Mexican national who is considering coming to Oregon to work.

PREVIEW

Review the information on previous waves of immigration to Oregon. Have students recall as much information as possible on the following topics:

- origins of immigrants
- where they settled
- reasons they left their homelands
- jobs they found in their new home

FOCUSED LEARNING

Step 1. Before class, prepare the handout and transparencies.

Step 2. Distribute the handout to students. Have students first review the categories given in the chart in Paso 1 and then read the text and fill in the first column of the graphic organizer (Figure 3.3). (The student organizer is also Transparency 1.)

Figure 3.3 Historical waves of immigration comparison chart. Excerpt from the student activity handout.

	SEGUNDA OLEADA (1980 AL PRESENTE)	PRIMERA OLEADA (1940–1980)
origen		
lugar(es) de asentamiento		
factores de expulsión		
factores de atracción		
trabajos		
lengua(s)		
presencia comercial		

Step 3. In pairs or as a whole class, have students review the answers to the comprehension questions. Use Transparency 1 to record student responses as you debrief the activity.

Step 4. In pairs or small groups, have students fill in the second column of the chart (Paso 2), using the information from the reading in the previous activity

(Unit 3, Activity 3). Then, have them report their responses back to the class. Use Transparency 1 to record student responses as you debrief the activity.

Step 5. Have students come up with comparisons, using the model and vocabulary given in Paso 2. Students can write one of their comparisons on the board to share with the class or share them with their group or partner for editing and revision. The following list presents terms that can be used for comparison.

Para comparar y contrastar

más ... que

menos ... que

tanto/a/os/as ... como

tan ... como

en comparación con

es/son igual(es)

a diferencia de

al igual que

Example   Al igual que en la primera oleada, en la seguna oleada los mexicanos venían principalmente del centro de México.

Step 6. Using library resources or the Internet, students should complete Paso 3, locating on a map the most common places of origin for Mexican immigrants to the U.S. (Zacatecas, Nayarit, Guanajuato, Jalisco, Oaxaca, Michoacán). Have them complete the graphic organizer (Figure 3.4) with the appropriate information. This step could be given as homework. Debrief answers as needed, using Transparency 2.

Figure 3.4 Places of origin for immigration comparison chart. Excerpt from the student activity handout.

	JALISCO	MICHOACÁN	OAXACA
la ubicación geográfica			
la población (número de habitantes, composición étnica, etc.)			
la actividad económica			

Step 7. Have students, individually or in groups, answer the follow-up questions posed in Paso 4:

1. Considera el tipo de trabajo que hacían los mexicanos en los décadas de 1940 a 1980. ¿Dónde vivían principalmente—cerca o lejos de los centros de población anglo? ¿Los inmigrantes tendrían mucho contacto con las poblaciones establecidas? ¿Qué impacto tendría esta distribución de población en las actitudes de las personas: favorece el sentimiento anti-inmigrante o la tolerancia?

2. Ahora, considera el contacto entre los inmigrantes latinos recientes y las otras comunidades en Oregon. ¿Qué factores fomentarían los sentimientos anti-inmigrante?

Step 8. For Paso 5, have students work in groups of three or four to study the following situation and, using what they have learned so far, make a recommendation. Have each group share its recommendation with the class, mentioning the key factors that group members considered in reaching their decision.

Lee el siguiente escenario y trabajando con dos o tres compañeros de la clase, contesten la pregunta usando información de la lectura.

Juan Gómez Ruiz es de un pueblo en el estado de Oaxaca, México. Vive con su esposa y tres hijos en una casa pequeña. Decide irse a Oregon para ganar un dinero extra durante los meses de la primavera. Habla un poquito de inglés. Los vecinos de su pueblo le dicen que los mejores trabajos están en las fábricas de procesamiento, pero que este año contratan a más personas para trabajar en la cosecha de papas.

¿Adónde le recomendarías a Juan que fuera? ¿Por qué sería un lugar ideal para él, según sus circunstancias? Tengan en cuenta los siguientes factores:

- su dominio del inglés
- los trabajos posibles
- los mexicanos ya residentes en las diferentes partes de Oregon
- las oportunidades futuras para Juan y su familia

EXPANSION

Have students use what they have learned in Steps 7 and 8 to compose a letter to Juan, giving him advice. Review the functional language for giving advice (e.g., *Te recomiendo que / es posible que* + present subjunctive, *sería mejor si* + past subjunctive, *¿Por qué no consideras...*).

You could also use the reading in a jigsaw activity. See the CD for ideas.

ACTIVITY 5 (DAY 7) # Símbolos mexicanos

As Mexican immigrants become more numerous and more permanently established in Oregon, it is not surprising to find concrete manifestations of their unique culture around the state. Cultural symbols take on special importance for immigrant communities because they give members of the community a focus for shared identity. Also, first-generation immigrants may fear that their offspring will become "Americanized," and symbols are used as tools against the incursion of North American mainstream culture in the immigrant community. In this activity, students use the format of a bingo game to learn about the most important Mexican cultural symbols and to search for examples in their community.

PREVIEW

Have students report any visible symbols or other evidence of other cultures or ethnic groups in their communities: stores, restaurants, or other businesses; logos, murals, or other public artwork; churches, temples, mosques, or other religious structures; popular festivals; housing types or decorations; and so on.

FOCUSED LEARNING

Step 1. Locate images of Mexican cultural symbols. Before class, prepare the handouts using these images and their descriptions.

Step 2. Have students read the information in Handout 1, associating the images with the phenomena described. This can be done in class or assigned as homework a day or two prior to playing the game in class.

Step 3. Make individual bingo boards from Handout 2 (one for each student) or give students a blank board and ask them to arrange the symbols as they wish on their board before beginning the game. The position of the symbols on the board should be randomized so that no two players have the same arrangement.

Step 4. Read the description of the different symbols, mixing up the order and perhaps slightly altering the exact description used (but still covering the same content). Using their individual bingo boards, and without looking at the written text, students should listen carefully to your description of the image and then cover the image being described with a chit.

EXPANSION

Have students do a scavenger hunt in the local community for these symbols. Point them to the Yellow Pages to find bakeries, restaurants, music stores, or radio stations with Mexican music or consumer goods that bear these images. Are any local streets associated with these symbols?

Assign each student (or each pair of students) one of the symbols to research in-depth as homework. Have them report back to the class orally or turn in their written research.

Have each student (or pair of students) come to class with an additional Mexican cultural symbol the following day. They should have the same type of information that was provided for the bingo images (the name, description, and geographical origin, and an example of the image).

In pairs, have students think of a few cultural symbols from the U.S., providing in Spanish the same type of information that was provided for the bingo images (the name, description, and geographical origin, and an example of the image).

Unit Extension Activities

Many of the individual activities have follow-up suggestions to expand on unit themes.

The unit as a whole is a case study; students will gain the tools necessary to approach the study of immigration in another region of the U.S.

After this unit, students would also be prepared to investigate the history of migration in Spain. In a very short time, Spanish society has undergone a transformation from a culture of emigration to one of immigration. Large numbers of Spaniards emigrated to other European countries and to the Americas in the early- to mid-20th century. Now in the 21st century, Spain has received thousands of immigrants from Africa, Latin America, and Eastern Europe.

Assessment

La historia de una familia mexicana: To synthesize and personalize all they have learned about Mexican immigration to Oregon, have students prepare an illustrated genealogical tree of a Mexican family (hypothetical or based on interviews with an immigrant family in the community) and present it to the class. Encourage an appealing visual format (posters with photos, drawings, and so forth, or a PowerPoint slideshow with digital photos).

An oral presentation based on a family tree elicits the language functions of past narration, extensive description, and comparisons between present and past time frames. The presentation should include descriptions of family members and their origins, their reasons for coming to the U.S., and an explanation of why they ended up where they did. Evaluate students on the completeness and accuracy of the historical and geographical information in their visuals and presentations.

Use the following list to guide students in their content. See the CD for follow-up ideas.

> ## Incluye la siguiente información
>
> - los miembros de la familia (nombres, edades, profesiones)
> - su origen (en México o en EE.UU.)
> - las razones por las cuales los antepasados se fueron de México (o de otro estado de EE.UU.)
> - por qué eligieron tu región para vivir
> - todos los lugares por los que han pasado antes de llegar a tu región
> - fotos, dibujos y otros objetos que se asocian con los diferentes miembros de la familia.

ASSESSMENT CRITERIA

A rubric for this unit is provided in appendix A. Not all the activities in this unit will elicit all the criteria listed in the rubric. Teachers should consider the nature of the task and choose the appropriate items from the rubric to evaluate. The target level of performance for these units ("meets standard") corresponds to Benchmark 5, or ACTFL Proficiency Level Intermediate Mid. Student production at a higher level exceeds the standard.

Content-Based Instruction in Japanese

Introduction

SACHIKO KAMIOKA

As described in the introduction to Units 1–3, the Center for Applied Second Language Studies (CASLS) at the University of Oregon has developed a series of content-based instruction units for both Spanish and Japanese. This section introduces you to three sample Japanese units.

These units teach students the history of the Edo period in Japan (1600–1868), one of the most fascinating times in Japanese history. After two centuries of bloody wars, a feudal warlord (*shogun*) took over the entire country at the start of this period, and the new centralized government built a highly organized feudal system that ushered in nearly 270 years of peace and stability. In the 19th century, this system collapsed, and Japan reopened its doors to the world after 200 years of seclusion.

The theme that links the three units presented here, the *Tokaido* or "Eastern Sea Road," refers to the major highway connecting Kyoto, the residence of the emperor, and Edo (Tokyo), where the shogun lived. The Tokaido was a thoroughfare where historical events took place and culture blossomed in the 17th to 19th centuries. The 53 post stations along the road were frequently illustrated in art forms such as the *ukiyoe* (literally, "pictures of the floating world"), Japanese woodblock prints that depicted how people traveled, worked, and lived during the period. The Tokaido is also a symbol of Japan's development. The route of the ancient eastern sea road, where feudal lords once traveled by palanquin, is now traversed by bullet trains, making this historical roadway an entry point for modern-day students to understand the Edo era and the political and economic development of Japan. It also brings important geographical content into Japanese language lessons.

Unit 4 introduces students to key historical realities of the Edo period. Students put Edo history into perspective by comparing coetaneous periods of Japanese history and U.S. history. Unit 5 allows students to access history through the art of the period. They study ukiyoe illustrating the range of social classes in the Edo period as well as typical activities of travelers on the Tokaido, thereby deepening their understanding of Edo society. Unit 6 invites students to imagine what traveling on the Tokaido was like in the Edo period through literary texts, arts, and popular culture. Students read the eyewitness journal of a German doctor, Engelbert Kaempfer, who traveled the road in the 18th century and accompanied feudal lords in their processions to Edo. Students personalize the material by developing a Web site comparing the lives of people in the Edo period with their own.

Travel the World's Great Highways

The theme of these Japanese MOSAIC units is the Tokaido, the great road connecting Edo and Kyoto. Almost every momentous event in feudal Japanese history could be witnessed along this road, making it a powerful organizing principle for a thematic unit.

Many cultures have similar thoroughfares that can serve as anchors for content-based units focusing on history, such as the Via Appia in Italy, the Silk Road through Asia, and the Champs Elysées in Paris. While these units are aimed at older students with relatively high language proficiency levels, using a great highway as an organizing principle for content-based language units could work equally well for younger or beginning learners. These learners could, for example, visit shops and inns on a make-believe highway and engage in simple transactions as part of a performance assessment at the end of a content-based unit organized around a famous road from any target culture.

The project described in this introduction is funded by the U.S. Department of Education Title VI program through CASLS at the University of Oregon.

Unit 4

Tokugawa Japan

Target Age: High school, university

Language: Japanese

ACTFL Proficiency Level: Intermediate High or above

Primary Content Area: World history

Connections to Other Disciplines: Geography, political science

Time Frame: 15 50-minute class periods

OBJECTIVES   Students will be able to:

- Demonstrate understanding of how the central government in the Edo period controlled the nation by highly organized and stable feudalism.
- Compare and contrast Japan and the United States from the 17th to the 19th centuries with respect to their political history and foreign relationships (e.g., Japan's seclusion policy vs. America's western expansion).
- Demonstrate understanding of how the United States approached Japan to demand reopening of the country and how Japan reacted.
- Compare and contrast the development of Japan and the United States during the last half of the 19th century (e.g., end of feudalism vs. end of slavery, accelerated industrial development in both countries).

DESCRIPTION   This is the first of three units focusing on the Edo era in Japan. This unit is designed for high school Japanese classes (fourth year and above) as well as university Japanese classes (third year and above). It is assumed that students will have a basic knowledge of American history and world history for the period covered (17th–19th centuries) before they begin work on this unit. While these units on the Edo era in Japan discuss using American history for comparisons, the lessons can be easily adapted using periods of history from other countries and regions.

Standards Addressed

NETS•S 3, 4, 5

STANDARDS FOR FOREIGN LANGUAGE LEARNING

Communication Standards 1.1, 1.2, 1.3
Cultures Standard 2.1
Connections Standard 3.1
Comparisons Standard 4.2

NATIONAL STANDARDS FOR HISTORY FOR GRADES 5–12

© National Center for History in the Schools, UCLA, http://nchs.ucla.edu

Standard 1: Chronological Thinking

A. Distinguish between past, present, and future time.

B. Identify in historical narratives the temporal structure of a historical narrative or story.

E. Interpret data presented in time lines.

G. Compare alternative models for periodization.

Standard 2: Historical Comprehension

A. Reconstruct the literal meaning of a historical passage.

B. Identify the central question(s) the historical narrative addresses.

C. Read historical narratives imaginatively.

D. Evidence historical perspectives.

E. Draw upon data in historical maps.

F. Utilize visual and mathematical data presented in charts, tables, pie and bar graphs, flow charts, Venn diagrams, and other graphic organizers.

G. Draw upon visual, literary, and musical sources.

Standard 3: Historical Analysis and Interpretation

A. Identify the author or source of the historical document or narrative.

E. Analyze cause-and-effect relationships and multiple causation, including the importance of the individual, the influence of ideas, and the role of chance.

Standard 5: Historical Issues—Analysis and Decision-Making

A. Identify issues and problems in the past.

C. Identify relevant historical antecedents.

In this unit, students explore the Edo period in Japan (1600–1868), and the comparative history of Japan and the U.S. from the 17th through the 19th century. The unit consists of four sections:

Section 1: Tokugawa Bakufu and Daimyo

Section 2: Seclusion and Expansion

Section 3: Arrival of Perry

Section 4: A New Era

The unit begins by providing students with the setting for the emergence of Tokugawa Ieyasu, a *shogun* (military dictator) who took over Japan and established the Tokugawa *bakufu* (military government) in 1600. Students will learn that prior to the Tokugawa period, Japan was a divided county with local *daimyo* (feudal lords) who fought each other in order to take control of the whole country. Students will discover in the lessons that follow how the Tokugawa bakufu sought to control the nation by ranking daimyo by blood ties and whether the daimyo had sided with Tokugawa Ieyasu in the Sekigahara War. The bakufu then located them in different sections of the country according to their rank. Students make a blank chronology table of Japanese and American history for their own use and for the class, which they may add to at the end of each activity.

In Section 2, students examine how the Tokugawa bakufu maintained its power and kept the country at peace for almost 270 years by exercising strong control over the daimyo and enforcing a seclusion policy toward the rest of the world. This period of peace and stability is contrasted with the history of 18th–19th century America, when the United States fought for its independence from England and began its expansion to the west.

In Section 3, students learn how Japan's long period of isolation ended when President Fillmore ordered naval officer Matthew C. Perry to lead an expedition to Japan to demand treaty relations in the mid-19th century. By studying paintings of the American war vessels (the "black ships") and portraits of Perry, students learn of the fear and anxiety Japan felt toward the West.

In the last section, students compare the development of the two countries during the last half of the 19th century. Social discontent and military activity in Japan ended 270 years of feudal rule, and the Tokugawa bakufu was replaced by a stronger centralized government. This is contrasted with the historical turning point of the United States when four years of civil war united the country under a federal government. During the last half of the 19th century, both Japan and the U.S. experienced accelerated industrial development and important political turning points in their history. Students will come to understand that although the two countries took different paths, both Japan and the United States experienced a critical moment of their history at the same time.

In a final group project, students produce a Web site that traces the comparative history of these two countries in the 17th–19th centuries. Each group identifies a social change that took place during that period which either marks a contrast between Japan and the U.S. (such as Japan's seclusion policy vs. American expansionism) or reveals a similarity between the two countries (industrial development in the late 19th century). Students gather visual materials that illustrate their main points, write a brief description of each illustration, and compile the images and text to make a simple Web page. Web pages from each group are then gathered together to make a class Web site on U.S.–Japan comparative history. As an extension, the class can connect with students studying history in Japan, exchange questions and answers about the Web site, and get feedback for making improvements.

CONNECTIONS TO
OTHER DISCIPLINES

Learning academic content in a second language leads language learners to a higher level of proficiency. One obvious reason is that students gain vocabulary that goes beyond the necessity of daily conversations. In this unit, students learn vocabulary for *history*, *geography*, *politics*, and *social science* such as lord, inland, social class, social system, and agriculture. Students are also exposed to abstract words such as control, change, and purpose. Learning academic content in a second language lets students engage in higher-level vocabulary in context and provides authentic reasons to learn and use the vocabulary.

Comparison of the history of two countries not only enables students to relate to the history of a foreign country but also promotes students' understanding of history, society, and human development. Students are encouraged to find similar patterns of human development in different parts of the world, as addressed in World History Standards for Grades 5–12: "(Students) focus their study on broad patterns of change that may transcend the boundaries of nations or civilizations." For more information and a complete list of the World History Standards, go to the Web site of the National Center for History in the Schools (www.sscnet.ucla.edu/nchs/).

SPOTLIGHT ON
TECHNOLOGY

Word Processing: Students use word processing software to make chronology tables and to prepare text for their Web site.

Internet: The lessons use visual aids (paintings, photos, maps) from various Web sites. Students use the Internet to find visual aids and information to include on their Web page. Students need to obtain permission if they want to include any copyrighted materials on their Web page.

Web Site Development Tools: Students can use HTML editor and image manipulation software to prepare their Web page.

Video Projection: If the classroom is equipped with a computer and video projection device, teachers can use them (rather than the board) to lead many of the activities and record student responses during class discussion. A projector may also be used for student presentations.

Presentation Software: Students can use software such as PowerPoint for their presentations.

TECHNOLOGY
RESOURCES NEEDED

Hardware
  computers with Internet access
  Web space on a server
  video projection device

Software
  word processing software
  HTML editor
  presentation software such as PowerPoint
  image manipulation software (optional)

SUPPLEMENTARY RESOURCES

Web Resources

Emuseum at Minnesota State University, 日本史年表, Timelines of Japanese
　　History (Japanese and English):
　　www.mnsu.edu/emuseum/prehistory/japan/japanese_history.html
Japan-guide.com: www.japan-guide.com/e/e2128.html
National Museum of Japanese History（国立歴史民俗博物館）れきはく＊子供
　　と親のページ日本の歴史を見よう:
　　www.rekihaku.ac.jp/kodomo/2/mitemiyo.html
子どもが見た「鎖国の窓　出島」長崎市立朝日小学校 (Children's view of
　　the "window of seclusion" on Dejima island, Nagasaki City, Asahi elementary
　　school): www.edu.nagasaki-u.ac.jp/private/fukuda/navi/asahi/index.htm
ペリー来航１５０年　慶応義塾大学三田メディアセンター展示委員会
　　(Perry's arrival 150 years later, Keio University Mita Media Center exhibition
　　committee): www.mita.lib.keio.ac.jp/lib_info/display_history/pamphlet/204.pdf

Literature Resources

Gordon, A. (2003). *The modern history of Japan: From Tokugawa times to the
　　present.* New York: Oxford University Press.
Pyle, K. B. (1978). *The making of modern Japan.* Lexington, MA: Heath.
Schirokauer, C. (1978). *A brief history of Chinese and Japanese civilization.*
　　New York: Harcourt Brace Jovanovich.
Varley, H. P. (1977). *Japanese culture: A short history.* New York: Praeger.

teaching
the unit

Tokugawa Japan

The following outline provides a summary of activities. Complete activities and
resources are found on the accompanying CD.

**ACTIVITY 1
(DAYS 1–2)**

Tokugawa Bakufu and Daimyo—1

PREVIEW

If possible, show students a segment of a Japanese movie or TV drama set during
the Sengoku period that shows two clans fighting each other. Good examples are
Akira Kurosawa's *Ran* (1985) and *Kagemusha* (1980). *Kagemusha* is a particularly
good choice, as it depicts the final years of the Japanese civil war period, just before
the Tokugawa bakufu takes power. Discuss with your students in English who is
fighting whom and why. Is there a central government? How do clans decide on
allies and enemies? If no video is available, use the picture scroll provided on the CD
(Transparency 2).

FOCUSED LEARNING

This is the first activity in a series of three. The focus of this activity is to provide students with the flavor of the era with a visual presentation. Students will study both the key historical concepts and the vocabulary to be used in this and the following activities.

The activity first takes students to 15th-century America when Christopher Columbus arrived. Show the picture of Columbus and the map of his expedition provided on the CD (Transparency 1) and ask students to imagine what Japan was like at the same time in history. Move on to a presentation of the historical background of the pre-Edo era using the picture illustrating samurai and daimyo, the Sengoku daimyo map, and the picture scroll depicting the Sengoku period (Figure 4.1, Transparency 2). Encourage students to ask questions using the teacher presentation sample script and explain that from the middle of the 15th century through the end of the 16th century, daimyo constantly fought each other for territory. Show the pictures of notable feudal lords who tried to unite the country: Oda Nobunaga, Toyotomi Hideyoshi, and Tokugawa Ieyasu (Figure 4.2, Transparency 2). Show also the picture of the Battle of Sekigahara and Edo Castle; explain that Tokugawa Ieyasu won the Battle of Sekigahara and gained control of Japan, becoming shogun and establishing the Tokugawa bakufu in Edo (Transparency 3).

With the transparency summarizing the key points (Transparency 4), explain how the Tokugawa bakufu controlled the country by ranking daimyo by blood and whether they sided with the Tokugawa family during the Sekigahara War, and by placing them in different sectors according to their rank.

Figure 4.1 Details from a picture scroll depicting the Sengoku period.

TEACHING TIPS

The names of three ranks of daimyo, 親藩 , 譜代, 外様, are difficult and it is not necessary for students to memorize them. You could substitute them with 一番の大名, 二番の大名, and 三番の大名, respectively, to simply show their ranks.

To make this history come alive, offer students some details and anecdotes about the lives and characters of the three famous generals. Discuss the famous poem that compares their characters:

鳴かぬなら殺してしまえほととぎす (信長)

鳴かぬなら鳴かせてみせよほととぎす (秀吉)

鳴かぬなら鳴くまで待とうほととぎす (家康)

If the nightingale won't sing, kill it. *(Nobunaga)*

If the nightingale won't sing, I'll make it sing. *(Hideyoshi)*

If the nightingale won't sing, I'll wait till it sings. *(Ieyasu)*

Figure 4.2 Feudal lords Oda Nobunaga, Toyotomi Hideyoshi, and Tokugawa Ieyasu.

ACTIVITY 2 (DAY 3)

Tokugawa Bakufu and Daimyo—2

FOCUSED LEARNING

This second activity in the Tokugawa Bakufu and Daimyo series expands on the information introduced in the previous lesson with a reading task. It is designed to teach students new vocabulary and content.

Prepare students for the reading task with pre-reading activities in which they match key vocabulary words with their English translations. Continue on to the reading task and have them read the passage explaining how the Tokugawa shogunate was established and how it controlled the nation by ranking daimyo and placing them in different sectors according to their rank. Check their comprehension through a true-or-false question activity and a multiple-choice task.

EXPANSION

Have students create a blank chronology table of Japanese and U.S. history for their own use. A larger version for a wall or bulletin board can be created for the class. Have them fill in the tables as they finish each unit activity with new historical events they have learned about.

ACTIVITY 3 (DAY 4)

Tokugawa Bakufu and Daimyo—3

PREVIEW

This last activity in the Tokugawa Bakufu and Daimyo series looks at the daimyo distribution in more detail. Using a blank map of Japan (Transparency 1), review the names of the four main islands of Japan (e.g., 北海道、本州) and the names of the regions of Honshu (e.g., 東北、関東).

Explain the first task on Handout 1 using Transparency 2. In pairs, have students speculate on the government's strategy for controlling the nation by coloring a blank map of Japan with three colors, representing the land governed by bakufu, the land controlled by the shinpan and fudai daimyo, and the land governed by the tozama daimyo. Have them create a two-column table and make a list in the first column explaining their rationale in Japanese. Students may share their speculations with the class.

FOCUSED LEARNING

Show students the daimyo distribution map (Transparency 3) and distribute Handout 2. Have students read a series of incomplete statements explaining the placement of daimyo around the country. To complete each statement, they must choose the most appropriate answer from the multiple choices. When they are finished, have them review their answers in groups, and then determine how accurate their speculations were using the second column in the table they created. In groups, have students speculate (in English) why the two "remote" types of daimyo were treated similarly.

As a follow-up, give students the quiz in the Assessment Ideas section on the CD in the next class hour.

TEACHING TIPS

The key to answering the multiple choice statements in this activity lies in how well students know and understand the basics of Japanese geography, particularly the locations and names of major cities and regions. Make sure that you spend adequate time with the map of Japan so that students are familiar with these names and their locations.

ACTIVITY 4 (DAYS 5–6)

Seclusion and Expansion—1

PREVIEW

Using the picture of Tokugawa Ieyasu and the daimyo distribution map (Transparency 1), review the establishment of the bakufu and its strategy for controlling the nation by asking students questions. Have them imagine the foreign policy the government enforced to keep the nation safe.

FOCUSED LEARNING

Show students pictures of 18th–19th century Japan and America and use the pictures to lead a discussion of the similarities and differences in the two nations' political history and foreign policy during this period. Using the image of Nagasaki Port

(Transparency 2), introduce *sakoku*, the Tokugawa bakufu's seclusion policy that almost totally cut Japan off from foreign relations and trade for more than 200 years. Then, show the images of the War of Independence (Transparency 3) and review how the U.S. gained independence from England and began its westward territorial and commercial expansion. Contrast the histories of the two countries.

EXPANSION

Lead students in a discussion of the kinds of commodities, technologies, and information that were imported and exported through Nagasaki Port.

ACTIVITY 5 (DAY 7) Seclusion and Expansion—2

FOCUSED LEARNING

In this lesson, students read a passage explaining Japan's seclusion policy and the development of the U.S. in 18th- and 19th-century America. Students are first given a scrambled sentence task in which they read the sentences from the text presented in a random order and are asked to put them in the correct order. Show the reading passage and continue on to the activities to check their reading comprehension and their understanding of the key events and concepts.

EXPANSION

To check the students' understanding of key events and concepts, have them create a two-column table and compare aspects of U.S. and Japanese history in the 18th and 19th centuries (e.g., foreign policy and trade relationships, territorial division and expansion, etc.).

As an assessment, have students choose a picture from the previous lessons and explain key historical events and concepts related to the picture.

Have the students add what they have learned to their chronology table of Japanese and U.S. history.

TEACHING TIPS

The reading material includes many kanji compounds (e.g., 安定, 独立, 西部開拓). If you think some of these compounds may be too difficult for your students, give them some kanji practice first. For example, explain the meaning of each character in a particular compound and then have them guess the meaning of the compound.

ACTIVITY 6 (DAY 8) Arrival of Perry—1

PREVIEW

The focus of this first activity in the series is to give a visual presentation using period paintings of Commodore Perry and his "black ships" and provide students with a general idea of the interaction between Japanese officials and Perry's men. To prepare students for this activity, review the seclusion policy by asking students questions using the teacher presentation sample script.

FOCUSED LEARNING   Using the visual aids and the teacher presentation sample script provided on the CD, talk about Perry's arrival in Japan. Have students engage in the discussion by asking questions about the picture of black ships and have them imagine the reasons for Perry's arrival.

TEACHING TIPS   To solicit students' active involvement in your presentation, show the picture of the black ships and ask students to describe and explain the scene rather than having them just listen to you passively. For example, you could ask students to look for clues that tell where these ships are from (the ships are flying American flags). Other questions to ask might include: What kind of ships are they? Why did they come? Which Japanese port did they first enter? What was the bakufu's reaction?

ACTIVITY 7 (DAY 9)

Arrival of Perry—2

PREVIEW   This second activity in the Arrival of Perry series provides a reading task for students to secure their understanding of Perry's arrival in Japan and the end of the seclusion policy and to master the new vocabulary related to the event. To prepare students for the activity, provide exercises to introduce new kanji in the reading text and to build students' ability to derive the meaning of compounds by examining what each character in a compound symbolizes.

FOCUSED LEARNING   After students have familiarized themselves with the new kanji, have them read the passage that explains the interaction between Japan and the United States in the 19th century and answer true-or-false questions. Next, have students refer to the map of Perry's expedition route to complete a multiple-choice exercise. As a final task, ask students to fill out the new vocabulary sheet.

EXPANSION   Have students add what they have learned to their chronology table of Japanese and U.S. history.

ACTIVITY 8 (DAY 10)

Arrival of Perry—3

PREVIEW   The focus of this last lesson in the Arrival of Perry series is to have students understand the mixed feelings of anxiety and curiosity the Japanese had toward the West.

FOCUSED LEARNING   Show the portraits of Perry and an illustration of Perry drawn by a Japanese artist at the time. Have students look at a list of descriptions and identify whether the descriptions match the illustration of Perry drawn by the Japanese artist (Figure 4.3, Transparency 1). Have students complete the sentences comparing the portraits and the illustration.

Have students discuss in groups why Japanese people drew Perry as they did. Students next read a passage explaining that Japanese people also drew numerous illustrations of the black ships, shipmen, and their belongings. Lead them to an understanding of how these drawings reflect Japanese attitudes about the West in the mid-19th century.

EXPANSION

In groups, have students make a skit illustrating Japan when the seclusion policy was in effect. Each student should play a different role, such as a shogun, a Dutch person, a foreigner trying to enter Japan, Perry, a samurai, an ordinary Japanese person, and so on. Have each group submit a script. Make corrections and return it to the group. Have the students memorize their lines and act out the skit in front of the class. Use this as an assessment.

Students may also update the chronology table.

TEACHING TIPS

Review the vocabulary and expressions used for describing people. Have students practice these expressions in groups before moving on to the discussion activity.

Figure 4.3 Portrait of Admiral Perry and an early Japanese portrayal of Perry, along with an excerpt from the student activity handout.

1. 日本人の描いたペリーはどんな顔をしていますか。あてはまるものを○で囲みなさい。

a. こわそうです。   b. やさしそうです。

c. はなが高いです。   d. 目が小さいです

e. ひげがたくさんあります。   f. うれしそうです

ACTIVITY 9
(DAYS 11–12)

FOCUSED LEARNING

A New Era—1

The focus of this lesson is to give a visual presentation illustrating the main incidents that changed the course of U.S. and Japanese history in the 19th century. Students should come to understand that although the two countries took different paths, Japan and the United States experienced a critical moment in their history during the same time frame.

Using the comic strips (Figure 4.4, Transparency 1), explain the development of the latter half of the 19th century in which social discontent ended the Tokugawa bakufu's 270 years of rule.

Talk about the establishment of a stronger centralized government and the new reforms undertaken by this new government. Show a map of 19th-century Meiji Japan (Transparency 2) and point out how the old *han* (clan) territories were replaced with territorial units called *to-do-fu-ken* (prefectures).

Using the map of the U.S. in the 19th century (Transparency 3) and the pictures of slavery and the American Civil War (Transparency 4), describe America's experience during the same time period. Focus student attention on the similarities between the two countries in the last half of the 19th century: accelerated industrial development and an important political turning-point.

Figure 4.4 Comic strips depicting the social changes in Japan at the end of the Edo period.

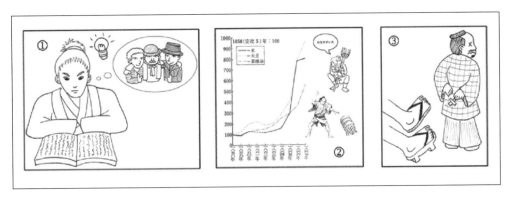

ACTIVITY 10
(DAY 13)

PREVIEW

A New Era—2

Have students complete a pre-reading task in which they match key vocabulary words.

FOCUSED LEARNING

Have students skim through the reading passage that explains the development of Japan and the U.S. during the latter half of the 19th century. Using the graphic organizer on the CD, help students identify the major similarities and differences between the U.S. and Japan during this critical period in both nations' histories (Figure 4.5).

EXPANSION

In groups, have students conduct Internet research to discover the reforms the Meiji government implemented to close the gaps between the Western powers and the Meiji government socially, economically, and militarily.

Have students complete their chronology table of Japanese and U.S. history.

Figure 4.5 Worksheet for identifying similarities and differences between the U.S. and Japan during the latter half of the 19th century.

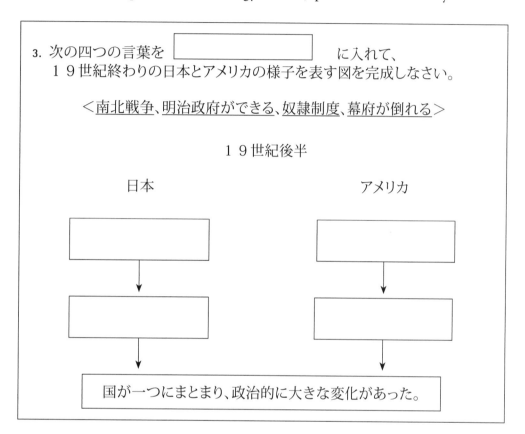

ACTIVITY 11
(DAYS 14–15)

Web Site on U.S./Japan Comparative History

PREVIEW

In the last activity of this unit, students develop a Web site and presentation demonstrating major aspects of 17th–19th century U.S./Japan comparative history. Prepare students for the project by reviewing the major points summarized on the transparency.

FOCUSED LEARNING

Have each group pick an aspect from the list they want to research. Ask them to illustrate similarities and differences between the two countries' histories with visual materials that support their point: pictures, maps, graphs, charts, tables, and so on. (Students can use the Internet to find visual aids and information to include on their Web page, but they need to obtain permission if they want to include any copy-righted materials.) Students should title the page, organize and arrange the materials, and provide a short description for each illustration. Have them draft the text using a word processing program. Collect their drafts and edit them. Have each group finalize their page and save it as an HTML file. Compile all the Web pages and make a class Web site.

Students should also prepare and deliver a presentation on their topic using presentation software such as PowerPoint.

TEACHING TIPS

To prepare students for this group project, review the most salient features of the word processing and Web development software they will be using. Be sure that students are familiar with how Japanese characters are handled by these types of software. If possible, form groups so at least one student in each group has experience in making a Web site. If creating HTML files is beyond many of the students' technology level, have them just create the text using the word processing software. Complete the rest of the steps yourself or ask volunteers to help you.

EXPANSION

If the class has a sister school in Japan, have students contact their peers there and ask them to visit the U.S./Japan comparative history Web site and give feedback. The Web project could, in fact, be organized as a collaborative effort between U.S. and Japanese students. Collaboration could happen at a variety of levels, depending on the time available and the language ability of students—from just sharing information to developing the whole Web site together.

UNIT
TEACHING TIPS

Have students learn new vocabulary in multiple ways. For example, introduce new vocabulary orally first with visual aids, then show them the vocabulary in written form in context, and then provide students with some kanji activities. For compounds, have students break down the word into parts and learn each part. Provide different types of vocabulary activities (e.g., matching, categorization, and illustration) and eventually have them use the vocabulary in communicative activities such as presentations and discussions.

Assessment

In this unit, the Web page that each group creates will serve as the basis for summative assessment. A scoring guide for the summative assessment is provided on the CD.

ASSESSMENT
CRITERIA

A rubric for this unit is provided in appendix A. The rubric contains an array of evaluation criteria, and not all may be applicable to each activity of this unit. Teachers should consider the nature of the task and choose the appropriate items from the rubric for evaluation.

Unit 5

Tokaido Travelers

OVERVIEW **Target Age:** High school, university

Language: Japanese

ACTFL Proficiency Level: Intermediate High or above

Primary Content Area: World history

Connections to Other Disciplines: Political science, geography, art

Time Frame: 10 50-minute class periods

OBJECTIVES Students will be able to:

- Identify the five main highways in Edo-period Japan.
- Demonstrate understanding of how the Tokugawa *bakufu* (central military government) used *sankin kotai* (an alternate attendance system) to control clans.
- Demonstrate understanding of how the Tokugawa bakufu governed the nation by utilizing *shinokosho* (a class system based on Confucian precepts).
- Identify forms of transportation, buildings, and occupations in the Edo period.
- Present an aspect of social transformation from past to present (e.g., transportation, technology, occupations, social systems).
- Express the spatial relationship between two locations.

DESCRIPTION This is the second of three units focusing on the Tokugawa era in Japan. Students are expected to have studied the previous unit (Tokugawa Japan) prior to this unit and know some of the key historical events and concepts of the Edo period. The unit is designed for high school Japanese classes (third year and above) as well as university Japanese classes (second year and above).

The unit begins with an introduction to the *Gokaido*, the five main highways in Japan during the Edo period. Students learn the routes and major cities along the Gokaido. Next, students are introduced to sankin kotai, the alternate attendance system instituted by the Tokugawa bakufu (central military government). This system

Standards Addressed

NETS•S	3, 4, 5
STANDARDS FOR FOREIGN LANGUAGE LEARNING	Communication Standards 1.1, 1.2, 1.3 Cultures Standard 2.1 Connections Standard 3.1

NATIONAL STANDARDS FOR HISTORY FOR GRADES 5–12

© National Center for History in the Schools, UCLA, http://nchs.ucla.edu

Standard 1: Chronological Thinking

    A. Distinguish between past, present, and future time.

    E. Interpret data presented in time lines.

    G. Compare alternative models for periodization.

Standard 2: Historical Comprehension

    A. Reconstruct the literal meaning of a historical passage.

    B. Identify the central question(s) the historical narrative addresses.

    C. Read historical narratives imaginatively.

    D. Evidence historical perspectives.

    E. Draw upon data in historical maps.

    F. Utilize visual and mathematical data presented in charts, tables, pie and bar graphs, flow charts, Venn diagrams, and other graphic organizers.

    G. Draw upon visual, literary, and musical sources.

Standard 3: Historical Analysis and Interpretation

    E. Analyze cause-and-effect relationships and multiple causation, including the importance of the individual, the influence of ideas, and the role of chance.

Standard 5: Historical Issues—Analysis and Decision-Making

    A. Identify issues and problems in the past.

---

of control mandated that every feudal lord (*daimyo*) in the country stay in Edo (the seat of the Tokugawa shogunate) biannually. The formal procession between their home territory and Edo required many followers and the maintenance of two official residences, placing a heavy financial burden on the daimyo. Students learn how this system helped the Tokugawa bakufu prevent clans from consolidating wealth and power in the provinces and thereby enhanced the stability of the military government.

The next activity is focused on the *Tokaido*, the most famous and well-populated road in Japan, connecting Edo and Kyoto. Fifty-three *shukuba* (post stations) were located along the Tokaido, where travelers and their horses rested during trips along this route. The names of these shukuba often contain *kanji* (Chinese characters) symbolizing nature (e.g., stone, sea, hill). Students learn these kanji as well as ways to express spatial relations and the distance between two locations. A new entertainment industry flourished on the Tokaido, alleviating travelers' pains. The pursuit of life's transient pleasures became one of the main themes of Japanese woodblock prints during this period. These prints are known collectively as *ukiyoe* (literally "pictures of the floating world"), and students learn about this art form through a series of activities that introduce students to the typical modes of transportation on the Tokaido (e.g., horse, palanquin), the facilities found along the way (e.g., restaurant, inn, tea house), and the occupations and social hierarchy of travelers and residents (e.g., courier, merchant, feudal lord).

This is followed by a reading activity that introduces students to shinokosho (literally "warrior-rulers, peasants, artisans, and merchants"), a social system based on Confucian precepts. Students learn how the system worked and how it helped the Tokugawa bakufu maintain absolute power for nearly 270 years. In the last activity, by comparing past and present Tokaido travelers, students are made aware of the vast changes in technology, society, and ways of life that have taken place in Japan over the past 150 years.

CONNECTIONS TO OTHER DISCIPLINES

The Tokaido (eastern sea route) connected Kyoto, the imperial capital, and Edo, the seat of the Tokugawa shogunate. This word, representing a spatial relationship, is also a symbolic word for a temporal relationship. The Tokaido symbolizes Japan's development from a feudal society into a modernized industrial country. The road where daimyo once traveled in palanquins carried by couriers in straw sandals now transports thousands of business people in bullet trains in 2 hours and 20 minutes. Fifty-three stations along the Tokaido where travelers and their horses rested have been transformed into factories, department stores, and office buildings. Mt. Fuji, located halfway between Tokyo and Kyoto, seems to be the only thing unchanged. By comparing past and present, this unit is designed to promote students' chronological thinking.

Learning academic content in a second language leads language learners to a higher level of proficiency. One obvious reason is that students extend their vocabulary beyond that used in daily conversation. In this unit, students learn vocabulary used in *history*, *geography*, *politics*, and *social science*, such as peasant, inland, social class, social system, and agriculture. Students are also exposed to abstract words such as *control*, *change*, and *purpose*. Learning academic content in a second language lets students engage in higher-level vocabulary in context and provides authentic reasons to learn and use the vocabulary.

SPOTLIGHT ON TECHNOLOGY

Word Processing: Students can use word processing software to make their presentation materials. They can also make tables and charts for the presentation.

Internet: The lessons use visual aids (paintings, photos, maps) from various Web sites. Students use the Internet to find information and graphics to include on their presentation. Students need to obtain permission to use copyrighted material.

Video Projection: If the classroom is equipped with a computer and video projection device, teachers can use them (rather than the board) to lead many of the activities and record student responses during class discussion. A projector may also be used for student presentations.

Presentation Software: Students may use presentation software such as PowerPoint for the culminating activity.

Photograph Manipulation Software: Students may use photo software to prepare images for their presentations.

TECHNOLOGY
RESOURCES NEEDED

Hardware
computers with Internet access
video projection device

Software
word processing software
presentation software such as PowerPoint
image manipulation software (optional)

SUPPLEMENTARY
RESOURCES

Web Resources
Asahi Internet service provider and community: http://asahi-net.jp/
五街道 (Gokaido): http://db.gakken.co.jp/jiten/ka/129690.htm
ももたろうの「お父さん」の東海道五十三次テクテク記 (The Tokaido's 53 Stations Tekuteku Journal by Momotaro's Father): http://homepage1.nifty.com/momotyan/Tokaidou/Tokai_Top.htm
東海道五十三次をゆく (Traveling along the Tokaido's 53 Stations): http://bruce.milkcafe.com/kaidou/know6.htm
なるほどデータforきっず ("Oh I See" Data for Kids): www.stat.go.jp/kids/datastore/
便利で役立つハウ・ツーもの「旅行用心集」 (The Convenient and Useful How-To Guide for Travel Precautions): www.dentsu.co.jp/MUSEUM/edo/tabi/ansin/ansin1464.html
Ando Hiroshige: The Fifty-Three Stations of the Tokaido Road: www.hiroshige.org.uk/
日本標準／日本標準教育研究所「学習サーチ」 (Nippon Hyojun/Nippon Hyojun Educational Institute for Teachers and Students, Learner's search page): www.nipponhyojun.co.jp/search/syakai/

Literature Resources
Kaempfer, E. (1998). *Kaempfer's Japan: Tokugawa culture observed* (edited, translated, and annotated by Beatrice M. Bodart-Bailey). Honolulu, HI: University of Hawaii Press. (Original work published 1727)
Traganou, J. (2004). *The Tokaido road: Traveling and representation in Edo and Meiji Japan.* New York: RoutledgeCurzon.

teaching
the unit

Tokaido Travelers

The following outline provides a summary of activities. Complete activities and resources are found on the accompanying CD.

ACTIVITY 1 (DAY 1)

The Gokaido

PREVIEW

Review the three ranks of daimyo taught in Tokugawa Japan (Unit 4). Show students a current map of Japan and point out the abundant railroad lines along the eastern shore of the main island of Honshu (Transparency 1). Distribute a blank map and have students speculate where roads were located in the Edo period and draw lines. Have some students draw their guesses on Transparency 2.

FOCUSED LEARNING

Show Transparency 3, the map of the Gokaido (Figure 5.1). Place Transparency 3 over Transparency 4, the map of the three ranks of daimyo (Figure 5.2). Help students to understand that the Gokaido mainly ran through the *bakufuryo* (military government sector), the most important sector for the government. Using the reading activity provided on the CD, have students identify the routes and major cities along the Gokaido and learn the key vocabulary words.

EXPANSION

Compare major cities on the Gokaido and on a modern map. Some (e.g., Tokyo, Kyoto) are still major cities. Others (e.g., Nikko) are now just tourist destinations. What makes some cities flourish over time while others fade away? Has this happened to American cities? Which American or Japanese cities will still be important 200 years from now? Which will fade away?

Figure 5.1 Map of the Gokaido.

Figure 5.2 Map of the three ranks of daimyo.

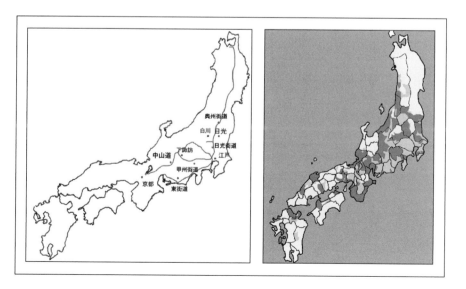

ACTIVITY 2 (DAY 2)

Sankin Kotai

PREVIEW

Show students Transparency 1, the *ukiyoe* (woodblock print) depicting a *daimyo gyoretsu* (procession), and use it to introduce important features of the daimyo gyoretsu.

FOCUSED LEARNING

Using the handout provided on the CD, lead students to a better understanding of sankin kotai, the alternate attendance system mandated by the Tokugawa bakufu. Display the handout questions and answer choices on a transparency, and discuss how the alternate attendance system worked and which governmental agendas were advanced through this system. Figure 5.3 shows an excerpt of this handout.

EXPANSION

Have students compare the goals and effects of the Tokugawa bakufu's alternate attendance system to modern governmental policies: how do national bureaucracies today try to control rivals for power, such as corporations, religious and special interest groups, and state and local governments?

Have students imagine a modern-day version of the daimyo gyoretsu, in which state governors and other political leaders would have to travel regularly and publicly to Washington, D.C. How would they travel? Who would go with them? Who would they visit there? This can be a class discussion, group activity, or written assignment.

Figure 5.3 Questions about alternate attendance and the Tokugawa bakufu. Excerpt from the student activity handout.

1. 大名は一年に一度江戸に行きました。江戸にはだれがいますか。
   a. 天皇
   b. 将軍
   c. 他の大名

2. 大名はどうして江戸に行ったと思いますか。
   a. 観光
   b. 新しい技術を見るため
   c. 幕府の命令

ACTIVITIES 3 AND 4
(DAY 3)

The Tokaido ACTIVITY 3
Where Is Hakone? ACTIVITY 4

PREVIEW

Before starting Activity 3, prepare kanji cards and categorization tables for groups of three students. Begin the lesson by reviewing the Gokaido and sankin kotai with the class. Review or preteach vocabulary that expresses spatial relationships between two locations. Introduce the Tokaido, the most important of the five main highways, connecting Edo and Kyoto (Transparency 1). Introduce as well the 53 shukuba (post stations) that were located along the Tokaido by showing students an ukiyoe that depicts one of the shukuba (Transparency 2).

FOCUSED LEARNING

After introducing the topic of shukuba, have students in groups of three begin the kanji exercises on the Activity 3 handout. Students must first categorize kanji by their meaning (Figure 5.4), then identify radicals and match kanji with their English translations. Finally, direct students to complete the shukuba matching task. Review the answers as a class.

Figure 5.4 Kanji found in the names of shukuba. Excerpt from the student activity handout.

1. The following kanji appear in the names of shukuba along the Tokaido. Categorize the kanji according to their meaning.

1. 沼	7. 津	13. 岡
2. 枝	8. 田	14. 藤
3. 谷	9. 坂	15. 土
4. 塚	10. 松	16. 草
5. 原	11. 崎	17. 石
6. 島	12. 海	18. 浜

Meanings related to water	Meanings describing physical features	Meanings describing botanical objects

Now begin Activity 4. Have students listen to the conversation between the Japanese teacher and her student (found on the Activity 4 CD file). In this conversation, the teacher and student discuss the cities along the Tokaido that used to be shukuba. The teacher describes the *sekisho* (checkpoints) at which travelers on the Tokaido were obliged to register.

After students have listened to the conversation twice, lead them in a discussion of the shukuba and sekisho: Why did the bakufu establish sekisho where they did? How did the sekisho help the central government monitor and control the movement of supplies and people throughout the country? What information or identification would travelers be expected to present at these checkpoints?

Finally, have students work in pairs to practice expressions that describe spatial relationships between two locations, and complete the fill-in-the-blank activity.

EXPANSION

Ask students to create stories in Japanese explaining how the various shukuba got their names. An example:

藤岡: むかし、藤原家の人がこの町を通った時、近くの丘 (岡) の上で詩を書きました。 "Once upon a time, a member of the Fujiwara family passed by and wrote a poem on the top of a nearby hill."

These stories can be entirely fictional, even humorous. The object is to give students a chance to practice both their storytelling skills and their kanji writing skills, which will help students to remember the names of the shukuba.

TEACHING TIPS

As students categorize characters by meaning, remind them to pay attention to radicals. In complex characters, the meaning is more often contained in the left part of the character, while the right part gives a hint on pronunciation.

ACTIVITY 5 (DAY 4)

Kaempfer's Journey on the Tokaido

PREVIEW

Introduce Engelbert Kaempfer using images provided on the CD (Transparencies 1 and 2). This German doctor accompanied a daimyo gyoretsu and traveled from Nagasaki to Edo in 1691. Review the Tokugawa bakufu's seclusion policy and attitude toward foreigners and foreign influence (covered in Unit 4).

FOCUSED LEARNING

Using the handouts of Kaempfer's travel schedule and the map, have students determine and record the details of his trip: When did he leave Mishima? When did he arrive in Edo? In which shukuba did he stay? How many kilometers per day did he travel? Figure 5 shows an excerpt from this activity.

Next, give students the short reading activity about Edo-era travel in general and Kaempfer's journey in particular. Reinforce the key vocabulary words that students learned in the previous activity.

TEACHING TIPS

To make these activities more interactive and communicative, find Kaempfer's travel schedule for a longer period of time (see Literature Resources), and divide the schedule into four sequences. For each sequence, develop worksheets like the ones in this lesson. Divide the class into four groups, and give each group one of the four sequences. When each group has completed their section of the schedule, rearrange the class into four new groups, making sure that each group has at least one representative from each of the original four groups. Then, have these new groups put the entire schedule into the proper sequence *without* looking at their worksheets, by asking each other questions and exchanging information orally. When they've come to a consensus, compare final sequences as a class.

Figure 5.5 Exploring Kaempfer's travel schedule on the Tokaido. Excerpt from the student activity handout.

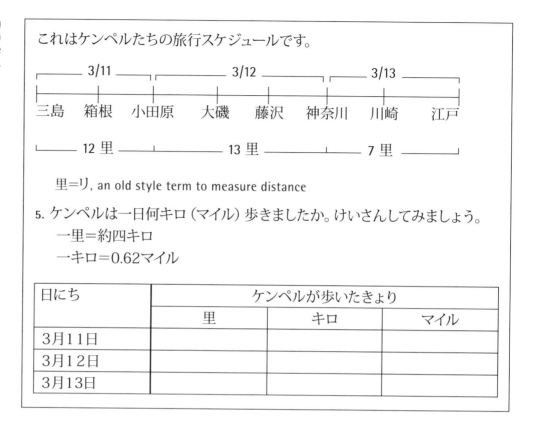

これはケンペルたちの旅行スケジュールです。

3/11		3/12		3/13
三島　箱根　小田原	大磯　藤沢	神奈川　川崎		江戸
12 里		13 里		7 里

里＝リ, an old style term to measure distance

5. ケンペルは一日何キロ（マイル）歩きましたか。けいさんしてみましょう。
一里＝約四キロ
一キロ＝0.62マイル

日にち	ケンペルが歩いたきょり		
	里	キロ	マイル
3月11日			
3月12日			
3月13日			

EXPANSION

Compare Kaempfer's travel journal with other famous travel journals, such as the account of the Lewis and Clark expedition. How are they similar or different?

Based on what students have learned about daimyo gyoretsu, have them write a fictional journal entry describing what it might have been like to be part of one of these processions.

ACTIVITY 6 (DAY 5)

Different Facilities and Occupations

PREVIEW

Have students brainstorm the following: What kinds of hotels are available to travelers today? Where do wealthy people stay? Where do common people stay? Who works to serve the needs of travelers, and what do they do for them?

FOCUSED LEARNING

Using four of the ukiyoe depicting representative shukuba provided on the CD, introduce some of the different facilities available to travelers in the Edo period and how people in different social strata traveled or helped travelers (Figure 5.6). Familiarize students with the range of occupations and social statuses that people occupied in Tokugawa Japan using the reading handout provided. When they have finished the reading, have students work in groups to identify the occupations of the individuals depicted in the ukiyoe. Lead a discussion about the facilities available on the Tokaido and the occupations that people pursued on it: Which of these facilities or occupations were surprising to students? Which would they prefer to work in, and why?

EXPANSION

Give students a list of modern people and have them decide which shukuba they would stay in (for example, the president of the United States, a teacher, a truck driver, a traveling salesman, a movie star, or an artist). Alternatively, assign the shukuba depicted in the ukiyoe to different groups of students and have them draw up a list of the kinds of modern people who might stay in them.

Show more ukiyoe and have students practice describing pictures.

TEACHING TIPS

Visual learners are more likely to focus on the ukiyoe, while analytical learners are more likely to focus on filling in the lists of facilities and occupations. Pair up students with these different learning styles so that each can benefit from the information gained by the other.

Figure 5.6 Ukiyoe depicting facilities for travelers during the Edo period.

ACTIVITY 7
(DAYS 6–7)

Social Hierarchy System

PREVIEW

Before starting this activity, ask students to describe the visual style and subject matter of typical ukiyoe.

FOCUSED LEARNING

Using Handout 1, introduce students to the social hierarchy system of the Edo period, shinokosho. Display the question and answer choices on Transparency 1, and have the class guess the correct answers. Each question is sequenced in such a way that students will gradually understand how the system worked and which governmental agendas were advanced through this system. Ask follow-up questions to promote students' imagination and reasoning skills. See Figure 5.7 for sample questions.

Next, give students the shinokosho reading activity, Handout 2. This will help students build on the vocabulary they learned in the previous activity.

As a post-reading activity, have students debate the purpose and effectiveness of the shinokosho system based on what they have learned, using Handout 3. Students should create graphs and compare the numbers of people in different occupations in the Edo period to current numbers today.

Figure 5.7 The social hierarchy system of the Edo period. Excerpt from the student activity handout.

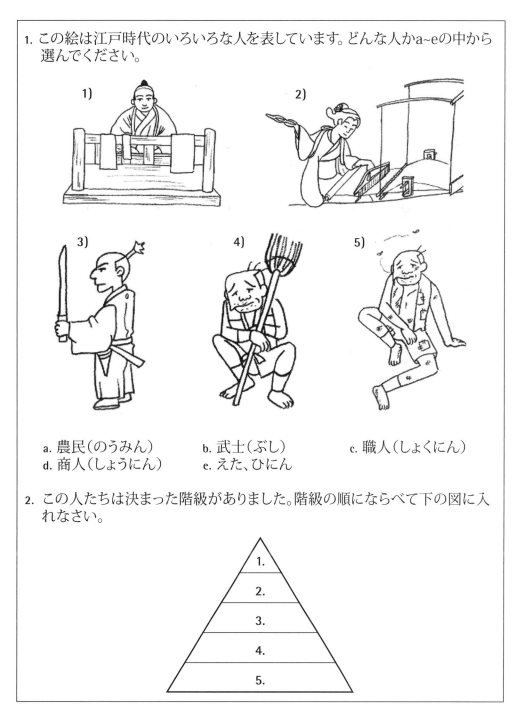

1. この絵は江戸時代のいろいろな人を表しています。どんな人かa~eの中から選んでください。

1)
2)
3)
4)
5)

a. 農民（のうみん）　　b. 武士（ぶし）　　c. 職人（しょくにん）
d. 商人（しょうにん）　　e. えた、ひにん

2. この人たちは決まった階級がありました。階級の順にならべて下の図に入れなさい。

1.
2.
3.
4.
5.

EXPANSION   Ask students to divide contemporary American society into four levels like the shinokosho. How do these social divisions compare? Which group would students like to be part of?

If time permits, ask students to divide modern Japanese society into four levels like the shinokosho. How do these social divisions compare both with the Edo system and with modern America? What accounts for the differences?

Discuss *eta* and *hinin*, such as the reasons why the bakufu made this social rank and how the discrimination against their ancestors continues in current times.

TEACHING TIPS   Discussions of class in America can be difficult. Be careful to keep the discussion in general terms so that no students feel they are being targeted or denigrated. If students have difficulty identifying different classes in America, refer them back to the previous activity in which different classes of people stayed in different shukuba.

ACTIVITY 8
(DAYS 8–10)

Tokaido Travelers in the Edo Period and Today

PREVIEW   Lead students in a quick review of the major elements covered in this unit: the Gokaido, shukuba and sekisho, bakufu politics, and social stratification in Tokugawa Japan.

FOCUSED LEARNING   Ask students to brainstorm scenarios describing how people typically travel from Kyoto to Tokyo today. Have students form groups and pick one scenario to develop more fully. For example, the scenario might involve a salaried worker with a wife and teenage son who goes to Tokyo for business. Students should compare this person's experience to that of business travelers on the Tokaido during the Edo period using the chart provided (Figure 5.8). Students should research their scenarios using the Internet and other resources and prepare a presentation in Japanese for the class using PowerPoint or other presentation software. After each group gives their presentation, the materials can be collected, organized, and displayed in the classroom.

EXPANSION   As an expansion activity (or as an option for the group presentation), encourage students to create a skit in which they act out a journey from Kyoto to Edo (Tokyo) in both modern and Tokugawa times.

If suitable for online viewing, materials created for these group presentations can be compiled, arranged, and added to the Web site developed in the previous unit on Tokugawa Japan.

Figure 5.8 Idea organizer for Tokaido travelers. Student handout.

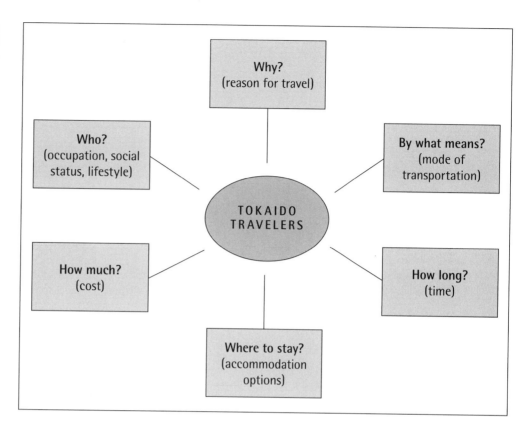

TEACHING TIPS

To prepare students for the group project, review the process for typing Japanese characters and pasting them in tables and charts. If possible, form groups so that at least one student in each group has experience in this area.

Assessment

In this unit, the group presentation will serve as the basis for summative assessment. The scoring guide for the summative assessment is provided on the CD.

ASSESSMENT CRITERIA

A rubric for this unit is provided in appendix A. The rubric contains an array of evaluation criteria, and not all may be applicable to each activity of this unit. Teachers should consider the nature of the task and choose the appropriate items from the rubric for evaluation.

Unit 6

Kaempfer's Journal

Target Age: High school, university

Language: Japanese

ACTFL Proficiency Level: Intermediate High or above

Primary Content Area: World history

Connections to Other Disciplines: Political science, geography, art, literature

Time Frame: 8 50-minute class periods

OBJECTIVES Students will be able to:

- Describe scenery and nature.
- Narrate past events and incidents.
- Express personal feelings and opinions.
- Compare and contrast the way people traveled in the Edo period and how people travel in the present time.

DESCRIPTION This is the last of three units on the Tokugawa era in Japan. Students are expected to have studied the previous two units (Tokugawa Japan and Tokaido Travelers) prior to tackling this unit, and should possess some basic knowledge of the Edo era. Students should also be familiar with basic expressions for describing things and expressing time and space transitions. This unit is designed for high school Japanese classes (third year and above) as well as university Japanese classes (second year and above).

This unit encourages students to explore Japanese history through literary texts, art works, and pop culture artifacts, and by making connections between historical events and their own contemporary experience. First, students are introduced to *Ryoko Yojinshu* (a travel guidebook written in 1810), Matsuo Basho (the most famous haiku poet and traveler of the 17th century), and *Tokaidochu Hizakurige* (*Traveling the Tokaido on Foot*, a comic travelogue written in 1802). Students use these primary source materials to learn how travelers in the Edo period prepared for their trip, what

Standards Addressed

NETS•S

3, 4, 5

STANDARDS
FOR FOREIGN
LANGUAGE
LEARNING

Communication Standards 1.1, 1.2, 1.3
Cultures Standard 2.1
Connections Standard 3.1
Comparisons Standard 4.2

NATIONAL
STANDARDS FOR
HISTORY FOR
GRADES 5–12

© National Center for History in the
Schools, UCLA, http://nchs.ucla.edu

Standard 1: Chronological Thinking

    A. Distinguish between past, present, and future time.

Standard 2: Historical Comprehension

    A. Reconstruct the literal meaning of a historical passage.

    C. Read historical narratives imaginatively.

    G. Draw upon visual, literary, and musical sources.

Standard 3: Historical Analysis and Interpretation

    A. Identify the author or source of the historical document or narrative.

    E. Analyze cause-and-effect relationships and multiple causation, including the importance of the individual, the influence of ideas, and the role of chance.

Standard 5: Historical Issues—Analysis and Decision-Making

    A. Identify issues and problems in the past.

    C. Identify relevant historical antecedents.

they brought with them, and what precautions they took and why. They are then encouraged to compare and contrast the past and the present on these issues.

Next, students read journal entries from *Kaempfer's Japan: Tokugawa Culture Observed*, a German travelogue modified and translated into Japanese. The author, Engelbert Kaempfer (1651–1716), was a German doctor who worked for a Dutch trading house in Nagasaki in the early 1690s. He accompanied the members of the trading house when they traveled to Edo (Tokyo) to see the Tokugawa shogun. Students will read four entries in which Kaempfer describes his travel adventures on the Tokaido. The journal reveals how people traveled and interacted with one another and nature along the Tokaido, reflecting the social and religious beliefs that held sway in Tokugawa Japan. Students review how the Tokugawa bakufu ruled the nation by utilizing different systems of control such as shinokosho and sankin kotai (both covered in Unit 5). Ukiyoe are used in this unit to give students a sense of the popular tastes and mores of the era and to encourage the learning of vocabulary used to describe scenery and nature. Students also practice narrating events and incidents and expressing their own feelings and opinions. Finally, students develop a picture-story show (*kamishibai*) based on an ukiyoe.

CONNECTIONS TO OTHER DISCIPLINES

This unit lets students engage with Japanese *history* through arts, literary texts, and pop culture. In other words, students step into the Edo period of Japan from different entry points and take multiple paths to explore and experience the era. This is different from studying history using a textbook written by a single author. This multi-faceted approach introduces students to various viewpoints and different aspects of history often omitted in textbooks.

Learning academic content in a second language helps language learners to develop a higher level of proficiency. One obvious reason is that students learn vocabulary that goes beyond the basic terms used in daily conversations. In this unit, students learn vocabulary for *history*, *geography*, and *political science*, such as peasant, castle, volcano, social class, and social system. Students are also exposed to abstract words such as incident, feeling, poor, and preparation. Learning academic content in a second language exposes students to higher-level vocabulary in context and provides authentic reasons to learn and use the vocabulary for communication.

SPOTLIGHT ON TECHNOLOGY

Word Processing: Students can use word processing software to prepare the script for their picture-story show.

Internet: The lessons use visual aids (prints, pictures, maps) from various Web sites. Students may use images from the Internet to create their final project, provided permission is obtained for copyrighted material.

Video Projection: If the classroom is equipped with a computer and video projection device, teachers can use them (rather than the board) to lead many of the activities and record student responses during class discussion. A projector may also be used for student presentations.

Photograph Manipulation Software: For the final project, students can use image manipulation software if they wish.

Presentation Software: Students can use presentation software for their picture-story show if they wish.

Video Editing Software: Students may use video editing software as a follow-up activity for the final project.

TECHNOLOGY RESOURCES NEEDED

Hardware
 computers with Internet access
 video projection device

Software
 word processing software (optional)
 image manipulation software (optional)
 presentation software (optional)
 video editing software (optional)

SUPPLEMENTARY
RESOURCES

Web Resources

Ando Hiroshige: The Fifty-Three Stations of the Tokaido Road:
www.hiroshige.org/hiroshige/tokaido/tokaido.htm

Japanese Prints at the Hood Museum of Art: Along the Tokaido Highway:
www.dartmouth.edu/~ukiyoe/tokaido/

Literature Resources

Ikku, J. (1995). Tokaidochu Hizakurige (Traveling the Tokaido on foot). In
Y. Nakamura (Ed.), *Nihon koten bungaku zenshu*, vol. *81*. Tokyo: Shogakkan.

Kaempfer, E. (1998). *Kaempfer's Japan: Tokugawa culture observed* (edited, translated, and annotated by Beatrice M. Bodart-Bailey). Honolulu, HI: University of
Hawaii Press. (Original work published 1727)

Traganou, J. (1995, September). Impact of railways on Japanese society and culture:
The Tokaido—Scenes from Edo to Meij eras. *Japan Railway & Transport Review,
13*, 17–27.

Vaporis, C. N. (1989). Caveat viator: Advice to travelers in the Edo period [includes
trans. of Yasumi Roan's 1810 Ryoko Yojinshu (The art of traveling or precautions
for travelers)]. *Monumenta Nipponica 44*(4), 461–484.

Kamishibai

Information and examples of kamishibai can be found at www.kamishibai.com.

Traditional kamishibai with beautiful illustrations and English translations on
the back can be ordered from: Kamishibai for Kids, PO Box 629, New York, NY
10025. 212-663-2471, 800-772-1228

teaching
the unit

Kaempfer's Journal

The following outline provides a summary of activities. Complete activities and
resources are found on the accompanying CD.

ACTIVITIES 1 AND 2
(DAY 1)

Ryoko Yojinshu ACTIVITY 1

Matsuo Basho ACTIVITY 2

PREVIEW

As a warm-up for Activity 1, have students brainstorm how they prepare for a trip:
what food and clothing do they take with them, what kind of identification and funds
do they need to carry, what problems might they encounter along the way, and how
do they prepare for the unexpected?

FOCUSED LEARNING

Introduce *Ryoko Yojinshu*, a traveler's guidebook written in 1810, using the picture of
the book provided on the Activity 1 CD file. Show students the list of suggestions for
travel preparation that have been selected from the book and translated into modern

Japanese. Ask students to indicate which of these things are still done in some form by travelers today, and which are not.

Then, show students the list of things that travelers in the Edo period did to avoid the problems and dangers they might encounter on the road. Have students match each activity with the appropriate problems or dangers (Figure 6.1).

Next, introduce Matsuo Basho (using the illustration of him provided on the Activity 2 CD file) and ask students to guess what Basho carried on his travels around Japan. Direct students to read the paragraph explaining what Basho carried with him, and have them discuss this paragraph in groups. What surprises them the most about the preparations Basho made for his travels?

Finally, show the images from the popular novel *Tokaidochu Hizakurige* provided on the CD. The two main characters in this book, Yaji-san and Kita-san, were comical figures who traveled around Japan in the Edo period. Using the fill-in-the-gap activity provided, have students write down what these characters carried with them when they traveled and why they did so.

EXPANSION

Have students work in groups to create a short skit depicting Edo-era travelers preparing for a trip along the Tokaido.

TEACHING TIPS

Have students work on the activities in pairs if the vocabulary is too difficult for them. The second activity assumes that students know the grammar points ようにする、から、とき, and と. Modify the sentences if your students have not learned any of these grammatical structures.

Figure 6.1 Avoiding the pitfalls of travel in Edo-period Japan. Excerpt from the student activity handout.

2. 江戸時代の人は旅行をしている時、どんなことに注意したと思いますか。それは、どうしてだと思いますか。a〜e の中から、選んでください。

a. お腹がすいていても、食べ過ぎないようにしました。(　)

b. 旅館に着いた時、出入り口を確かめました。(　)

c. 疲れていても、道端で寝ないようにしました。(　)

d. 五、六人以上のグループで旅行しないようにしました。(　)

e. 荷造りをするときは、着物を油紙[7]で包みました。(　)

1) 虫にさされるからです。

2) 火事の時、すぐ逃げられるからです。

3) 川をわたる時、ぬれるからです。

4) 食べ過ぎると、かごや馬から落ちるからです。

5) みんなの都合が合わないと、いろいろ不便だからです。

ACTIVITY 3 (DAY 2)

Crossing the Tenryu River

PREVIEW

Reintroduce Engelbert Kaempfer using his portrait (Transparency 1) and the script in the Teacher Presentation Sample Script section on the CD. (Kaempfer is introduced in the previous unit, Tokaido Travelers. If your students have not done Unit 5, Activity 5, have them complete it before doing this activity.)

FOCUSED LEARNING

Using Handout 1, check to see how much students remember of Kaempfer's journey: why he traveled, how he traveled, how far he traveled and how much time it took, and the distance he traveled each day.

Using Handout 2 and the ukiyoe depicting three *shukuba machi* that Kaempfer passed through on his journey, have students speculate how many residential homes each town or village had, what other buildings besides residential homes existed on the route, what travelers did for their meals, and how they crossed rivers (Figure 6.2).

Direct students to do the reading activity provided on the CD (Handout 3). To help them with this challenging text, have them circle the names of rivers and draw squares around the names of towns and villages. Show them the map of the Tokaido and have students identify the towns mentioned in the passage. Ask them to select the illustration that best matches the route Kaempfer took on that day. Then, have them use the information in the reading to determine which of their speculations in Handout 2 were correct.

EXPANSION

The Tokugawa bakufu did not create bridges for big rivers like the Tenryu. Have students discuss the government's reasons for not doing so. Review the sekisho and other ways that travel was controlled by the bakufu.

Have students imagine what sorts of people lived and worked in the buildings Kaempfer describes. While all social classes—*bushi* (warriors), *shonin* (merchants), and *nomin* (peasants)—might be found in the shrines and gates along the Tokaido, only bushi lived in the castles.

TEACHING TIPS

For some students, the vocabulary level of the reading passage will be very challenging. If necessary, simplify and condense the text and make it more approachable by changing difficult and obscure words into simpler expressions and shortening descriptive information.

Figure 6.2 Kaempfer travels the Tokaido. Excerpt from the student activity handout.

a. 町（村）には家が何けんあるか。

＜想像＞	＜旅行記からわかること＞

b. 家の他にどんな建物があるか。

＜想像＞	＜旅行記からわかること＞

ACTIVITY 4 (DAY 3)

Fire in Kakegawa City

PREVIEW

Show students the ukiyoe of Kakegawa city (Transparency 1) and introduce the reading material with the script provided on the CD.

FOCUSED LEARNING

Distribute Handout 1 and ask students to read the passage carefully.

Give students adequate time to complete the reading. To help them understand this difficult passage, ask them to match the list of natural phenomena-related vocabulary in task 1 on the handout with the appropriate pronunciation and meaning. Then, have students put the four pictures in task 2 that illustrate events Kaempfer experienced in Kakegawa in the correct chronological sequence (Figure 6.3).

Check the students' understanding of the vocabulary words and grammar points underlined in the text, particularly those words expressing the time relationship between two events such as その時, "it was then," and ～うちに, "in the meantime." Review time-related vocabulary such as とつぜん, "suddenly," and あっという間に, "in an instant," and ask students to use these words in a sentence. Review the use of そう (predictions and suppositions), ～てくる, and the conditional と. Check the students' understanding of these expressions with a fill-in-the-blank activity based on a text that narrates a series of events.

EXPANSION   Have students practice these terms in pairs or groups by narrating a series of events that happened to them recently using the target vocabulary.

TEACHING TIPS   When you introduce the words related to natural phenomena, have students guess the meaning from the kanji characters. To help students memorize the kanji characters, have them draw pictures illustrating how the kanji is made.

When working on the fill-in-the-blank activity, visual learners can be encouraged to turn the story into a comic strip with four illustrations.

Figure 6.3 Kaempfer visits Kakegawa. Excerpt from the student activity handout.

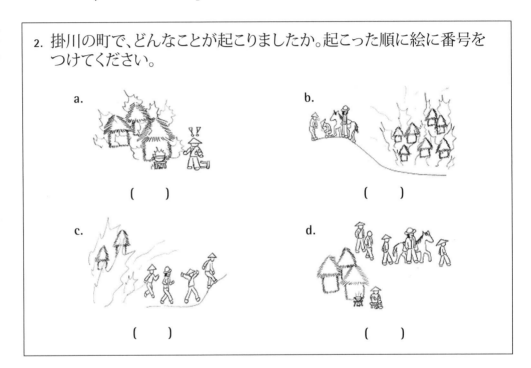

ACTIVITY 5 (DAY 4)

Mt. Fuji

PREVIEW   Tell students that they are going to read a section of Kaempfer's journal in which he describes Mt. Fuji. Show the ukiyoe and photo of Mt. Fuji provided on the CD and have students speculate on the features of Mt. Fuji that might have attracted Kaempfer's attention. Write their ideas on the board (or use a computer and projection device), grouping similar features together and gathering a range of responses.

FOCUSED LEARNING   Give students adequate time to read the text, and then divide them into groups to discuss how close their speculations were to Kaempfer's description of Mt. Fuji. Have each group report to the whole class. With the true-or-false and short answer activities provided, check their comprehension. Complete the lesson with a discussion activity.

EXPANSION

The reading describes how Edo-era people climbed Mt. Fuji to worship the god of wind. Talk about similar mythologies surrounding mountains and the ways that humans relate to them (Mt. Olympus in ancient Greece, Mt. Sinai in the Bible, Pike's Peak in the Old West, etc.).

TEACHING TIPS

To encourage students to use the target vocabulary when speculating about Kaempfer's description of Mt. Fuji, ask them questions that will elicit the descriptions that appear in the reading (e.g., Are there trees and bushes?).

ACTIVITY 6 (DAY 5)

A Poor Village

PREVIEW

Tell the students that the last journal entry they are going to read starts with 元吉原は貧しい町で ("Motoyoshiwara is a poor village"). Tell them that in this passage, Kaempfer describes the village and his interactions with local children. In pairs, have them speculate on how he describes these children.

FOCUSED LEARNING

Have students read the passage on the handout once. The first task asks students to discover from reading the text out how close their speculations were. The next three tasks will help students interpret the text. In task 2, students review a list of actions and events and decide whether they involved Kaempfer or the children (Figure 6.4). In task 3, students scan the text and underline phrases that illustrate the poverty of the village, and discuss them in groups. The fourth task asks students to find and describe how travelers on the Tokaido carried money, and then draw a picture illustrating it. Task 5 has the students working in pairs to review shinokosho and deepen their understanding of the system.

Figure 6.4 Kaempfer describes a poor village. Excerpt from the student activity handout.

2. 次の行動をしたのはケンペルですか。子供達ですか。あてはまるものを○で囲んでください。(こうどうする: to take an action)

　a. 馬やかごにかけよって来る。　　　　　　（ケンペル、子供達）

　b. とんぼがえりをしてはねまわる。　　　　（ケンペル、子供達）

　c. 金をねだる。　　　　　　　　　　　　　（ケンペル、子供達）

　d. 金を投げる。　　　　　　　　　　　　　（ケンペル、子供達）

　e. 金をあらそって拾う。　　　　　　　　　（ケンペル、子供達）

EXPANSION   The poverty described in the text—particularly among peasant children—was very common in the Edo period. Review the shinokosho class system and what it meant for peasants, who far outnumbered the other classes. Have students discuss the social, political, and environmental dimensions of this poverty. What governmental agendas were served by keeping peasants poor? Was any assistance available? Were peasants doomed to remain poor or did some escape poverty? If so, how did they succeed?

ACTIVITY 7 (DAYS 6–8)

Picture-Story Show

PREVIEW   Review the four journal texts using the ukiyoe that depict the villages described by Kaempfer, and ask students to summarize what he experienced.

FOCUSED LEARNING   Working in groups, students make a *kamishibai* (picture-story show) that narrates an event and describes nature in the same way that Kaempfer does in his journal. Have them write a script and prepare pictures, using image manipulation software if they wish. If students use images from the Internet, they must obtain permission for copyrighted material. Give feedback on the script and have them practice the story. Have each group present their kamishibai to the class.

EXPANSION   These picture-story shows can be posted on the Web site created in Unit 4, Tokugawa Japan. Each picture-story can also be turned into a movie using video editing software, with students narrating the story and voice-acting. If you have a sister school in Japan, ask the students there to watch the picture-story show and give comments.

TEACHING TIPS   Show students a kamishibai to demonstrate how it works. Have the students pay attention to the timing for changing pictures. Arrange groups so that each group has at least one student who is good at illustrations and one student who is good at using technology.

Assessment

In this unit, the kamishibai project will serve as the basis for summative assessment. Evaluation should be based both on the script for the picture-story show and on the presentation in class. A scoring guide for the summative assessment is provided on the CD.

ASSESSMENT CRITERIA   A rubric for this unit is provided in appendix A. The rubric contains an array of evaluation criteria, and not all may be applicable to each activity of this unit. Teachers should consider the nature of the task and choose the appropriate items from the rubric for evaluation.

Content-Based Language Teaching with Technology

Introduction

LAURENT CAMMARATA AND DIANE J. TEDICK

Who as a foreign language teacher hasn't dreamed of making language learning a meaningful and fun experience? Who hasn't thought about bringing in content related to learners' interests and experiences and imagined what that might do to the overall dynamic of the language classroom? And who as a teacher hasn't wanted to weave his or her own passions into the language curriculum? The foreign language curriculum can bring in so much more than language! But this is possible only if a teacher uses a curricular approach that integrates language with content that is interesting to learners. Content-based instruction (CBI) is just such a curricular approach.

CBI echoes the voices of philosophers in education, such as Rousseau and Dewey, who have emphasized the importance of developing instruction that is meaningful to the students here and now—instruction that creates bridges between subject matter content and the learners' real-world experiences. CBI is also supported by the latest research in the fields of education, cognitive psychology, and second language acquisition. It has been identified as a key curricular approach in second/foreign language education (e.g., Brinton, Snow, & Wesche, 2003; Grabe & Stoller, 1997; Mohan, 1986), and it is very effective in a range of language settings, including immersion (e.g., Genesee, 1987, 1994; Johnson & Swain, 1997), English as a second language (e.g., Snow & Brinton, 1997), and more traditional foreign language contexts (e.g., Stryker & Leaver, 1997).

NOTE

The CoBaLTT program is funded by the U.S. Department of Education Title VI program through CARLA (www.carla.umn.edu/index. html) at the University of Minnesota. CoBaLTT staff members are Director Diane J. Tedick, Graduate Program Associate Laurent Cammarata, and Marlene Johnshoy, who provides technology instruction and Web support for the program.

The purpose of the Content-Based Language Teaching with Technology (CoBaLTT) professional development program is to help K–16 foreign language teachers become familiar with CBI and to provide tools to enable them to integrate this curricular approach into their teaching. The biggest challenge of weaving cognitively appropriate and meaningful content into existing foreign language teaching practice is that most curricula currently in place focus only on language (functions, grammar, vocabulary). The CoBaLTT program proposes a curricular framework that helps teachers learn how to integrate content and language.

The program combines a year-long professional development program with support from a Web Resource Center (www.carla.umn.edu/cobaltt/) to guide teachers through the process of planning CBI lessons and units. Through face-to-face instruction and online instructional modules the participants learn about:

- Key principles and rationales for CBI
- National standards and their relationship to CBI
- Curriculum development for CBI
- Instructional strategies for CBI
- Performance assessment for CBI
- Technological applications to support CBI

Each of these areas is taught through online instructional modules that provide readings (along with guided reading templates) and other activities for learning the concepts and supporting CBI instruction. CoBaLTT participants work through the modules and participate in face-to-face instruction throughout the year as they develop "mini" CBI units. They utilize the CoBaLTT curriculum framework, which is designed to aid them in developing the units. Following a CBI curricular organization, the units include a number of lessons that explore connected topics that all relate to an overarching main theme. The CoBaLTT curriculum framework is divided into three major sections: a unit overview section, a section for developing detailed lesson plans, and a unit assessment section (Figure 1). It is presented in an online template that includes many help windows to guide the curriculum development process.

Use These Units for Many Levels

The CoBaLTT units presented here were developed by teachers for specific needs, but the concepts and ideas are applicable to a wide variety of contexts and levels. The Le Moyen Âge en France unit, for example, could be adapted for use by middle school learners in immersion settings. The same themes of political, historical, and cultural change in the Middle Ages could be applied to German, Spanish, or Italian classes as well. Similarly, the Yo Soy el Agua unit, developed for elementary-school Spanish immersion students, could easily be adapted for either middle school or even high school learners of any language.

Figure 1. Example of the CoBaLTT curriculum template.

UNIT OVERVIEW

Lesson Title:

Submitted by:

Language:

Unit Cultural Theme or Academic Content Area:

Target Audience:

Grade:

Proficiency Level:

Standards:

Communication: ☐ 1.1 ☐ 1.2 ☐ 1.3

Cultures: ☐ 2.1 ☐ 2.2

Connections: ☐ 3.1 ☐ 3.2

Comparisons: ☐ 4.1 ☐ 4.2

Communities: ☐ 5.1 ☐ 5.2

Unit Time Frame:

Unit Overview:

Context:

General Unit References and Resources:

Figure 1 *(continued)*.
Example of the CoBaLTT
curriculum template.

LESSON TEMPLATE

Lesson Title:

Content Objectives:

    Content: Students will...

    Cultural: Students will...

Language Objectives:

    Content Obligatory: Students will...

    Content Compatible: Students will...

Learning Strategies: Students will...

Time Frame:

Materials Needed:

Description of Task:

    Preview phase (pre-activities):

    Focused learning phase (during-activities):

    Expansion phase (post-activities):

Formative Assessment:

Handouts / Attachments:

UNIT ASSESSMENT

Unit Title:

Submitted by:

Time Frame:

Materials Needed:

Description of Tasks:

Attachments Rubrics/Checklists:

Once units are complete, they are made available to other teachers through a database at the CoBaLTT Web Resource Center. The complete published units come with everything needed for other teachers to be able to use them right away such as downloadable attachments of materials. activities, and assessment rubrics.

The framework puts special emphasis on helping teachers develop clear objectives for each lesson of the unit. This is a departure from the focus on "unit objectives" in this publication. Therefore, we distinguish the two in the CoBaLTT units showcased in this volume by referring to unit *goals* in contrast to lesson *objectives*. Unit goals for both content and language are written broadly to identify the long-range aims of the unit as a whole. Lesson objectives, in contrast, are stated concretely and in detail so that teachers are clear about the content and cultural concepts they are teaching as well as the language that should be emphasized in individual lessons. Following the framework set forth by Snow, Met, and Genesee (1989), language objectives are organized into two categories—content-obligatory (i.e., necessary for learning about the content) and content-compatible (i.e., additional language that complements the content and enhances students' language learning). Lesson objectives also highlight specific learning strategies that may be important for the lesson. To ensure that teachers successfully integrate content and language in their lessons, it is important that they write clear and precise objectives that are assessable. The CoBaLTT unit framework is quite prescriptive, as it helps teachers who are new to CBI. It also serves to provide a standard framework for every unit so that they are written in enough detail for other teachers to use. Units culminate with final performance assessment projects and accompanying rubrics to assess students' language use and content knowledge.

NOTE

For more information on the CoBaLTT Project, go to the Center for Advanced Research on Language Acquisition at the University of Minnesota (www.carla.umn.edu/cobaltt/).

This volume contains three CoBaLTT units, one for the elementary Spanish immersion context, one for French for middle school students, and one for French at the high school level. The print material includes a summarized version of each unit, and the accompanying CD provides the complete version with all the necessary handouts and rubrics. We adapted all three of the units from their original versions to incorporate an additional focus on technology. These three units and others available at the Web site are designed to be manageable even if access to technology is not sufficient to allow for effective integration of it in the curriculum. We invite you to visit the CoBaLTT Web Resource Center (www.carla.umn.edu/cobaltt/) to learn more about this project and about ways to integrate language and content instruction. It's free and geared toward teachers who are interested in learning more about CBI as well as teacher educators who teach about CBI.

REFERENCES

Brinton, D. M., Snow, M. A., & Wesche, M. (2003). *Content-based second language instruction* (2nd ed.). Ann Arbor, MI: University of Michigan Press.

Genesee, F. (1987). *Learning through two languages: Studies of immersion and bilingual education.* Cambridge, MA: Newbury House.

Genesee, F. (1994). *Integrating language and content: Lessons from immersion.* (Educational Practice Report No. 11). Santa Cruz, CA, and Washington, DC: National Center for Research on Cultural Diversity and Second Language Learning.

Grabe, W., & Stoller, F. L. (1997). Content-based instruction: Research foundations. In M. A. Snow & D. M. Brinton (Eds.), *The content-based classroom: Perspectives on integrating language and content* (pp. 5–21). New York: Longman.

Johnson, K., & Swain, M. (1997). *Immersion education: International perspectives.* New York: Cambridge University Press.

Mohan, B. A. (1986). *Language and content.* Reading, MA: Addison Wesley.

Snow, M. A., & Brinton, D. (Eds.). (1997). *The content-based classroom: Perspectives on integrating language and content.* New York: Longman.

Snow, M. A., Met, M., & Genesee, F. (1989). A conceptual framework for the integration of language and context in second/foreign language instruction. *TESOL Quarterly, 23*(2), 201–216.

Stryker, S. B., & Leaver, B. L. (1997). *Content-based instruction in foreign language education: Models and methods.* Washington, DC: Georgetown University Press.

Unit 7

Le Moyen Âge en France

Target Age: High school

Language: French

ACTFL Proficiency Level: Intermediate Mid to Intermediate High

Primary Content Area: World history

Connections to Other Disciplines: Geography, architecture, art, literature, political science

Time Frame: 5 weeks

UNIT GOALS   Students will:

- Explore the history of France during the Middle Ages (about 476 to 1453 A.D.).
- Learn about major events during the Middle Ages.
- Investigate the topics of governance and leadership, challenges (war, famine, disease), and cultural and artistic creations.
- Learn about the effect of events, people, and works of literature and art on medieval society.
- Address the question of why medieval heroes and artistic creations are still considered important today.
- Understand and use the present tense and past tenses (*imparfait, passé composé,* and *passé simple*) to engage in a variety of reading, writing, and speaking activities.
- Use a variety of learning strategies to extend academic skills.

DESCRIPTION   This unit is designed for a traditional fourth-year high school French class, including students who have studied French only in traditional classrooms as well as students who have completed an immersion program through the elementary and middle school years.

Standards Addressed

NETS•S   3, 4, 5

STANDARDS   Communication Standards 1.1, 1.2, 1.3
FOR FOREIGN Cultures Standards 2.1, 2.2
LANGUAGE   Connections Standards 3.1, 3.2
LEARNING   Communities Standard 5.1

In French IV at Edina (Minnesota) High School, students use the first half of the textbook *Trésors du Temps*, by Yvone Lenard, which provides an introduction to French history from prehistoric days to the end of the 16th century. The lessons in this unit utilize and enhance the materials in *Trésors du Temps*. During the course of this unit, students explore the history of France during the Middle Ages (about 476 to 1453 A.D.). As they learn about major events during this time frame, they investigate the topics of governance and leadership, challenges (war, famine, disease), and cultural and artistic creations. They learn about the effect of events, people, and works of literature and art on medieval society, and address the question of why medieval heroes and artistic creations are still considered important today.

CONNECTIONS TO   Topics in *geography, architecture, art, literature,* and *political science* can all be
OTHER DISCIPLINES explored through the content introduced in this unit. Each of these content areas is easily and naturally connected to the study of *history*. It is difficult to imagine, in fact, how students could learn about the Middle Ages in France without knowing something about the geography of medieval Europe or the geopolitical tensions at play at the time. Art and scripture were the two major means used to record knowledge during the Middle Ages, so they become important domains in this unit. The evolution of architecture and the building of cathedrals—projects that often lasted hundreds of years and involved generations of builders—represent an observable trace of the incredible social transformation that marked the transition between the Dark Ages and the Renaissance.

SPOTLIGHT ON   *Web Browsers and Asynchronous Communication Software:* The Internet has opened
TECHNOLOGY   many new possibilities that are particularly meaningful to teachers who want to implement CBI. It provides endless access to authentic materials, one of the biggest challenges identified by CBI instructors. Using e-mail, students can also go beyond the limited communication that occurs within the classroom environment and connect with experts to gather information regarding particular topics.

Word Processing Software: Word processing software such as Word can provide an opportunity for students to work on newsletters and journals for publication. Publishing brings another dimension to learning, as it gives students an opportunity to communicate to real audiences for meaningful purposes. This software also offers the ability to transpose documents into HTML format, which allows for online publication without requiring learners to possess programming knowledge.

Concept Mapping Software: Concept mapping software such as Inspiration can expand learners' ability to conceptualize and organize their knowledge, and can help them outline and plan more complex oral and written projects—an important academic skill for all content areas. Because this software requires learners to visually map their thinking processes, it can also help support different intelligences and learning styles.

Multimedia Authoring Tools: Using computer technology can increase opportunities for creation and expression. If computers are available and loaded with appropriate presentation software such as PowerPoint, students can integrate images, music, and other multimedia elements from the Internet into their work. Focusing on presenting for a particular audience and making information clear and appealing is a skill that high school students should practice extensively because they will benefit from it in the future.

TECHNOLOGY
RESOURCES NEEDED

Hardware
computers with Internet access (optional)
overhead or LCD projector
Web space on a server (optional)

Software
Internet browsing software and e-mail capabilities (optional)
word processing software (optional)
concept mapping software such as Inspiration (optional)
multimedia authoring tools such as PowerPoint (optional)

SUPPLEMENTARY
RESOURCES

Web Resources
De la fortification: http://sabreteam.free.fr/fortif2.htm
Liens vers des sites sur le Moyen Âge:
    http://his.nicolas.free.fr/Histoire/Liens/LiensHMAge.html
Le Moyen Âge:
    http://his.nicolas.free.fr/Histoire/Panorama/MoyenAge/MoyenAge.html
Les premiers châteaux forts:
    www.jecris.com/histoire/les-chateaux-du-moyen-age.html
La tour de Guinette: www.mairie-etampes.fr/visite/texteguinette.htm
Un voyage de plusieurs siècles en Gaule:
    http://perso.wanadoo.fr/jean-francois.mangin/

Literature Resources
Barroy, M.-H. (1984). *L'histoire de France par les mots croisés.* Paris: Éditions Retz.
Caselli, G. (1981). *La vie privée des hommes: Le Moyen Âge.* Paris: Hachette.

Caselli, G. (1998). *La vie privée des hommes: Des Celtes aux chevaliers du Moyen Âge.* Paris: Hachette Jeunesse.

Chamot, A. U., Barnhardt, S., El-Dinary, P. B., & Robbins, J. (1999). *The learning strategies handbook.* White Plains, NY: Addison Wesley Longman.

Gibbons, P. (2002). *Scaffolding language, scaffolding learning.* Portsmouth, NH: Heinemann.

Lenard, Y. (1997). *Trésors du temps.* New York: Glencoe/McGraw-Hill.

Mathiex, J. (1981). *Outils: Histoire de France.* Paris: Hachette.

Miquel, P. (1983). *La vie privée des hommes: Histoire des Français.* Paris: Hachette.

Nembrini, J.-L. (1996). *Histoire.* Paris: Hachette Livre.

teaching
the unit

Le Moyen Âge en France

The following section provides a brief synopsis of each activity. A more detailed description of the lesson activities, formative assessment strategies, and handouts is provided on the accompanying CD.

Introduction au Moyen Âge en France

ACTIVITY 1
(DAYS 1–3)

PREVIEW

To facilitate the introduction of this theme, begin by focusing on building background, an instructional strategy that is key to developing effective content-based units. First, organize the class into groups of four students. To help learners connect their background knowledge to the topic, access students' prior knowledge about the Middle Ages in France by asking them to brainstorm in groups answers to the following question: What do you know about the Middle Ages in terms of leaders and governance, challenges, cultural and artistic products, and values and beliefs?

Encourage groups to share their ideas with the class, and have a class secretary place the ideas on large poster paper. This will help the class establish a lexicon with key terminology, which will be written on a separate poster (this will target the content obligatory language objectives set for the lesson—see the CD for a detailed description). Add words to the list throughout the course of the unit.

A variation for teachers with access to computers and concept mapping software such as Inspiration is described on the CD.

FOCUSED LEARNING

This task requires students to find dates that correspond with particular events and then place this information on a timeline. Indicate chapters in textbooks (and Web sites, if desired) where students can locate the information. To complete this task, students must consult the textbooks (and Web sites) to find the dates, then copy their information onto a timeline. When done, have students share their findings with the class in an oral presentation.

EXPANSION

Students will use a graphic organizer to categorizes the information on the timeline. The categories are political and religious leaders, challenges, and artistic and cultural creations. See Figure 7.1.

Figure 7.1 Graphic organizer for Le Moyen Âge en France.

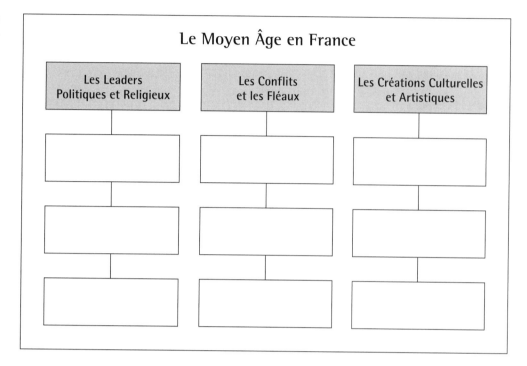

After students have completed their graphic organizers, lead a discussion that explores the following questions:

- What is the relationship between the three categories? (*Quel est le rapport entre les leaders, les conflits et les fléaux tels que la guerre et la peste, et les créations artistiques?*)

- In your opinion, given the constant wars and other challenges, what were the responsibilities of medieval leaders? (*À votre avis, étant donné les guerres continuelles et les autres conflits/épreuves de l'époque, quelle était la responsabilité des leaders au Moyen Âge?*)

TEACHING TIPS

Many variations of this activity are possible, depending on the knowledge base and reading level of the students. The most useful strategy to help students understand the reading has proven to be student skits, including props, a narrator, and a written summary. These skits can be done at any time during the unit, even throughout the unit, to enhance understanding.

ACTIVITY 2
(DAYS 4–8)

Les conflits et les fléaux au Moyen Âge

PREVIEW

The lesson begins with a review of the list of challenges established during the Expansion phase of Activity 1. You may wish to display Handout 1 at this time. Have students speculate on possible causes and effects for these challenges. Note the discussion points on an overhead transparency (or have a student do so).

FOCUSED LEARNING

Divide the students into groups of four and distribute Handout 1. Assign each group a topic to research (chosen randomly from this list of challenges). If computers are available, dedicate some class time to online research. Encourage students to explore historical Web sites to research their topic. Students will use their findings to complete a graphic organizer and write a one-paragraph summary in the past tense (using Handout 2; see Figure 7.2).

Figure 7.2 The challenges of the Middle Ages: Handout for graphic organizer and one-paragraph summary.

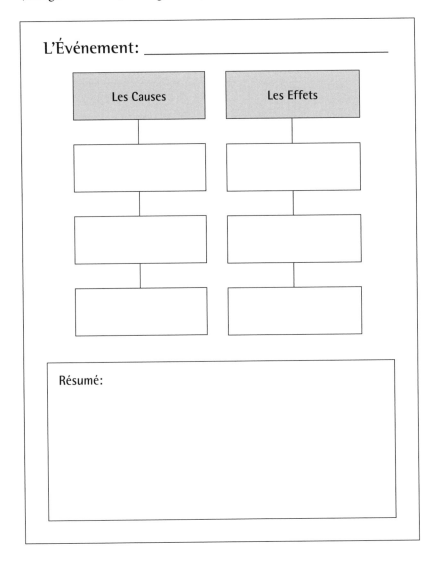

This task culminates in a jigsaw activity that requires students to reform in different groups. Within the new groups, one member of each of the previous groups will present to the others. Following the presentations, have each group identify similarities and differences among the events described and answer this question: Why was this event a challenge for people living in the Middle Ages in France? (*Pourquoi est-ce que cet événement représentait une épreuve pour les Français au Moyen Âge?*)

EXPANSION Ask a speaker from each group to present the group's list of similarities and differences as well as the group's answer to the discussion question. Then have the class brainstorm a list of current events that have similar causes or effects. An extension that incorporates the use of technology is described on the accompanying CD.

TEACHING TIPS As a variation for this activity, the entire group could work on a single event, such as the plague or the 100 Years' War. Students should work first in small groups, and then share their knowledge with the class as the teacher makes notes on the graphic organizer using an overhead or LCD projector.

ACTIVITY 3 (DAYS 9–12)

La féodalité

PREVIEW Begin class with a discussion of this question: What do you know about feudalism in medieval France? (*Que savez-vous de la féodalité en France au Moyen Âge?*) Note the ideas on a large sheet of paper. In the course of this conversation, introduce relevant content obligatory vocabulary. See the CD for a detailed description of the lesson's objectives.

FOCUSED LEARNING For the first task, students will read several texts describing the structure of feudalism, a fortified castle, and life in a castle in the Middle Ages. They may also read a text about knights, if you wish to also assign this. These texts are provided as Handouts 1 and 2 on the accompanying CD. Students will gain language practice during the course of this task by answering questions about the text, writing definitions for words, and rewriting sentences using different tenses. These reading and writing exercises may be completed over a period of several days. Students will also search for images and descriptions of *châteaux forts* (fortified castles) on the Internet.

For the second task, in class over a period of two days (less or more as needed), students in groups of four will complete the following:

- Self-correct the verbs they have written in the imperfect tense. The teacher will display text with verbs in the imperfect tense on an overhead transparency.
- Read the texts aloud with verb changes.
- Read and discuss the answers to the questions and the definitions of the words they have previously written.

EXPANSION   After the two tasks have been completed, hold a class discussion (or divide the class into two or three discussion groups). Review the challenges of the Middle Ages explored in Activity 2. Prompt students with questions, such as: How did feudal society and the fortified castle help people meet those challenges? What are some similarities and differences between the role of government and leaders in the Middle Ages and the present?

As an assessment, ask student groups to create a graphic organizer on a large sheet of paper to explain how society was organized during the Middle Ages. Have groups present their results to the class.

As a homework assignment, ask students to write a paragraph explaining how feudal society and châteaux forts helped people meet the challenges of life in the Middle Ages. Have them also analyze the disadvantages of this governance model.

ACTIVITY 4
(DAYS 13–17)

Des créations artistiques au Moyen Âge

PREVIEW   Begin the lesson with a brainstorming session in which students explore possible answers to the following questions:

- What are some examples of different types of artistic creations? (Examples include books, such as *Life of Pi*; movies, such as *The Day After Tomorrow*; and paintings, such as Monet's *Water Lilies*.)
- Why do people create art? (Possible answers include for personal expression, to entertain, to instruct, and to celebrate the actions of a famous person.)
- What is the role of art in a society?

FOCUSED LEARNING   Divide students into groups of three to five and distribute a list of skit ideas and resources (Handout 1). Assign a topic from the list or allow groups to choose their own. Then distribute a description of the task and a checklist (Handout 2). Have students research their topic. If computers are available (or a session in a computer lab can be scheduled), have students search the Internet for specialized Web sites that have images of medieval art work. Students will then be required to prepare and deliver a dramatic presentation to acquaint the class with their art piece as well as the role and importance of this cultural or artistic creation for society then and now.

Ideally, the presentation would be prepared and performed with the help of computer technology and software such as PowerPoint. If this option is selected, students may begin the task of gathering the material in class and then complete the PowerPoint presentation outside class as a group homework assignment.

EXPANSION   Lead a summary discussion, prompting students with this question: During a time when famine, the plague, wars, and invasions affected the daily lives of people, how did artistic creations improve people's lives?

TEACHING TIPS   It is interesting to expand this question to the present as well: how do artistic creations enrich our lives today?

ACTIVITY 5   # La vie de Charlemagne
(DAYS 18–20)

PREVIEW   Begin the lesson by asking students what they already know about kings and emperors to activate their background knowledge: What is a king? What is an emperor? What is the difference? Review with the class your previous discussions about the role of leaders in the Middle Ages and record (or ask a student to record) these ideas. As a final point of discussion, ask students what they already know about Emperor Charlemagne of France.

After the discussion, introduce the following homework assignment: students will read about the life of Charlemagne in the textbook *Trésors du Temps*. This will provide the necessary background for the following day's work. Students will be required to write down five main ideas from the text to share with their group the following day.

FOCUSED LEARNING   This phase of the activity has two parts: a presentation of key vocabulary terms and a dictogloss exercise. The whole class will first participate in the development of a vocabulary list, and then students will listen to and reconstruct the dictogloss text. These tasks are explained in great detail on the CD.

EXPANSION   The lesson concludes with a discussion in which students review and reflect on the facts of Charlemagne's life . This will help students prepare for the final assessment activity of the unit, which is to deliver a presentation about an important historical figure from the Middle Ages. The task requires students to work in small groups to discuss various questions about Charlemagne (available in detail in both English and French on the CD). Assign roles, such as recorder, speaker, task facilitator/time-keeper, and language coordinator. The recorder takes notes for the group. Following the small group work, the whole class discusses the questions. First, ask the speaker from each group to present the group's response to one of the questions, and then encourage the class to add comments.

TEACHING TIPS   Some students find this reading exercise to be quite challenging, so you may wish to have them use a pre-reading strategy to help with their comprehension. For instance, before beginning the Focused Learning, ask students to scan the textbook passage quickly to find the main points.

UNIT EXTENSION
ACTIVITIES

Have students discuss their personal concept of a hero: what qualities and/or actions make someone a hero? Have them give examples of personal heroes who are well known (e.g., Martin Luther King) as well as people they know well who are heroes for them (e.g., a parent or grandparent). Have students discuss these issues in small groups (four or five per group), followed by a large group discussion. Have each group create a list of characteristics of people they admire. Finally, ask students to write an essay describing a person they admire.

UNIT TEACHING
TIPS

Be flexible! Don't hesitate to adapt every lesson to the needs of your students. Keep students accountable for all the work they do. Use student skits to encourage and increase understanding. Incorporate games to help students retain vocabulary, dates, and other information. This is a vast topic, so don't hesitate to pare down the material and activities to suit the needs of your class.

ACTIVITY 6
(DAYS 21–27)

Assessment

DESCRIPTION
OF TASK

The final assessment of this unit is in the form of a culminating project, a type of assessment that places emphasis on the learning process and that is particularly well suited to CBI because it involves synthesis of content knowledge and language use in multiple modalities. For this task, students will be required to demonstrate knowledge of a key figure from the Middle Ages by introducing themselves as that person and presenting that historical figure's background and importance. They will answer the question "Why am I remembered today?" In answering this question, they will describe the person's life and accomplishments. If possible, they will do their presentations in the context of a school event to which other classes are invited.

Students will choose their historical figure (or names may be drawn at random) from a list provided by the teacher (Handout 1). They will then spend several days in class working on the research and writing. The remainder of the research and writing will be done at home.

Students will use the description of the project, checklist, and rubrics for the oral and written presentations to complete this task (Handouts 2, 3, and 4). They will hand in the written version of their presentation, and deliver their completed speeches to the class.

Finally, students will take a multiple-choice quiz put together by the teacher from questions prepared by the presenters.

TECHNOLOGY
ALTERNATIVES

The final presentation could be prepared and performed with the help of computer technology and software such as PowerPoint. One possibility is for students to conduct their research and gather their presentation material in a computer lab equipped with Internet connections (or at home if all students are equipped, which is rarely the case). If you decide to incorporate technology in your lesson plan, you will need to create a rubric to evaluate this use.

Also, you may encourage students to use asynchronous and synchronous communication to contact experts in the field (historians, scholars, etc.) or to post questions on specialized Web discussion boards. Include this in the rubric as a chance to gain extra points for the zealous students who always want to do more. All traces of communication will need to be recorded and presented to the teacher as proof that such attempts were made. You may wish to reward any attempts, successful or not, but give maximum points only to exchanges that resulted in the student receiving useful information.

Finally, consider publishing the final projects online (for instance, placing them on the school server, if available) to be shared with others and to stimulate future projects by modeling exemplary work.

TEACHING TIPS There are several things you can do to manage this process effectively. If possible, deliver a model presentation of a historical figure to help the students visualize exactly what is expected. As they begin their own work, set clear deadlines for each step of the process. In addition, remind students not to cut and paste from the Internet. They need to put all information into their own words. You could also allow students to do the project in pairs, with one student interviewing the historical figure. Remind students that they may not read their presentations, but must perform them.

ASSESSMENT CRITERIA Have students complete checklists as a self-assessment. Use the rubrics to evaluate their performance.

Rubrics for the assessment tasks in this unit are provided in appendix A.

Unit 8

Les Stéréotypes des Français

OVERVIEW

Target Age: Middle school

Language: French

ACTFL Proficiency Level: Intermediate Low to Intermediate Mid

Primary Content Area: Cultural studies

Connections to Other Disciplines: Social studies and psychology

Time Frame: 8 40-minute class periods; several 20-minute homework assignments

UNIT GOALS

Students will:

- Develop an awareness of how preconceived notions affect the way human beings live and experience the world they inhabit.
- Reflect on the many ways that stereotypes are created and maintained.
- Develop a sensitivity to issues related to cultural diversity and become more aware of the many prejudices that we human beings all carry within us.
- Identify common stereotypes Americans hold regarding other cultures and explore their insidious remodeling of actual realities.
- Use the present tense and past tenses (*passé composé* and *imparfait*) to engage in a variety of reading, writing, and speaking activities.
- Use a range of learning strategies to organize information, work cooperatively, and expand critical thinking skills.

DESCRIPTION

This unit is intended for a traditional fourth-year middle school French class. These fourth-year students are typically in the eighth grade and have completed the equivalent of one year of high school French. This means that they have mastered much general and basic survival vocabulary, including colors, numbers, clothing, food, geographical terms, and parts of the body, the house, and the town. They can recognize simple cognates. They can write sentences in the present tense without much

Standards Addressed

NETS•S   1, 3, 4, 5

STANDARDS
FOR FOREIGN
LANGUAGE
LEARNING

Communication Standards 1.1, 1.2, 1.3
Cultures Standards 2.1, 2.2
Connections Standards 3.1, 3.2
Comparisons Standard 4.2
Communities Standard 5.1

prompting. They are familiar with grammatical concepts central to basic French, such as gendered nouns, subject/verb agreement, adjective agreement, and correct word order.

This unit comprises four major lessons, which are distinct yet cumulative. In Activity 1, the students lay the groundwork for their examination of French stereotypes by generating those stereotypes themselves. They may draw, write, or find examples of what they think are "typical" French things. In Activity 2, they are required to change perspective—instead of being the examiners, they are the examined culture. Students look at various stereotypes of Americans, as shown through Web sites and books about Americans. Thus, in Activity 2, they begin to examine stereotypes and their relationship with truth. In Activity 3, they shift again to the role of examiners of French culture—the teacher shows movies, books, pictures, and Web sites that might reflect the same stereotypes the students generated in Activity 1. This lesson will demonstrate concretely to the students that the image they have of French people is created and maintained by strong forces in American culture. In Activity 4, learners explore those French stereotypes in more detail in order to understand their origins and relationships with daily life and reality in France today. These lessons culminate in a final multimedia presentation project in which small groups of students working collaboratively examine a cultural myth, a generalization, and a cultural reality of French people and show their relationship to French society today.

CONNECTIONS TO
OTHER DISCIPLINES

In this unit, students explore their own views toward the French and other nationalities' views toward Americans, connecting their learning to the discipline of *social studies*. These lessons delve into issues of cultural and social identity: What does it mean to be French? What does it mean to be American? Students will be led toward the understanding that within every culture lies tremendous individual variation. This unit can, therefore, serve as a logical trampoline to explore threads related to the field of *cross-cultural psychology*, which focuses on the intricate link between individual behavior and the cultural context within which it occurs, as well as on the diversity of human behavior.

SPOTLIGHT ON
TECHNOLOGY

Web Browsers: Students will use the Internet to explore questions about the origins of various stereotypes as well as to utilize the many reference materials available online to clarify terms with which they might not be familiar. More advanced students can seek out French-language publications and sources that address French and American stereotypes.

TrackStar: TrackStar allows teachers to easily compile a list of resources for students to access online. It is designed to help students explore a variety of sites related to a particular topic, and can be used as the starting point for online lessons and activities. Using this resource, teachers can collect Web sites, enter them into TrackStar, and add annotations for their students in order to create interactive online lessons called "Tracks." This online resource allows teachers to either create their own Track or use one of the hundreds of thousands already made by other educators, which are accessible online free of charge. Teachers can search the database by subject, grade, or theme and standard.

Word Processing Software: Word processing software such as Word can provide an opportunity for students to work on newsletters and journals for publication. Publishing brings another dimension to learning, as it gives students an opportunity to communicate to real audiences for meaningful purposes. This software also offers the ability to transpose documents into HTML format, which allows for online publication without requiring learners to possess programming knowledge.

Multimedia Authoring Tools and Web Publishing Software: Students will create a multimedia presentation that will be shared with others in the classroom, and can be published online, using software such as PowerPoint or HyperStudio. This activity will help learners develop skills in technology, language, and cooperative work.

Asynchronous Communication Software: Using e-mail, students can go beyond the limited communication that occurs within the classroom environment and connect with others to gather information regarding particular topics.

TECHNOLOGY
RESOURCES NEEDED

Hardware
   computers with Internet access
   television and videocassette or DVD player

Software
   Internet browsing software
   TrackStar (free online software)
   word processing software
   presentation software such as PowerPoint or HyperStudio
   Web publishing software (optional)
   e-mail capabilities (optional)

SUPPLEMENTARY
RESOURCES

Web Resources

Information on Stereotypes

Dynamique interculturelle et stereotypes:
www.mediation-interculturelle.com/IMG/pdf/TXT-Stereotypes.pdf
Although likely to be too advanced for middle school students, this Web site serves as an excellent resource for teachers of French and for more advanced learners. It provides information in French about stereotypes.

Nationalities and Their Stereotypes:
http://iteslj.org/Lessons/Counihan-Stereotypes.html

Stereotypes on Germans and Americans (a look at stereotypes from several perspectives): www.serve.com/shea/vorurtei.htm

TrackStar lesson on French stereotypes (type in track number 28811):
http://trackstar.4teachers.org/trackstar/

Articles in English about French Culture and News

About.com: http://gofrance.about.com

U.S. News and World Report: www.usnews.com

French Newspapers

Le Journal Français: www.journalfrancais.com

Le Monde: www.lemonde.fr/

L'Express: www.lexpress.fr/info/

Libération: www.liberation.com

Paris Match: www.parismatch.com

French Television Broadcasts

France 2: www.france2.fr/

France 3: www.france3.fr/

France 4: www.france4.fr/

France 5: www.france5.fr/

RFO: www.rfo.fr/

TFI: www.tf1.fr/

French Webcams

La Chaîne Météo: www.lachainemeteo.com

TF1: http://webcams.tf1.fr/webcam/

Learning Tools

TrackStar (free online software): http://trackstar.4teachers.org/trackstar/

Literature Resources

American Council on the Teaching of Foreign Languages (ACTLF). (1999). *Standards for foreign language learning in the 21st century.* Yonkers, NY: Author.

Faul, S. (1999). *Xenophobe's guide to the Americans.* London: Oval Books.

Short, D. (1993). Assessing integrated language and content instruction. *TESOL Quarterly, 27*(4), 627–647.

Yapp, N., & Syrett, M. (1999). *Xenophobe's guide to the French.* London: Oval Books.

teaching the unit

Les Stéréotypes des Français

The following section provides a brief synopsis of each activity. A more detailed description of the lesson activities, formative assessment strategies, and handouts is provided on the accompanying CD.

ACTIVITY 1 (DAYS 1–2)

Stereotype Simulation

PREVIEW

On the first day of the unit, have students complete a checklist to self-assess their knowledge of Web technology applications (the checklist is provided as Handout 1 on the accompanying CD). Then begin the lesson with a blank piece of paper and a pencil in the hand of each student. Instruct the students to close their eyes and imagine a typical French person in their heads. Then ask some guiding questions to help learners explore their stereotypes of the French (e.g., What do typical French people usually wear?).

Once you have covered the physical appearance of French people, turn to their surroundings. Where are these "typical French people"? What possessions do they have with them? What are they doing? For an example of what this brainstorming process produced in one class session, see Handout 2 on the CD.

FOCUSED LEARNING

After the image has been formed, have students write down everything they have imagined about the typical French person. If the students finish early, they can draw a picture of the person as well.

The students should then reveal their work and see how many people produced similar descriptions. Any shared items of description should be put on the board, with the teacher translating into French as needed. Then introduce students to the concept of stereotype and explain that it often refers to commonly held perceptions of a people or a culture.

Next, on another section of the board, ask students more specific impressions about the French (e.g., Where do they work? Where do they live? What are some hobbies?).

EXPANSION

On the next day of class, begin the final task of the lesson, organizing the stereotypes into the *Guide d'analyse des stéréotypes* chart (Handout 3; see Figure 8.1). This chart is organized in a 3 x 3 grid with the following categories: products, practices, and perspectives; and positive, negative, and neutral. Carefully explain each area to the students. Students should then, as you circulate the room, try to fit each of the stereotypes listed the previous day into the chart. For example, the stereotype of the French smoking all the time would be "negative" and "practice." France associated with good food would be "positive" and "product."

Have students start this handout in class and finish it for homework. Collect, grade, and keep this sheet to hand back during Activity 3: America Views France.

Figure 8.1 Handout for analyzing stereotypes.

Guide d'analyse des stéréotypes

Nom _____

	POSITIF	NÉGATIF	NEUTRE
Produits			
Pratiques			
Perspectives			

TEACHING TIPS

The brainstorming session on the first day of the activity can provide interesting insights into the students and how they perceive other cultures. A student in one class defended passionately the fact that French people were known for their use of gondolas, and this after a year of French study! It also lends insight into the motivations of some students in studying French; stylish girls usually picture their typical French person as a model decked out in the latest styles; a snowboarder once imagined snowboarders in the Alps; one rap aficionado imagined a rapper!

ACTIVITY 2 (DAY 3)

Stereotypes of Americans

PREVIEW

Begin this lesson with a collective reading of excerpts from the book *Xenophobe's Guide to the Americans*. This English book is one of a series that claims on the cover to take "an irreverent look at the beliefs and foibles of nations, almost guaranteed to cure Xenophobia." Nonetheless, the book does reflect some common stereotypes about Americans, without being overly negative or disparaging. In beginning this lesson with a group reading, steer students in the direction of constructive commentary. The sections entitled Attitudes and Values, Eating and Drinking, and Leisure and Pleasure should all elicit appropriate reactions. If this book is unavailable, similar documents may be used. The first link of the TrackStar on French stereotypes listed below can be a suitable replacement.

FOCUSED LEARNING

After students have completed the reading, have the class collectively discuss their impressions of the text and the stereotypes described within, with each student sharing his or her thoughts in French. This initial guided discussion should adjourn to the computer lab, where students will log on to the TrackStar lesson on French stereotypes. To do so, instruct the students to access http://trackstar.4teachers.org/trackstar/ and type in track number 28811 (see Figure 8.2).

Figure 8.2 The TrackStar lesson on stereotypes.

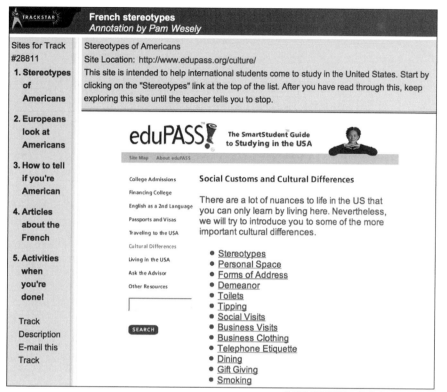

© 1995–2006 ALTEC at the University of Kansas

The first link is a set of instructions given to foreign students planning to study in the United States. This is a very unbiased and fair document, and it is included to reinforce (or replace!) the comments in the *Xenophobe's Guide*. After students have explored the first site, they should (on a cue from the teacher) move on to the second link. This link is much more controversial, and students may have more of a reaction to it. At this point, distribute another *Guide d'analyse des stéréotypes* (Handout 1) to the students and encourage them to fill it out using the stereotypes of Americans listed on the second site. Once they have finished the task, they should continue to the third link, which is another set of stereotypes of Americans (and French and Australians), which they can also add to their chart. By the end of the class period, they should try to have every box on the chart filled with at least one stereotype.

EXPANSION The final task in this lesson is a discussion of stereotypes and their relationship with the truth. Once students are back in the classroom, have them look at the American *Guide d'analyse des stéréotypes*, which they just filled out. They should then attempt to categorize each stereotype into one of three categories, based on their interpretation of its relationship with the truth: a cultural myth (it is not true at all, or it is no longer true), a generalization (it is true maybe for some members of the culture but not for all), and a cultural reality (it is pretty much true for all members of the culture). Instruct students to underline or highlight the stereotypes in three different colors to reference the three categories. Have the class collectively discuss their categorizations. Encourage students to express their agreement or disagreement, and to provide reasons to support their opinions. At the end of this lesson, collect, grade, and keep this sheet.

TEACHING TIPS   More mature students might be able to start this lesson with a brainstorming exercise similar to that used for the French in Activity 1. This is not recommended for younger students, however, because they are probably not aware of stereotypes of Americans and would find this exercise frustrating.

Students may be argumentative about, horrified by, or begrudgingly accepting of the stereotypes about Americans that are discussed. This activity in particular seems to heighten student awareness of cultural stereotypes, and some students may even become "experts" on the topic.

ACTIVITY 3 (DAY 4)   America Views France

PREVIEW   The preview for this lesson is a student assignment. First, hand back to students their *Guide d'analyse des stéréotypes* for the French (from Activity 1). Then send students out to find examples of stereotypes of the French in the American media, particularly ones that reflect items from their *Guide d'analyse*. Prompt them by mentioning Disney movies, television commercials, or shows in which French is spoken or the French people are portrayed. Each student must find at least one good example. Give them several days to complete this assignment, during which time other classroom work can be undertaken.

FOCUSED LEARNING   Once examples have been collected, have students informally present the images they found of the French in the American media. During and after their presentations, have the class fill out the *Présentations* worksheet (Handout 1; see Figure 8.3), which will assure their attention and their analysis. In order to do this sheet, they will need to keep their French *Guide d'analyse* nearby. After these presentations, round out the examples with any images you have collected. Pass back the students' original image of the "typical French person" from Activity 1. Each student should mark on the *Présentations* handout how many of the American images are mirrored on their original "typical" sheet.

EXPANSION   As a follow-up activity, discuss with the class reasons why the parallels between their personal stereotypes and the portrayal of French in the American media exist. Collect three things at the end of the lesson: the "typical French person" brainstorming list from Activity 1, the *Guide d'analyse* of the French, and the *Présentations* sheet.

Figure 8.3 Excerpt from Handout 1, *Présentations.*

Présentations

Nom _____

ÉLEVE	ORIGINE	DESCRIPTION	CLASSIFICATION	COMMENTAIRE

TEACHING TIPS

For this activity, you could require the students to find more than one example of a stereotype of the French. You could then refrain from presenting any examples yourself, and make the exchange and discussion more student-centered and student-run.

ACTIVITY 4
(DAYS 5–8)

Truth and Stereotypes

PREVIEW

Before class, select several video news clips for student viewing (see the CD for resources). Then have students watch the clips on their computers and rank them on a piece of paper in order of "Frenchness." This exercise will introduce students to the idea that some stereotypes are indeed visible and important in France, although other images and beliefs exist as well.

As a variation on this activity, ask students to explore and rank either TF1 Webcam feeds (http://webcams.tf1.fr/webcam/) or La Chaîne Météo Webcam feeds (www. lachainemeteo.com). You could also ask students to explore French Web sites and try to identify those that seem to be typical of France and those that seem atypical. Even if such an activity isn't as dynamic or interesting as watching videos, it still remains a practical alternative that can yield similar language learning experiences, especially during this phase of the lesson.

FOCUSED LEARNING

This task engages students in analyzing French stereotypes. To do this, redistribute their *Guide d'analyse des stéréotypes* of the French from Activity 1. Have students return to the TrackStar lesson and move on to item 4 to discover how much truth, if any, exists in these stereotypes. These articles are reports and informed analyses of French culture, ostensibly written in a way that avoids stereotypes. As the students read these articles, they should fill out Handout 1, *La vérité des stéréotypes* (see Figure 8.4), which asks them to classify stereotypes of France into categories of cultural myth, generalization, and cultural reality. Since students already did this with the American stereotypes in Activity 2, they should be able to work efficiently with only a short review.

Figure 8.4 Excerpt from Handout 1, *La vérité des stéréotypes.*

La vérité des stéréotypes

Nom _____

LES MYTHES CULTURELS	LES GÉNÉRALISATIONS	LES VERTIÉS CULTURELLES

EXPANSION

As a follow-up task, engage students in a more involved exercise based on the previous activity and on material to which they have been previously exposed. In small groups, have students complete Handout 2, *Les articles et les stéréotypes*, which will help them gain a deeper understanding of the complexity of stereotypes through the analysis of Web sites. This will also teach them analysis techniques, which they can take with them into the final project. Collect the handouts at the end of class.

EXTENSIONS

Students with more knowledge of French could conduct an interview in French—either through e-mail or face to face—of a French person (from France or another French-speaking country) about their perceptions of Americans. Questions could range from the concrete (What clothing does a typical American wear?) to the abstract (Why do you think these stereotypes of Americans exist?), depending on the proficiency of the student. The student could also question the French person about some of the stereotypes that Americans have of the French.

Questions about these stereotypes could be included in a final exam or a year-end summative assessment. Students could be given stereotypes of the French and be required to categorize them in French as positive/negative/neutral or products/practices/perspectives. This would verify that they understood the main concepts of the unit.

Students could also conduct surveys about stereotypes of the French with students and adults in the school who do not speak French. The French students could then prepare presentations of these findings, including graphic representations. Although the survey would have to be in English, the presentation and graphs could be in French, perhaps using PowerPoint.

TEACHING TIPS More mature students could seek out English sources that address French stereotypes themselves. Articles in English about French news can be found through the search engines at any American publication sites, particularly those of local papers and *U.S. News and World Report* (www.usnews.com). Advanced students could read French newspaper articles. See additional sources on the CD.

A note of caution regarding the temporary nature of certain online materials: Accessing news channels is very easy, since most major French news broadcasts are freely accessible through the Internet in a digital format. These are updated daily and are made available shortly after the actual TV broadcast. However, generally speaking, news broadcasts are available only for a limited period of time and are replaced by more recent material on a regular basis. Teachers should take this into account and plan accordingly.

This unit both introduces students to the idea of stereotypes and allows them to discuss cultural stereotypes more openly and with less fear. Once the subject of the long-standing, widely accepted stereotypes that Americans have of the French has been broached, students have license to examine the stereotypes, challenge them, and ultimately see how they function in American ways of viewing the world.

This unit lends itself well to interdisciplinary work, including English, ethics, and history. As they work through the unit, students become more reflective concerning the truth of stereotypes they have about other cultures. Students develop their ability to read current media using critical techniques they have developed in these activities. In turn, students bring their new understanding of stereotypes to other classes, all while learning a lot about the French culture and its realities.

**ACTIVITY 5
(DAYS 9–14)**

Assessment

**DESCRIPTION
OF TASK**
Divide students into groups of three or four, or have students select their groups. The final project consists of a 10-minute group oral presentation conducted with the support of multimedia (PowerPoint or similar presentation software), with a minimum of nine slides. Using multimedia technology will give students an opportunity to develop presentational skills for future professional or academic

settings. Ask students to be creative in their use of technology and utilize whatever media they see fit (digital sound/videos, graphics, effects, etc.) to support their presentation. The use of multimedia will need to be well thought out and not detract from the content of the project. To ensure that learners develop appropriate presentational skills using these tools, provide guidelines and a formal explanation in class (see Handout 1, *Directions for the Final Project*). Each student should take up a particular responsibility for the final project, which will be part of the student's grade.

The presentation requires students to teach others what they have learned during the course of the unit. Assess students on the content as well as the language. Their presentation will need to follow a particular outline (see the CD for details) that will be discussed in class.

ASSESSMENT CRITERIA

The final grade of this unit will be based on individual scores for Activities 1, 2, 3, and 4, and on a group score for the final project, Activity 5. Students will also be evaluated on their particular contribution to the final project.

The grade for the final project will cover the following:

- the oral presentation
- the slideshow accompanying the oral presentation
- the written commentary that accompanies each slide, supplying the script, the name of the person responsible for the slide, and the justification for the multimedia elements selected

Rubrics for the assessment tasks in this unit are provided in appendix A.

Unit 9

Yo Soy el Agua

Target Age: Elementary school

Language: Spanish

ACTFL Proficiency Level: Novice High to Intermediate Low

Primary Content Area: Science and language arts

Connections to Other Disciplines: Biology, environmental studies

Time Frame: 5–6 45-minute class periods

UNIT GOALS

Students will be able to:

- Identify different forms of water in nature.
- Recognize different uses of water.
- Identify ways to take care of water.
- Comprehend and use the present tense to form and respond to simple questions and to report information.
- Use a variety of learning strategies to expand critical thinking skills.
- Develop basic skills in Internet browsing and word processing.
- Use multimedia technology to enhance their creativity and power of expression.

DESCRIPTION

The unit is designed for first-year (elementary-level) students of Spanish, and should be taught during the last trimester of the school year. By that time, students will have been exposed to the Spanish language for at least seven months. They should be able to follow directions in Spanish, work on cooperative learning activities, express ideas using complete sentences, ask questions seeking clarifications, express feelings, use the first person singular of basic verbs, and use graphic organizers. Students will also have been exposed to particular themes such as natural phenomena and weather, and will have covered topics such as temperature and seasons.

Standards Addressed

NETS•S   1, 5

STANDARDS
FOR FOREIGN
LANGUAGE
LEARNING

Communication Standards 1.1, 1.2, 1.3
Cultures Standards 2.1, 2.2
Connections Standard 3.1

This unit introduces children to a number of concepts related to water. First, students activate and build on prior knowledge as they explore various places where water is found (e.g., lakes, rivers, swimming pools). In the second activity, students differentiate between water found naturally (e.g., in a lake) and artificially (e.g., in a swimming pool). The third activity focuses on the uses of water and its importance for human life. Next, students learn about the various states of water (solid, liquid, gas). In the final activity, students learn what people can do to conserve water and care for this natural resource. Throughout the lessons, students are exposed to songs and books about water. The unit culminates with an assessment that asks pairs of students to create a nonfiction question-and-answer book about a specific representation of water. Technology options are offered for several of the lessons, including the assessment task.

CONNECTIONS TO
OTHER DISCIPLINES

The exploration of water easily converges with the topics of *natural science*, *biology*, and *environmental studies*, specifically issues related to "human rights" versus "earth rights."

SPOTLIGHT ON
TECHNOLOGY

Web Browsers and TrackStar: Students can develop basic Internet browsing skills while accessing preselected Web sites listed on a Web page created with TrackStar, a free online service and resource that allows teachers to create interactive online lessons. Using TrackStar will help to ensure that young learners are not exposed to inappropriate or unsuitable material.

Word Processing Software: Learners can begin to develop word processing skills as early as Grades K–2 with software such as Kid Pix, which includes an interface adapted to learners of this age (offering graphic menus with rollover tool descriptions to assist emergent readers and help movies for more advanced use of the software). This software provides features similar to those included in more complex word processing software (spelling checkers in English and Spanish, the ability to format documents and to add graphics and sounds) but with an ease of use that is adapted to the level of instruction.

Multimedia Authoring Tools: In recent years, software companies have provided teachers with multimedia software that is specifically dedicated to supporting learning experiences in Grades K–5, such as Kidspiration and Kid Pix. These programs can help learners develop skills in creativity, organizing and presenting ideas, reading and writing, using technology as productivity tools (by checking spelling, formatting documents, etc.), and listening and speaking. Multimedia software can be used by students to create books with texts, images, sounds, voice recording, and other creative features. The latest version of the Kid Pix software includes a Spanish language mode that offers a spelling checker, help screens, foreign language character support, and menus in the target language.

Concept Mapping Software: Concept mapping software such as Inspiration and Kidspiration can expand learners' ability to conceptualize and organize their knowledge, and can help them outline and plan more complex projects—an important academic skill for all content areas. Because this software requires learners to visually map their thinking processes, it can also help support different intelligences and learning styles.

TECHNOLOGY RESOURCES NEEDED

Hardware
computers with Internet access
projection device (optional)
television (optional)
Web space on a server (optional)

Software
Internet browsing software
TrackStar (free online service; optional)
word processing software (optional)
multimedia authoring tools specifically designed for K–5, such as Kid Pix (optional)
concept mapping software such as Inspiration or Kidspiration (optional)

SUPPLEMENTARY RESOURCES

Web Resources

Royalty-Free Images for Instructional Use
Classroom Clipart: http://classroomclipart.com
Copyright Free Photos: www.copyrightfreephotos.com
Educypedia: www.educypedia.be/
elearning Free Clip Art: www.thelighthouseforeducation.co.uk/clipart.htm
Google: http://directory.google.com/Top/Computers/Graphics/Clip_Art/Pictures/
Pics4Learning: http://pics.tech4learning.com
Princeton Online Clip Art: www.princetonol.com/groups/iad/links/clipart.html

Because online resources are often temporary, some of the Web sites in this list might no longer be available. If this is the case, you will need to identify new sources. To obtain royalty-free images for instructional use, use an Internet search engine such as Google and appropriate keywords.

Learning Tools

An editable KWPL chart (by CoBaLTT): www.carla.umn.edu/cobaltt/modules/
index.html?strategies/gorganizers/index.html

TrackStar (free online service): http://trackstar.4teachers.org/trackstar/

Literature Resources

Background Information

Chamot, A., & O'Malley, J. M. (1994). *The CALLA handbook: Implementing the cognitive academic learning approach*. Reading, MA: Addison-Wesley.

Cloud, N., Genesee, F., & Hamayan, E. (2000). *Dual language instruction: A handbook for enriched education*. Boston: Heinle & Heinle.

Espino-Calderón, M., & Minaya-Rowe, L. (2003). *Designing and implementing two-way bilingual programs*. Thousand Oaks, CA: Corwin Press.

Kucer, S., Silva, C., & Delgado-Larocco, E. (1995). *Curricular conversations: Themes in multilingual and monolingual classrooms*. York, ME: Stenhouse.

Nebraska Department of Education. (1997). *Nebraska K–12 foreign language frameworks: Challenge for a new era*. Lincoln, NE: Author.

Texts Used in Lessons

Delacre, L. (1992). *Arroz con leche: Canciones y ritmos populares de América Latina*. New York: Scholastic. (Book and audiocassette.)

Fowler, A. (1993). *Y aún podría ser agua*. New York: Children's Press.

Marzollo, J. (1999). *Soy el agua*. New York: Scholastic.

Morris, A. (1996). *Agua*. Glenview, IL: Harper Collins Educational Publishers.

Vendrell, C. S., & Parramón, J. (1983). *El agua*. Woodbury, NY: Barron's Educational Series.

teaching the unit

Yo Soy el Agua

The following section provides a brief synopsis of each activity. A more detailed description of the lesson activities, formative assessment strategies, and handouts is provided on the accompanying CD.

ACTIVITY 1 (DAY 1)

Yo soy el agua

PREVIEW

During the introductory phase of this lesson, use a KWHL chart to write down students' ideas about water and help them activate their background knowledge regarding the topic (Handout 1; Figure 9.1). As a class, have students brainstorm what they already know about water (K). Then have students formulate questions or statements about what they want to learn or want to know about water (W). Finally, have students list activities that identify how they can learn about the topic such as paying attention, listening, experimenting, or asking questions (H). Later in the unit (Activity 5), they will return to the chart and fill in the final column with information related to what they learned (L). A variation of this chart is KWPL—Know, Want to know, Predict, and Learned.

Figure 9.1. A KWHL chart.

KWHL			
Nosotros sabemos que...	Nosotros queremos saber...	Nosotros aprenderemos si...	Nosotros aprendimos que...

Adapted from models included in the Nebraska K–12 Foreign Language Frameworks.

This activity could also be done using Inspiration or Kidspiration. With one of these programs, you could create a KWHL chart using pictures and words and display it by connecting your computer to a television or projection device. (See Handout 2 and Figure 9.2.)

Figure 9.2 A KWHL chart created using Inspiration.

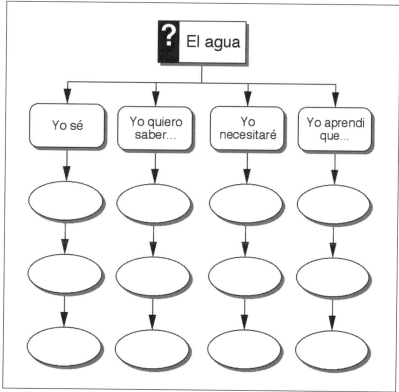

Adapted from models included in the Nebraska K–12 Foreign Language Frameworks.

FOCUSED LEARNING | During this phase, read the book *Soy el agua* (I am water) aloud to students. If some students are able to read the book by themselves, ask one of them to be the reader. Following the reading, ask comprehension questions to help students review the content of the reading, such as *¿Cuál es el título del libro?* (What's the title of the book?), *¿De qué nos habla el libro?* (What is the book about?), and *¿Dónde se encuentra el agua?* (Where do you find water?). Write down the answers, and add any new ideas to the KWHL chart.

EXPANSION | Begin this phase by having students sing the song *Yo soy el agua* (I am water). Handout 3 has the song lyrics, which you could distribute to the class and project for students as they sing.

Next, give each student a flashcard with a form of water. Ideally, there would be two of each water form. You can use the flashcards on Handout 4 or prepare your own using images you've located on the Internet. Have students take turns presenting their card, saying *Yo soy...* and then the form of water. (For instance, *Yo soy la lluvia; Yo soy el lago; Yo soy el hielo.*)

Have students look for partners with the same water representation by asking *¿Quién eres tú?* (Who are you?) or *¿Eres tú el hielo/el río/la lluvia?* (Are you the ice/the river/the rain?).

Instruct students who have the same picture to form pairs and get ready to sing by raising their cards. Once all the students have found their partner and have their flashcards in the air, have them sing *Soy el agua* again.

TEACHING TIPS | The KWHL chart should remain in a visible place throughout this unit. It would be very beneficial to refer to the chart during future activities.

A folder of poems and songs is a good resource to have on hand. Students could decorate and file the printed material throughout the year.

ACTIVITY 2 (DAY 2) | **El agua en el medio natural y el agua en el medio artificial**

PREVIEW | Review Activity 1 by asking questions like *¿Sobre qué hablamos ayer?* (What did we talk about yesterday?) and *¿Qué aprendimos ayer?* (What did we learn yesterday?), and by referring to the KWHL chart created in Activity 1. Sing the song *Yo soy el agua* as a class.

Introduce two new words—*natural* and *artificial*—and explain the new concepts using a graphic organizer called a T-chart to facilitate learners' understanding (Handout 1; see Figure 9.3).

Figure 9.3 Excerpt from Handout 1, the *Natural and Artificial* T-chart.

T-Chart: Natural and Artificial	
Natural	**Artificial**

Explain the differences between the terms *natural* and *artificial* through analogies (authentic hair color vs. dyed hair color; real flowers vs. artificial flowers). This would be a good time to introduce the idea of human intervention (*las personas intervienen/ las personas lo hacen*) and lack of human intervention (*las personas no intervienen/ las personas no lo hacen*). Following the explanation, provide many more examples (pictures of a river and a pool, a bird and an airplane, a volcano and a stove) and model how to categorize them in the T-chart by explaining why that category has been chosen (e.g., *El río es natural porque el hombre no interviene/el hombre no lo hace* [The river is *natural* because man doesn't intervene/man doesn't make it.]).

FOCUSED LEARNING

During this phase, introduce a new T-chart, with agua (water) as the theme and with two columns: *medio natural* and *medio artificial* (Handout 2; see Figure 9.4).

Figure 9.4 Excerpt from Handout 2, the *El agua* T-chart.

T-Chart: El Agua	
El agua en medio natural	**El agua en medio artificial**

Have students form pairs and give each pair two flashcards, one with a picture of water in an artificial medium and the other with a picture of water in a natural medium. Have students work together to categorize the pictures using the T-chart. Then ask students to present the set of flashcards, naming the representation of water and explaining why the water was categorized as natural or artificial.

EXPANSION   In this final phase of the lesson, lead a whole class discussion that reinforces the learning, classifying all the examples of water as either natural or artificial. Add all the ideas to a master El agua T-chart, to be used in Activity 3.

ACTIVITY 3 (DAY 3)   Usos del agua

PREVIEW   After briefly reviewing Activity 2, have students reflect on the importance of water for human beings by asking questions such as *¿Crees que el agua es importante para nosotros?* (Do you believe that water is important for us?) and *¿Por qué?* (Why?). Write down all the answers. These will provide a foundation for the next part of the lesson.

FOCUSED LEARNING   Introduce the book *El agua* by explaining that it talks about why water is important in human lives, as well as different ways people use water. Then ask students to answer comprehension questions, such as *¿De qué nos habla este libro?* (What is this book talking about?) and *¿Qué información nos da el libro?* (What information is the book giving us?). Write down students' answers and clarify the various uses of water.

EXPANSION   During the final phase of this lesson, students will be required to represent two uses of water. Have students form groups of three. Each group should have a writer, a reader, and an actor or actress. Have students select two uses of water and then complete the following: the writer will write about the two uses using sentence strips, which the reader will read to the whole class while the actor or actress acts out each use. After the presentations, have students paste their sentence strips onto a big piece of paper to create a class poster.

ACTIVITY 4 (DAY 4)   Estados del agua

PREVIEW   Begin the activity by having students sing the song *Yo soy el agua*. This time, encourage students to mime each representation with body movements.

FOCUSED LEARNING

After they have acted out the song, ask students if they think that water is always in the same state, *¿Encontramos el agua siempre en la misma forma o en el mismo estado?* Introduce new terminology to the class and present the graphic organizer (Handout 1; Figure 9.5) with the three phrases *estado líquido* (liquid state), *estado sólido* (solid state), and *estado gaseoso* (gas state).

Figure 9.5 Excerpt from Handout 1, *Estados del agua*, a graphic organizer for categorizing states of water.

Estados del agua		
Estado sólido	Estado líquido	Estado gaseoso

Show flashcards with examples of each state of water and identify basic characteristics of each state. Ask guiding questions such as *¿Cómo es el agua en este estado?* (What is the water like in this state?).

EXPANSION

During the final phase of this lesson, read the book *Y aún podría ser agua* and emphasize the importance of water. The story will provide new examples of each state. Use each new example to expand the graphic organizer by adding the new information to it. Following the reading, distribute Handout 1 and have students form pairs to create a poster for display. Students will cut out different representations of water from magazines and paste the pictures into one of the three columns in the graphic organizer. Afterward, have each group make an oral presentation to the class.

You could alter this activity to incorporate technology by having learners create their own graphic organizer using concept mapping software such as Inspiration or Kidspiration, which is adapted to their age level (see Figure 9.6). (Refer to the accompanying CD for a detailed description of this alternative activity.)

Figure 9.6 A graphic organizer created by students using Inspiration.

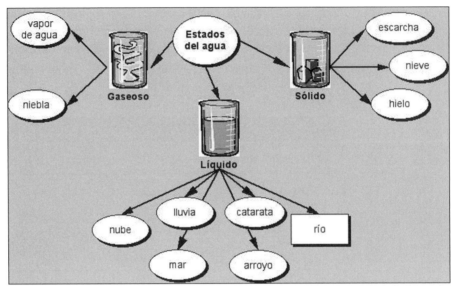

Diagram created in Inspiration by Inspiration Software, Inc.

ACTIVITY 5 (DAY 5)   ## ¡Cuidemos el agua!

PREVIEW   Once again, begin class with students singing *Yo soy el agua* and showing different representations of water with body movements. Then display the KWHL chart from Activity 1. As a class, go through the chart to recall initial ideas and to complete the final column (L, Learned), noting information that students have learned during the unit.

FOCUSED LEARNING   During this phase of the lesson, show pictures of places where students could observe a lack of water or polluted water. Ask guiding questions to help students explore important issues regarding water shortage and water pollution, such as *¿Qué podemos observar en esta figura?* (What can we observe in this picture?) and *¿Quién será el responsable de este problema?* (Who is responsible for the problem?). Ask students to brainstorm solutions.

EXPANSION   This lesson will conclude with students working in pairs to create a Save the Water poster with a catchy phrase like *¡A cuidar el agua!, ¡Cuidemos el agua!, ¡Viva el agua!,* or *¡El agua es tu amiga!* and an illustration showing one way to take care of water. After completing the activity, have students present their poster to the class.

A similar activity could be completed with concept mapping software such as Inspiration or Kidspiration, or multimedia software such as Kid Pix, if available. Students could brainstorm their solutions using the concept mapping software and create their posters, complete with catchy phrases and illustrations, using Kid Pix.

UNIT EXTENSION ACTIVITIES

Students could present their posters from Activity 5 to different classes inside the school.

Instead of posters, students could create pamphlets or small booklets to provide practical advice and guidelines to promote water conservation. They could also create a song to illustrate the different ways they have identified to conserve water.

Teachers could utilize a problem-based learning approach to language instruction, which presents learners with complex and authentic problems that may not have any clear-cut solutions, or questions that do not have readily available answers. Water conservation is a good topic for such discussions because preserving water often means questioning what we take for granted and breaking old habits (some examples: human hygiene versus water pollution, industry/energy use versus water pollution). The teacher could present students with simple cases that reflect current problems related to water preservation. Such an activity would obviously need to be tailored to the students' cognitive level, and scaffolding should be carefully planned to facilitate the reflection process. Such a task, even if challenging for this age group, could provide students with the means to take on the role of "explorers" and "thinkers."

UNIT TEACHING TIPS

In first-grade classrooms, it's especially important to establish clear routines.

Start using graphic organizers as early as possible so that students can become familiar with them. Encourage learners to use more advanced features and formats as they move toward increasingly more complex activities.

Students need lots of practice working in small groups. The teacher needs to establish rules and give very clear directions so students know what they are supposed to do. It helps to assign a different role to each student in the group so that they have a concrete understanding of exactly what's expected of them. For example, one student could serve as the recorder of ideas, another as illustrator, and another as time keeper and task facilitator to make sure that the group stays on task. There should also be one student who serves as a language facilitator, who can be provided with a sheet of paper with language phrases in Spanish that the group is likely to need for carrying out the task. This will help prevent students from using English unnecessarily. In addition, before small group work, the teachers should review with students the language forms they will need for carrying out the task.

ACTIVITY 6 (DAYS 6–8)

Assessment

DESCRIPTION OF TASK

Students will work in pairs to create a nonfiction question-and-answer book about a specific representation of water. Give students a picture with a representation of water. Then model how to create a book based on different questions about their pictures (see Handout 1). Explain the format of the book: writing the question on the top of the page and the answer on the bottom of the page. The middle of the page should be used for an illustration. Introduce the rubric (Handout 2) and one or both checklists (Handouts 3 and 4) so students can understand what is expected of them.

Allow students time at the end of the unit to present their projects to the class. Ideally, the projects would be posted on the Internet to share with family members, the school community, or other interested parties, and to serve as a model for future projects of this kind.

A similar project could be conducted with multimedia software such as Kid Pix, utilizing text, images, sounds, voice recording, and other creative features. The activity would be similar to the paper-and-pencil one described above, except for a few minor revisions (refer to the accompanying CD for a more detailed description).

If the technology option is used, students can also complete the checklist on their technology use (Handout 5). A checklist to assess technology use is more appropriate than a rubric for the age level of the learners targeted in this unit.

ASSESSMENT CRITERIA

Have students complete checklists as a self-assessment. Use the rubric (Activity 6, Handout 2) to evaluate their performance.

A rubric for the assessment task in this unit is provided in appendix A.

National K–12 Foreign Language Resource Center

Introduction

MARCIA HARMON ROSENBUSCH

The units in this section were created by teachers who attended, or served as leaders for, summer institutes sponsored by the National K–12 Foreign Language Resource Center (NFLRC) at Iowa State University. The NFLRC, which aims to improve student learning of foreign languages at the elementary and secondary school levels, provides professional support for foreign language educators through ongoing research projects, summer institutes, and publications such as the units contained in this section.

Several NFLRC summer institutes have focused on the development of thematic units in the K–12 classroom and others have addressed the use of technology in education. The units in this section are the work of foreign language educators who were part of one or more of these NFLRC summer institutes and represent a rich intertwining of thematic teaching enhanced by technology. While a key component of the institutes is the development of a learning community, and the concept of thematic teaching has been enriched by the work and ideas of all of the institute participants, these units were primarily designed by the following authors: Nancy Gadbois (Unit 10), Michele Montás (Unit 11), and Karen Willetts-Kokora (Unit 12).

These units provide examples of thematic teaching that integrate language, culture, and subject content as inspired by Helena Curtain and Carol Ann Dahlberg's seminal work, *Languages and Children—Making the Match* (Curtain & Dahlberg, 2004). Additionally, the units relate classroom teaching to the national student standards in foreign language education (American Council on the Teaching of Foreign Languages, 1996). All the units have a cultural focus and exemplify the incorporation of meaningful cultural concepts in classroom teaching. The units address subject content that is developmentally appropriate and provide opportunities for students to enhance their understanding of the second language. All units utilize similar teaching strategies that include the use of the target language throughout the class by teachers and students, and the use of techniques that appeal to students with diverse learning styles, foster students' ability to think critically and creatively, and facilitate students' ability to work cooperatively in a variety of groupings.

The francophone West Africa unit is designed to enrich the literary and cultural knowledge of the francophone world for upper level secondary students of French; the unit on Carole Fredericks's music, designed for middle and high school students of French, exemplifies cultural assimilation and human achievement; and the unit focused on the children's book *La peineta colorada*, which clarifies the concept of slavery, is designed for middle school students of Spanish. The latter unit is an adaptation of a lesson in a published thematic unit with the same name as the book (Montás & Cannon, 2003). All of the units can be and have been adapted to other levels of instruction. We hope that these units inspire foreign language teachers to refocus and revitalize their teaching by incorporating technology-rich thematic units into their own K–12 classrooms.

REFERENCES   American Council on the Teaching of Foreign Languages (ACTLF). (1996). *Standards for foreign language learning: Preparing for the 21st century*. Yonkers, NY: Author.

Curtain, H. A., & Dahlberg, C. A. (2004). *Languages and children—Making the match* (3rd ed.). Boston: Pearson Education.

Montás, M., & Cannon, L. (2003). *A thematic unit: La peineta colorada*. Rosenbusch, M. & Haas, M. (Eds.). Ames, IA: National K–12 Foreign Language Resource Center, Iowa State University.

Carole's story is a wonderful example of cultural assimilation and human achievement. From humble beginnings in Western Massachusetts, Carole evolved into a consummate artist, humanitarian and citizen of the world

—Connie Fredericks-Malone

Unit 10

Carole Fredericks: Music Is Only the Beginning

Unit author Nancy Gadbois teaches in the inner-city urban district where Carole Fredericks was born and attended school. Although the school's technology where Nancy teaches will soon be upgraded, she manages with limited access to incorporate multimedia whenever possible. She has described her work on Carole as the highlight of her career. Her students concur.

OVERVIEW

Target Age: Middle school through post-secondary

Language: French

ACTFL Proficiency Level: Novice to Intermediate Low

Primary Content Area: Foreign Language, Music

Connections to Other Disciplines: U.S. and world history, popular culture

Time Frame: 1–3 weeks, depending on the depth of the individual project and the intent of the teacher

OBJECTIVES

Students will be able to:

- Listen to and interpret several French-language songs and music videos of the late Carole Fredericks.
- Read interviews with and stories about Carole Fredericks in the target language.
- Interview each other on music in general using the target language.
- Use presentation and telecommunications hardware and software to present what they have learned about Carole to others at school and to the community at large.

DESCRIPTION

In this lesson, students will learn about the life and work of multicultural singer and humanitarian Carole Denise Fredericks of Springfield, Massachusetts. Students

Standards Addressed

NETS•S   3, 4, 5

STANDARDS
FOR FOREIGN
LANGUAGE
LEARNING

Communication Standards 1.1, 1.2, 1.3
Cultures Standard 2.1
Connections Standards 3.1, 3.2
Comparisons Standards 4.1, 4.2
Communities Standards 5.1, 5.2

will listen to her music, view her music videos, and read authentic press clippings and reviews of the singer in the target language. Carole rose to the top of the music charts in both Europe and West Africa in the 1990s, but until recently was virtually unknown in the U.S. She was truly an international musician and star who sang bilingually in French and English and often collaborated with Wolof language artists. During the course of this unit, students will be asked to interpret her music and the stories about her life and work, and present what they have learned to their classmates and the community at large.

This lesson plan can be adapted for use with a variety of age groups, from seventh graders through post-secondary students. Different aspects of the lesson can be shortened or expanded, depending on the age and proficiency level of your students. Ideally, this unit should be taught in a modern language lab with student headsets. However, this unit has been successfully taught in a classroom with only two computers, no lab set-up, and a boom box with no headsets. A classroom equipped with laptop carts will work perfectly for many of the tasks. Activities can also be modified to suit your students' technical facility.

CONNECTIONS TO
OTHER DISCIPLINES

The musical selections in this unit invoke the *U.S. and world history* themes of apartheid, genocide, and equal rights for all. One song discusses the choices that must be made in extreme circumstances, such as in Germany during the Holocaust or South Africa during apartheid. Themes of hunger, children's and women's rights, and the plight of the world's less fortunate populations are also addressed.

This unit also explores the *arts, music,* and *popular culture.* The artists' love of their instruments is often highlighted in music videos, as it is in the videos employed in this unit. The interviews and press releases that students will read in this unit discuss musical themes and inspirations and the choices made during the production of songs and videos.

SPOTLIGHT ON
TECHNOLOGY

Web Browsers: Students will use the Internet to read and interpret interviews with Carole Fredericks and her fellow musicians in several target-language newspapers. They will also study the official English- and French-language Web sites dedicated to Carole, and investigate the Wolof language online.

Word Processing, Presentation, Publishing, and Digital Video Editing Software: Students will create reports on the music and life of Carole Fredericks, and use PowerPoint, Publisher, or digital video editing software to create presentations that they can share with the wider community of learners.

Asynchronous Communication Software: Using e-mail, students can go beyond the limited communication that occurs within the classroom environment and connect with others regarding particular topics.

TECHNOLOGY RESOURCES NEEDED

Hardware
computers with Internet access (preferably broadband)
CD player
DVD/VHS player

Software
Internet browsing software
word processing software
presentation software (e.g., PowerPoint)
digital video editing software
publishing software (e.g., Microsoft Publisher)
asynchronous communication software (optional)

SUPPLEMENTARY RESOURCES

Web Resources
About.com (review of *Tant qu'elle chante, elle vit!*, a collection of curricular resources built around six of Carole Fredericks's music videos): http://french.about.com/cs/listening/fr/tantquellechant.htm
American Association of Teachers of French (AATF; Carole Fredericks curricular materials): www.frenchteachers.org
Annenberg Media (assessment strategies; teaching foreign languages in K–12; music video online, *A nos actes manqués*): http://learner.org
CaroleFredericks.net (the official French-language site): www.carolefredericks.net
CDF Music Legacy (the official English-language Web site dedicated to Carole Fredericks, with numerous learning resources including ordering information for *Tant qu'elle chante, elle vit!*, an integrated package of language-learning activities, worksheets, and a VHS tape or DVD containing six of Carole's music videos including "Un, deux, trois," "Qu'est-ce qui t'amène," and "Respire"): www.cdfmusiclegacy.com
La chaîne de l'espoir (humanitarian organization): www.chaine-espoir.asso.fr/
Les Enfoirés and the presence of Carole Fredericks: http://ericouaibe.ifrance.com/ericouaibe/enfoires/historique.htm
L'Humanité (online report): www.humanite.presse.fr/journal/2001-06-11/2001-06-11-245607
Jose Feliciano: www.josefeliciano.com
Lyon People (homage to Carole Fredericks from the city of Lyon): www.lyonpeople.com/news/p1frederiks.html
MassLive.com (story about Carole Fredericks's family): www.masslive.com/search/index.ssf?/base/living-0/1139647910310110.xml?nnae

NPR: French Lessons Keep Singer's Legacy Alive (National Public Radio story on Carole, with links to audio streams of "Un, deux, trois," "Qu'est-ce qui t'amène," and "Respire" and a video stream of "Un, deux, trois"): www.npr.org/templates/story/story.php?storyId=3857380

Parler d'Sa Vie (interview with Carole Fredericks): www.parler-de-sa-vie.net/ecrits/interviews/19931229.txt

Parler d'Sa Vie (Jean Jacques Goldman/Carole Fredericks interview): www.parler-de-sa-vie.net

Les Restos du Coeur (humanitarian efforts of Carole Fredericks): www.restosducoeur.org

Shine: Carole Fredericks (French informational fan site): www.shine.fr.st/

Tralco-Lingo Fun (where you can purchase the *Couleurs et parfums* CD, including "Respire," with lesson plans and a "Respire" PDF lesson sample based on the music video; click on "Carole Fredericks" link on the left menu): www.tralco.com/thome.htm

Wolof Online: www.wolofonline.com

teaching
the unit

Carole Fredericks: Music is Only the Beginning

The following describes 10 days of activities that focus on Carole Fredericks and her music (many additional learning activities can be found on the CDF Music Legacy site, www.cdfmusiclegacy.com). Each lesson is identified by title (e.g., Researching Carole Fredericks) and activity number (e.g., Activity 1).

Because many of the materials for this unit are online, this unit lends itself to being student-directed.

ACTIVITY 1
(DAYS 1–2)

Researching Carole Fredericks

Students will research online information about Carole Fredericks, both in English and in French. Depending on the level of detail expected, this work may take two (or more) days to complete.

PREVIEW

Prepare an outline of research expectations, including a timeline, to guide the students and keep them on topic.

FOCUSED LEARNING

Step 1. Provide students with a list of questions about Carole Fredericks's life and work to guide their research. The following suggestions are based on the information available on the French-language Web site CaroleFredericks.net. These questions are also provided on the CD as Handout 1.

- D'oú vient Carole?
- Quelle est la date de sa naissance?
- Parlez un peu de sa famille.
- Quelle sorte de musique a-t-elle chantée?
- Elle était membre de quel trio célèbre?
- Oú est-elle décédée, et quand?
- Elle est enterrée dans quel cimetière?
- "Qu'est-ce qui t'amène" a été tourné où aux Etats-Unis?
- Parlez un peu de cette gare.
- Que savez-vous du road-movie "Respire"?

While these questions may seem basic, interpreting them and finding answers on a target-language Web site can be quite challenging. Adjust the difficulty level of the questions to fit the proficiency level of the class.

Step 2. Direct students to explore the two official Web sites dedicated to Carole Fredericks to learn about her life and music, with the list of research questions as their guide.

- CDF Music Legacy (English): www.cdfmusiclegacy.com
- CaroleFredericks.net (French): www.carolefredericks.net

Step 3. After an appropriate amount of time, bring students back to the whole class and discuss what they have discovered about Carole Fredericks's life and music. The format of this discussion and the range of topics covered will depend on the age and proficiency level of the French class. Topics may include the importance of her life, her journey abroad, her impact on the world, and her untimely death in 2001.

ACTIVITY 2 (DAY 3)

Interpreting "Un, deux, trois"

Work on the next several days will center on "Un, deux, trois," a song from *Fredericks Goldman Jones*, Carole's 1990 debut album. Free audio and video streams of the song and music video are available on the NPR site (www.npr.org/templates/story/story. php?storyId=3857380), or they can be purchased as part of a larger set of curricular materials and videos titled *Tant qu'elle chante, elle vit!* from the American Association of Teachers of French (AATF) at www.frenchteachers.org. Students will listen to the song, examine the lyrics, and view and interpret the music video.

PREVIEW

Prepare the song for listening in class. If using the free streaming audio file (best if the classroom has broadband access to the Internet), prepare the computer and speakers and navigate to the NPR site using your Web browser. If using the CD, VHS tape, or DVD purchased from AATF, prepare the appropriate playing equipment. Begin the lesson by asking students to speculate what a song called "Un, deux, trois" might be about, basing their answers on what they have learned about Carole Fredericks.

FOCUSED LEARNING

Step 1. Play the song "Un, deux, trois" to the class.

Step 2. Divide the class into pairs and give each pair a copy of the cloze exercise (Handout 1; available on the accompanying CD). The cloze exercise requires students to fill in the blanks to complete the song lyrics.

Step 3. Review the answers to the cloze exercise and distribute the song lyrics (Handout 2). Then, have students work in pairs to translate and interpret the song's lyrics. The pairs should look for cognates to help them translate and grasp the meaning of the text.

Step 4. When students finish their translations, guide them to the additional online resources listed in the Supplementary Resources section of this lesson, and ask them to find and read articles related to Carole's humanitarian work.

ACTIVITY 3 (DAY 4)

Interpreting the Music Video for "Un, deux, trois"

Students will present their interpretations of "Un, deux, trois" to the class and arrive at a consensus regarding its major themes. The class will then view the music video for this song and analyze how those themes are portrayed and played out in the video.

PREVIEW

Prepare the music video for viewing in class. If using the free streaming video file (best if the classroom has broadband access to the Internet), prepare the computer and projection device ahead of time. If using the VHS tape or DVD purchased from AATF, prepare the appropriate playing equipment. Begin the lesson by asking students to speculate what they might see in the video, based on their knowledge of the song and what they have learned about Carole Fredericks.

FOCUSED LEARNING

Step 1. Have students share their translations and interpretations of the lyrics to "Un, deux, trois," seeking a consensus on its major themes. Use the questions on the song's lyrics (Handout 1, provided on the CD) to guide this discussion.

Step 2. Play the video of "Un, deux, trois" one time through, and have students discuss their initial reactions: What did they see? What did they like? Where was the video filmed? What surprised them about the video or Carole Fredericks's performance?

Step 3. Play the video a second time, asking students to pay close attention to the ways that the video depicts, implies, or plays off the major themes that they have identified in the song's lyrics.

Step 4. Complete the analysis of the music video with a whole-class discussion.

Step 5. Introduce the group presentation assignment that students will be working on over the next several days. Break the students into pairs (or larger groups, if necessary) and have them select a format for their presentation, such as a slideshow (using presentation software), a video (using digital video editing software), or a publication (using a publishing program).

ACTIVITY 4
(DAYS 5–8)

Creating the Group Presentations

Students will work in pairs (or larger groups) to create a project that introduces Carole Fredericks to another group of French students in their own or a different school, or to their parents, or to the community at large.

PREVIEW

Review the discussions of the past two days, and give students a copy of the rubrics that will be used to assess their performance on the group presentation project (Handout 1).

FOCUSED LEARNING

Step 1. Have students analyze the rubrics for both the oral presentation and technology tasks and make sure they understand what is expected of them as they complete their projects.

Step 2. Direct students to begin designing storyboard outlines or layouts for their project. Also, have them brush up on the technical skills needed to complete their particular project: a slideshow, a video, or a publication. Completing this project may take several days, depending on the technical facility of the students and the amount of class time they can devote to this project.

Step 3. As students work on their presentations over the next several days, encourage them to review the rubrics periodically, refine their outlines, and invite peer evaluations of their work-in-progress.

ACTIVITY 5
(DAYS 9–10)

Delivering the Group Presentations

PREVIEW

Prepare the classroom for the group presentations.

FOCUSED LEARNING

Step 1. Have each pair or group share their presentation with the class.

Step 2. After each presentation, ask students to peer-evaluate the projects anonymously, based on the rubrics given to the whole class.

Step 3. Collect these evaluations at the end of each class period (if presentations extend over more than one day).

UNIT EXTENSION
ACTIVITIES

Students can be asked to present their work to another French class at school, or to nearby elementary or middle school French students. Student presentations can also be video recorded for sharing beyond the school setting.

Students may also contact (by e-mail) members of the Fredericks family, including sister Connie Fredericks-Malone, at www.cdfmusiclegacy.com.

Although this unit is dedicated to Carole Fredericks, any popular musical icon who would interest today's students could be studied in a similar manner. One example might be Jose Feliciano, one of the original "crossover" artists in American music, whose Web site (www.josefeliciano.com) offers his music in several formats. His site also hosts a bilingual historical timeline of his career, including highlights as well as disappointing moments. Students can follow his career and track the historical events that have affected his music and the world in general.

UNIT
TEACHING TIPS

Before you start, clearly identify your desired outcomes and consider alternative assessment strategies that will better engage your learners. To help you with this process, visit http://learner.org, where you can view a digital video that covers three different types of foreign language assessment. Select Foreign Languages from the drop-down menu, choose any grade level, select Go, scroll to the bottom of the page, and click on "Teaching Foreign Languages K–12: A Library of Classroom Practices."

Click on the Web site entry link arrow and scroll to the location on the page where the assessment video link is located. Select that link and then click on "analyze the video," which will allow you to see the video on demand. All worksheets created for this project are downloadable. The site is free of charge, but will require you to supply some basic information to access resources. The video describes assessment strategies for all three communicative modes: Interpretive, Interpersonal, and Presentational.

Because students are generally enthusiastic about any technology, and also love music, this project is almost guaranteed to be of high interest. This unit has been used in classes that are large, and have included learners of all styles as well as gifted and special needs students. Although logistics and limited technology access can occasionally be a hindrance, you would never know this by the excitement generated when the mobile cart is wheeled into the classroom.

Be aware that some students may need help when using technology to create their projects. Many students, even those who may also be enrolled in technology classes, may have no idea how to perform foreign language–specific tasks such as inserting accents or using online translation services. Never assume anything!

ASSESSMENT

Several forms of evaluation may be used to assess student performance. These may include the following:

Activity 1. Teachers can create a "treasure hunt" worksheet based on the two official Web sites, and use these for formative assessment.

Activities 2 and 3. The students' translations and responses to the interpretive questions about the meaning of the lyrics to "Un, deux, trois" can be used for assessment purposes. Teachers can also assess student comprehension of the online articles they read during these activities.

Activity 4. Formative evaluation of the group presentations-in-progress should be based on the two rubrics handed out to students. Frequent feedback should be provided to students while they are working on their projects to help them improve their final presentations.

Activity 5. The culminating activity may include both student and teacher evaluations of the final presentation.

ASSESSMENT
CRITERIA

Rubrics for this unit are provided in appendix A.

A Technology-Rich Unit from *La peineta colorada*

Unit author Michele Montás adapted this unit from Lesson 5 in *A thematic unit: La peineta colorada* (Montás & Cannon, 2003). Since this unit was published, Montás began teaching in a technology-rich school and has explored integrating technology into her lessons. As a result of her recent experiences, this unit now clarifies how technology can transform the teaching of a thematic unit in a middle school foreign language classroom.

OVERVIEW

Target Age: Middle school, Grades 5–8

Language: Spanish

ACTFL Proficiency Level: Novice High to Intermediate Mid

Primary Content Area: World literature

Connections to Other Disciplines: History, geography, music, home economics

Time Frame: 1–2 weeks

OBJECTIVES

Students will be able to:

- Explore and discuss the influence of the African heritage in Latin America and in their communities.
- Develop an awareness of important historical and social events through music and video.
- Explore the concepts of slavery, freedom, friendship, and solidarity.
- Use the Internet and software to collect, organize, analyze, and report information.
- Enhance Spanish vocabulary and skills in the Interpersonal, Interpretive, and Presentational communicative modes.

Standards Addressed

NETS•S	3, 4, 5
STANDARDS FOR FOREIGN LANGUAGE LEARNING	Communication Standards 1.1, 1.2, 1.3 Cultures Standard 2.2 Connections Standard 3.1

DESCRIPTION

This unit is intended for use in a middle school Spanish class with students who have had previous exposure to Spanish and are at the Novice-High to Intermediate-Mid level of proficiency on the Student Oral Proficiency Assessment (SOPA) rating scale developed by the Center for Applied Linguistics (Thompson, Kenyon, & Rhodes, 2002). However, the lessons could easily be adapted to upper or lower levels. The unit could also be extended several weeks, depending on the amount of time the teacher has with the students, the pace of the class, and the supporting materials the teacher decides to integrate with the unit to enrich the students' learning experience.

La peineta colorada (*The Red Comb*), by Fernando Picó (1991), with illustrations by María Ordóñez, is a children's story from Puerto Rico, set in the 19th century. The story tells how a young girl and an older woman work together to save a runaway slave from a rich man who earned his living chasing and capturing runaway slaves (*cimarrones*). The author based the story on anecdotes and historical facts he found in the general archives of the mid to late 1800s in Puerto Rico. The tale captures the importance of teamwork as well as the spirit and the wit of a Latin American community. It also touches on the strong influence women can have in a community in spite of their traditionally submissive roles.

The unit presented here focuses on these questions:

- *¿Quién es el cimarrón?* (Who is a runaway slave?)
- *¿Cómo es un palenque?* (What is a slave dwelling like?)

CONNECTIONS TO OTHER DISCIPLINES

This unit connects to the disciplines of *geography, social studies, music, home economics, art,* and *language arts*. This story revolves around the following cultural components: the African influence in Latin America through slavery, family, community, solidarity, friendship, food, social traditions, oral tradition (storytelling), and women's role in society.

SPOTLIGHT ON TECHNOLOGY

Web Browsers: Using an Internet search engine, students search for images that depict the meaning of words used to clarify aspects of slavery.

Projection System: The teacher uses a projection system to share aspects of the lesson with the class; students use the projection system to share their work with the class.

Video Recording: Students view the video to become familiar with the history of slavery in the Americas.

Audio Recording: Students become familiar with music created by the slaves by listening to an audio recording as they view pictures of *cimarrones.*

Concept Mapping Software: Both the teacher and students use concept mapping software to organize and display text and illustrations.

Word Processing Software: Students use word processing software to record their responses to questions posed by the teacher. The teacher may also use a word processing program to create the questions and to graph student responses in table format for analysis.

Presentation Software: Both the teacher and students use presentation software to organize and display text and illustrations.

Paint or Draw Program: Students use a paint or draw program to create their illustrations of a *cimarrón* and a *palenque.*

Timeline Software: Timeline software such as TimeLiner can be used to help students organize and present material.

TECHNOLOGY
RESOURCES NEEDED

Hardware
   computers with Internet access
   projection system
   video and audio recordings and equipment

Software
   Internet browsing software
   concept mapping software (e.g., Inspiration)
   word processing software
   presentation software (e.g., PowerPoint)
   paint or draw program
   timeline software (optional)

SUPPLEMENTARY
RESOURCES

Web Resources
   The Changing of the Guard: Puerto Rico in 1898 (a history of slavery in Puerto
      Rico with photographs and maps): www.loc.gov/rr/hispanic/1898/bras.html
   History of Puerto Rico (a timeline of the history of Puerto Rico):
      http://welcome.topuertorico.org/history.shtml
   Resistance in Paradise (a history of Puerto Rico's African heritage):
      www.cosmos.ne.jp/~miyagawa/nagocnet/data/prhistory.html

Literature Resources

Benitez, M., & Milagros Gonzalez, L. (1992). *La tercera raiz: Presencia Africana en Puerto Rico*. San Juan: Centro de Estudios de la Realidad Puertorriqueña (CEREP) / Instituto de Cultura Puertorriqueña (ICP). Catalog from an art exhibit with several essays focusing on various aspects of African heritage in Puerto Rico and an extensive bibliography on materials related to the topic of the African influence on Puerto Rican culture.

García, S. (1997). *Coloréame*. (Available from the Asociación Profesional de Artesanía y Folclor, 623 Calle Artico, Puerto Nuevo, Puerto Rico 00920.) Coloring books containing a collection of words of African descent and drawings of various cultural products and practices influenced by African culture in Puerto Rico.

González, L. M., & Quintero-Rivera, A. G. (1991). *La otra cara de la historia: La historia de Puerto Rico desde su cara obrera 1800–1925*. Rio Piedras, Puerto Rico: CEREP. Traces the history of the labor force in Puerto Rico. Excellent photographs.

Jacobs, F. (1992). *The Tainos: The people who welcomed Columbus*. New York: Putnam & Grosset Group.

Kennedy, J. H. (1991). *Relatos latinoamericanos: La herencia africana*. Lincolnwood, IL: National Textbook Company. A cultural reader for intermediate students of Spanish.

Montás, M., & Cannon, L. (2003). *A thematic unit: La peineta colorada*. Rosenbusch, M. & Haas, M. (Eds.). Ames, IA: National K–12 Foreign Language Resource Center, Iowa State University.

Perez Martinez, A., & Diaz Cubero, J. H. (1980). *El mundo y mi isla: Estudios sociales para cuarto grado* (7th ed.). Madrid, Spain: Cultural Centroamerica, S.A.

Picó, F., & Ordóñez, M. A. (1991). *La peineta colorada*. Caracas, Venezuela: Ediciones Ekaré.

Thompson, L., Kenyon, D., & Rhodes, N. (2002). *A validation study of the student oral proficiency assessment (SOPA)*. Ames, IA, and Washington, DC: Iowa State University, National K–12 Foreign Language Resource Center and the Center for Applied Linguistics.

Video Resources

Bozzi, M. R. (Director). (1992). *Palenque: Un canto* (The African heritage of a Colombian village) [Film]. New Day Films. (Available from The Latin American Resource Center, Stone Center for Latin American Studies, Tulane University, New Orleans, LA 70118, 504.862.3143, or http://stonecenter.tulane.edu/LARCIndex.htm.)

Dratch, H. & Rosow, E. (Directors/Producers). (1997). *Roots of rhythm: A worldwide celebration of Latin Music, from Africa to the Caribbean and America with Harry Belafonte* [Film]. PBS. (Available from www.amazon.com or www.pbs.org.)

Ferrand, C. (Director). (1983). *Cimarrones* [Film]. Cinema Guild. (Available from The Latin American Resource Center, Stone Center for Latin American Studies, Tulane University, New Orleans, LA 70118, 504.862.3143, or http://stonecenter.tulane.edu/LARCIndex.htm.)

James, A. (Director), & Singer, R. (Producer). (2001). *Bomba: Dancing the drum* [Film]. Searchlight Films. (Available from City Lore, New York, www.citylore.org.) A film on Puerto Rico's leading family of traditional music and dance.

La presencia africana en Hispanoamérica [Film]. (1988). International Film Bureau. (Available from The Latin American Resource Center, Stone Center for Latin American Studies, Tulane University, New Orleans, LA 70118, 504.862.3143, or http://stonecenter.tulane.edu/LARCIndex.htm.) This 30-minute video was created as a classroom resource for beginning-level Spanish students.

Spielberg, S., Wilson, C., & Allen, D. (Producers), & Spielberg, S. (Director). (1997). *Amistad* [Film]. Dreamworks Pictures and HBO Pictures. The film documents the story of 53 Africans who seized the Spanish slave ship on which they were being transported in the 1800s.

Audio Resources

Allen, R. (Ed.). (1988). *Voices of the Americas: Traditional music and dance from North, South, and Central America, and the Caribbean* [Concert and cassette series]. (Produced by the World Music Institute, 109 West 27 Street, New York, NY 10001.)

Libertad, T. (1994). *Africa en América* [CD]. Sony International. (Available from www.amazon.com.) CD collection of afroamerican and afrocaribbean music.

teaching the unit

A Technology-Rich Unit from *La peina colorada*

Each of the following lessons is identified by title (e.g., Describing the Cimarrones) and activity number (e.g., Activity 1). A translation of Spanish is provided here to assist the reader, but need not be provided in the classroom.

ACTIVITY 1 (DAYS 1–2)

Describing the Cimarrones

PREVIEW

To prepare for watching the video *Cimarrones*, students learn descriptive words while creating concept maps based on images of cimarrones.

Use a video display device to project scanned pictures of cimarrones, and insert each picture into its own concept map using a program such as Inspiration. Create empty word bubbles around the image for the students to fill in.

To find images to display, search online for "runaway slaves," "middle passage illustrations," "sugar cane field workers," and similar terms. Project the images as you play selections from the *Africa en América* CD in the background.

FOCUSED LEARNING

Step 1. Break the students into small groups. Give each group a different concept-map file, with a different image in the center. Ask the groups to list as many descriptive words as they can by typing the words in the bubbles you have already created around the image. You may want to guide the class by asking questions such as:

¿El es rico o es pobre? ¿El hombre en el dibujo es esclavo o es libre? ¿Dónde vive él, en el monte o en el pueblo? (Is he rich or poor? Is the man in the picture a slave or free? Where does he live, in the woods or in the town?)

You may also use this exercise to introduce vocabulary, such as *limpio* versus *sucio*, *fuerte* versus *débil*, and *tranquilo* versus *nervioso* (clean versus dirty, strong versus weak, and calm versus nervous).

Step 2. Have each student group project its finished concept map to the class. Encourage students to explain their descriptions and word choices.

Step 3. As the students project and report their concept maps, categorize their descriptive vocabulary by parts of speech (nouns, verbs, adjectives) in a Word document table.

Step 4. After students deliver their reports, project the Word table and discuss it. This will serve as a review and summary of the students' work on descriptions. Have the students copy the table and the vocabulary, divided into parts of speech, in their notes.

Creating Picture Sentence Stories of the Cimarrones

ACTIVITY 2 (DAYS 3–4)

PREVIEW

To review new vocabulary and further clarify the concept of cimarrones, randomly assign vocabulary words to small groups or pairs of students, who will then use Internet search engines to find illustrations to clarify their meaning. For instance, students will look for images to illustrate *tener hambre, valiente, escapar* (to be hungry, courageous, to escape).

FOCUSED LEARNING

Step 1. When students have found a set of images, have them write one or more sentences using the target vocabulary, working to connect all of the sentences to tell a story.

Step 2. Students should then illustrate each sentence with the images they have found, and share their stories and images using presentation software such as PowerPoint. Students can project and present their work in class or print and post it.

For instance, a group of students working with tener hambre, valiente, and escapar should find illustrations for each, and then sequence them to express something like Figure 11.1.

Figure 11.1 An example picture sentence story.

El esclavo es valiente. El esclavo escapa porque tiene hambre.

EXPANSION

Students can also be asked to use their downloaded images to form picture sentences that other students can decode to practice the new vocabulary. They can create their illustrated sentences in a Word document, print it, and pass copies around. Students can also create their illustrated sentences using PowerPoint and display their pictures for other students to decode.

TEACHING TIPS

Show students a sample sequence of illustrations that form a sentence when combined. Once students have seen a model (such as the one illustrated in Figure 11.1), they will have a better idea of what the final product should look like.

ACTIVITY 3 (DAY 5)

Responding to the Cimarrones Video

PREVIEW

Tell students that they will be watching the *Cimarrones* video two times. The first time, students should watch it to become familiar with its content. The second time, students will answer a questionnaire about it with a partner.

FOCUSED LEARNING

Step 1. Show the *Cimarrones* video twice.

Step 2. Assign pairs of students to respond to the questionnaire by opening a word processing document you have prepared that provides the questions followed by answers that have missing words (Handout 1, see Figure 11.2). Student partners should discuss and write in the answers to these questions.

Step 3. At the end of the questionnaire, student partners should respond to the final, open-ended question by writing down two things they found interesting in the video.

Figure 11.2 Excerpt from Activity 3, Handout 1.

Preguntas para el video

LAS PREGUNTAS	LAS RESPUESTAS
1. ¿En dónde tomó lugar la acción del video?	La acción del video _____ en _____. *verbo*
2. ¿Qué año era en el video?	En el video _____ el año _____. *verbo*
3. ¿En qué se basaron los datos del video?	Los datos del video _____ en _____. *verbo*
4. ¿En qué año llegaron los conquistadores al Perú?	Los conquistadores _____ al Perú en _____. *verbo*

TEACHING TIPS

Make sure you go over the meaning of each of the questions on the questionnaire with the students so that they can focus on the information they need to fill in. Also, explain to students that they are to use the verbs in the questions to fill in part of the blanks when they are writing their answers.

ACTIVITY 4 (DAY 6)

Reviewing the Cimarrones Video

PREVIEW

Review what was covered the day before, and then replay the *Cimarrones* video once again.

FOCUSED LEARNING

Step 1. After showing the video again, have students share their answers to the questionnaire with the whole group. Have students take turns asking and answering the questions on the questionnaire.

Step 2. Ask students to share any historical facts they found of interest in the film from their responses to the open-ended question.

Step 3. Record, tabulate, and project their responses to summarize the discussion on historical facts of interest.

Step 4. You may choose to print and post this summary.

TEACHING TIPS

When you ask the students to share their comments on what they found interesting in the video, give them chunk phrases to get them started in Spanish, such as:

> *Yo pienso que el número de africanos que capturaron fue interesante porque es un número muy grande. Yo creo que la parte donde los cimarrones pelean fue curiosa porque no matan al conquistador. Yo (no) estoy de acuerdo con _____ porque _____.*

> (I think that _____ was interesting because _____. I believe that the part where _____ was curious because _____. I (don't) agree with _____ because _____.)

You may also wish to highlight the verbs in the questions and answers to discuss the preterit.

ACTIVITY 5 (DAY 7)

Understanding the Story of the Cimarrones

PREVIEW

Review the comments recorded the day before.

FOCUSED LEARNING

Step 1. Watch the video one more time.

Step 2. Project a sentence about the cimarrón that is divided into three parts, and demonstrate how the pieces can be rearranged to form a complete sentence.

Step 3. Distribute Handout 1: *Lee y organiza.* (See Figure 11.3)

Step 4. Have students work in pairs to number the sentence parts in the correct order to form a complete sentence.

TEACHING TIPS
Have students share each of the sentences in the correct order aloud. Ask other groups to decide whether they agree or disagree with the order of the sentence shared. You may also ask students to work individually to illustrate some of the sentences on the board and have other students guess which of the sentences have been illustrated. This reinforces comprehension and the structure of sentences in Spanish.

Figure 11.3 Excerpt from Activity 5, Handout 1.

Lee y organiza

Organiza las frases para escribir oraciones lógicas y completas.

1. _____ era un esclavo que se escapaba
   _____ un cimarrón
   _____ y se escondía y vivía en los montes

2. _____ y no tenía muchas cosas
   _____ como ropa ni zapatos
   _____ el cimarrón era pobre

3. _____ por lo general el cimarrón
   _____ y tenía muchas marcas de cicatrices y golpes viejos
   _____ estaba sucio y descalzo (sin zapatos)

4. _____ los cimarrones vivían peleando
   _____ tenían miedo
   _____ y muchas veces

ACTIVITY 6
(DAYS 8–9)

Illustrating the Story of the Cimarrones

FOCUSED LEARNING
Step 1. Have students use a draw or paint program to create a drawing of a cimarrón and a palenque.

Step 2. Provide students with the template for the worksheet (Handout 1: *Ilustración gráfica y descripción*) through file-sharing and have them paste the images in their worksheet. Then have students write a description of each.

Step 3. When done, students should print and post their work.

Step 4. Provide an opportunity for students to review the work of their peers by creating a gallery walk in which students circulate around the room viewing the work.

UNIT EXTENSION
ACTIVITIES
Have students work in groups with vocabulary related to the unit and the information they have gathered and discussed from the video to write a short script that reenacts a portion of the video. This reenactment should demonstrate their understanding of what a cimarrón is and what the lives of cimarrones were like.

To make connections with the social studies curriculum, students could do research to find stories of runaway slaves in the U.S. and compare those stories with the one presented on the video. They could summarize their findings using a Venn diagram created in Word or by creating a PowerPoint presentation.

Students could summarize the sequence of events and what they have learned about the history of slavery in a timeline using software such as TimeLiner or Inspiration. Students may also be able to create a timeline chart using the diagram or organization chart options in Word.

UNIT
TEACHING TIPS

When preparing students to watch the video, make sure to go over each of the questions on the questionnaire and check for comprehension, clarifying any words students may not understand.

The video moves slowly in some sections, so you may want to be prepared to fast-forward portions in which there is no dialogue.

When teaching verbs, it is always a good idea to use pantomime to help students gain an understanding of the meaning of each verb. Having them play charades helps students remember the vocabulary with greater ease. As you introduce the verbs, combine them into longer stretches of language to form sentences that you know they will come across in the story or in the video summary activities. This will help them assimilate the language with more ease. Take time to go over each activity with students and whenever possible show them models of what you are expecting so that they can focus on showing what they know and what they can do with the new language to express their ideas.

Some students will likely move faster than others through these activities. Prepare back-up activities for these students so that students who work at a slower pace will have adequate time to complete the handouts.

Whenever possible, prepare a PowerPoint presentation to introduce new vocabulary, and make a copy of the presentation available to students so that they can review the terms at their own pace outside of class.

ASSESSMENT

Teachers can choose one or more of the following tasks to assess student learning in this unit:

- Teachers can prepare a quiz to assess students' understanding of the events in the video. Teachers can use questions from the Activity 3 questionnaire to prepare the quiz.
- Teachers can use Activity 6 as the assessment task. They can also use the rubrics provided in the appendix to help them grade students' work.
- Teachers can use any of the unit extension activities listed as assessment tasks, and write rubrics to help them evaluate students' work.

ASSESSMENT
CRITERIA

Rubrics for the assessment tasks in this unit are provided in appendix A.

Un veillard qui meurt, c'est une bibliothèque qui brûle.
(For each elder who dies, a library burns.)

—Amadou Hampaté Bâ

Unit 12

The Culture and Literature of Francophone West Africa

This unit was developed by Karen Willetts-Kokora, an author for *Foreign Language Instructional Guides for Upper Levels of French* for the Montgomery County Public Schools (MCPS). It is part of the French 5 theme Discovery and History. The MCPS secondary curriculum for Upper Levels 4–6 is content-based foreign language instruction within thematic units. This unit is an expansion of the original material and has been written with a focus on technology integration. The lessons now include several opportunities to participate in technology-enhanced tasks to assist teachers in integrating various technology tools seamlessly into their instruction. The activities teachers choose to implement in class may depend upon which technology resources are available in their school.

OVERVIEW

Target Age: High school, Grades 9–12

Language: French

ACTFL Proficiency Level: Intermediate Mid to Intermediate High

Primary Content Area: Cultural studies

Connections to Other Disciplines: Geography, history, music, folklore, literature

Time Frame: 4 weeks

OBJECTIVES

Content Objectives

Students will be able to:

- Identify West-African francophone countries and capitals on a map.
- Present information about the geography, history, government, economics (including products), and languages of a selected francophone West African country.
- Explain the CFA monetary system (le franc de la Communauté Financière Africaine) and discuss important cultural symbols and information depicted on

Standards Addressed

NETS•S 3, 4, 5

STANDARDS
FOR FOREIGN
LANGUAGE
LEARNING Communication Standards 1.1, 1.2, 1.3
Cultures Standards 2.1, 2.2
Connections Standards 3.1, 3.2
Comparisons Standards 4.1, 4.2
Communities Standard 5.1

CFA bills (including art, animals, clothing, lifestyles, plants, and other cultural objects).

- Compare CFA money with the Euro from a cultural and historical point of view.
- Describe major West African instruments and state how music is integral to the African oral tradition.
- Read and understand sample folktales from francophone West Africa (with a focus on Bernard Dadié from Côte d'Ivoire).
- Investigate the use of African languages in traditional folktales and the role of the *griot*, or storyteller.
- Examine connections to European folktales and discuss how messages or morals in the stories reflect various traditional cultural values.

Language Objectives

Students will be able to:

- Practice the use of prepositions with geographical terms, countries, and capitals.
- Correctly identify and write past tenses of a variety of verbs (*passé composé, imparfait, passé simple*).
- Develop a repertoire of African-specific French vocabulary.
- Increase use of a variety of transition words, adverbs of time, and expressions included in traditional tales.
- Write an original folktale using vocabulary, structures, and other features typical of this genre.

Technology Objectives

Students will be able to:

- Conduct Internet research using authentic French language Web sites.
- Use software to organize, classify, and present findings.
- Collaborate electronically with other students and with the teacher.
- Use software to develop a presentation or a Web site to share their projects with the class.

DESCRIPTION This unit touches on a variety of aspects of francophone West Africa and is written for upper-level secondary students of French (whose proficiency is Intermediate Mid to Intermediate High) to enrich their literary and cultural knowledge of the francophone world outside of Europe. Textbooks in French are often very Eurocentric; thus, this unit could supplement a variety of high-school French courses. Lessons include basic geography, history, and country profiles. Information on the West African monetary system, oral tradition, musical instruments, and typical African poems and folktales is provided. The unit time frame is approximately four weeks, but teachers may select smaller portions of activities or expand the lessons to meet their own objectives.

The unit begins with a review of the geography of francophone West Africa. A country profile of Côte d'Ivoire or Sénégal is presented, with students then asked to investigate another county's geography, history, government, economy, ethnic groups, and languages. Students will conduct Internet research and present their findings orally to the class. They may also use presentation software, publishing software, or a Web site development program at the teacher's discretion.

The next activities provide an overview of the CFA franc and the monetary system. Students are asked to visually analyze CFA currency and consider the cultural aspects of the animals, plants, peoples, and typical African objects and art printed on the money. A comparison can then be made with the Euro and the cultural information represented on these bills. Again, research will be conducted online. Students may use concept mapping software (e.g., Inspiration) to organize their findings. Students may also use electronic communication tools (e.g., e-mail) to collaborate and interact with peers and the teacher about their findings or to report results.

Poems and two traditional folktales by Bernard Dadié of Côte d'Ivoire follow a section on the role of the *griot*, or storyteller, and musical instruments in African oral tradition. One of the tales includes examples of Baoulé, an Ivoirian language and an important ethnic group. Teachers may wish to expand this example to other African languages, especially if Haitian or African students are in their class. Web sites of various African instruments, music, artists, and languages can also be explored.

Students are then asked to compare African and European folktales to investigate cultural differences. Numerous Web sites of traditional African and European tales are available, some with sound recordings of the tales in French (see Supplementary Resources).

The last section provides students with an opportunity to write their own folktale and thus demonstrate the language skills and cultural knowledge acquired in this unit. As a culminating project or summative assessment, students can videotape or make a sound recording of their original tale. If digital video cameras are available, students may incorporate original video clips into their presentations. They may also choose to publish a collection of the classes' tales using a word processor or publishing tool. Students could also present their original stories (or dialogues made from them) to other French classes, at a French club meeting, or at a cultural event at the school or in the community.

The complete unit, including lesson plans, student handouts, visual aids, teacher keys, and assessment ideas, is included on the accompanying CD.

CONNECTIONS TO
OTHER DISCIPLINES

Students will study *geography* and *history* through their exposure to francophone areas outside of continental Europe and will have the opportunity to study one or more of these regions in more depth. Teachers can expand the content provided in this unit to include a discussion of the role of France and other colonizing countries in the history and current day-to-day life of francophone Africa.

An exploration of *literature* and *oral tradition* is naturally suited to the topic of francophone West Africa. While oral tradition in Africa is and was carried out in numerous local African languages, students will have the occasion to read poems and folktales translated by African authors into the French language. The griot, or story-teller, is essential to oral tradition and the recognition of African life events, such as rites of passage and funerals. Teachers may expand these lessons to include chapters from recommended AP French literature books, such as *L'Enfant noir* (Camara Laye) and *Une si longue lettre* (Miriama Bâ).

Music is an integral part of oral tradition and contemporary life in francophone Africa. In this unit, students are given the opportunity to advance their understanding of *music*, as well as *ethnomusicology* and *African languages*. One lesson provides background information on typical African instruments. Students could expand their knowledge and interests by exploring traditional musicians such as Lamine Konté and Daili Djimo Kouyate or more contemporary African singers such as Youssou N'Dour and MC Solaar. Many of the artists sing in local African languages, as well as in French. Students could preview some lyrics provided on Web sites to explore how African languages are written. A study of the musical systems and "drum language" is also possible if the teacher has local colleagues or specialists to assist in developing an interdisciplinary lesson.

SPOTLIGHT ON
TECHNOLOGY

Web Browsers: While many resources are provided within the unit, students will need to find additional information on the Internet to expand their knowledge base and their language learning. Using authentic Web sites in French will help students develop reading and comprehension skills. In this unit, students will conduct Internet research to obtain historical and cultural information.

Projection System: The teacher can use a projection system to share aspects of the lesson with the class.

Database and Encyclopedia Software: Numerous informational databases and multimedia encyclopedias are available (although some are online and may require a subscription through a school's media center). Popular resources include *Gale Student Resource Center* (culture and country information), *SIRS Researcher, ProQuest* (foreign language newspapers and magazines), *Grolier's Multimedia Encyclopedia,* and *Britannica Online School Edition.* Students should learn to select and evaluate various information resources, not just Internet resources, as part of a media literacy unit.

Synchronous and Asynchronous Communication Software: Students can enhance their receptive and productive language skills by using e-mail, chats, instant messaging, and other communication technologies to exchange information, comments, opinions, or analyses of various topics under study in this unit. Discussions may take place on a virtual discussion medium available on a school's local area network (LAN). For example, students may conduct peer-review feedback on draft assignments by posting to a virtual discussion board such as Blackboard. Student may also use Yahoo! Groups for communal e-mails for group projects. Keep in mind, however, that e-mails, chats, and instant messaging may be difficult for teachers to monitor.

In addition, students may contribute to "blogs," or online journals, to exchange information, even with French students abroad (several popular Web sites are posted for French-speaking "bloggers"). Communication with native speakers of the language will enhance students' language skills, although, again, it may be difficult for teachers to "control" or monitor blogs.

It is interesting to note that a "paralanguage" or "Net language" has developed in both French and English, changing many words and spellings in electronic communications. Students enjoy exploring and using these new terms in activities.

Word Processing Software: Student assignments, assessments, and creative projects may require the production of various authentic text types (e.g., essays, letters, or personal journal entries). In addition, tables, graphs, and charts will enhance the organization and logical presentation of word processed documents. Word processing programs also provide the possibility of easily transposing documents into HTML format for Web sites.

Presentation Software, Publishing Programs. and Multimedia Authoring Tools: Student projects and presentations (such as class newsletters, journals, or brochures) can be enhanced by the use of programs such as Microsoft Publisher, PowerPoint, HyperStudio, or more powerful multimedia authoring tools. These multimedia programs allow students to be more creative with graphics, sounds, music, and video clips incorporated into their presentations. Many of these authoring programs also provide a way to save projects as HTML documents to import into Web sites. If students have access to a digital camera with video/still capabilities, they may capture images and edit them into their presentations. Multimedia software includes: (for Mac) iMovie, FinalCut Pro; (for PC) AVID, Adobe Premiere.

Concept Mapping Software: Concept mapping software such as Inspiration can expand learners' ability to conceptualize and organize their knowledge, and can help them outline and plan more complex oral and written projects—an important academic skill for all content areas. Because this software requires learners to visually map their thinking processes, it can also help support different intelligences and learning styles.

Graphics Software: Graphics software such as a draw or paint program can be used to illustrate ideas. These tools appeal to visual learners.

Web Publishing Software or Web Editors: Students who are more advanced technology users may produce their projects on a Web site. Many free HTML editors, Web editors (e.g., Netscape Composer), and site builders are widely accessible. For free programs, teachers may consult: www.thefreecountry.com/webmaster/htmleditors.html.

Students who are experienced in JavaScript may enhance their Web sites by improving layout of the Web pages or the navigation of the site and by adding special graphical effects or dynamic Web page content.

TECHNOLOGY
RESOURCES NEEDED

Hardware

computers with Internet access
projection system
CD-audio player (for musical selections not on the Internet)
digital video/still camera (optional)
voice recording equipment (optional)

Software

Internet browsing software
databases and encyclopedias (some may be accessed online)
synchronous and asynchronous communication software
word processing software
presentation software, publishing programs, and multimedia authoring tools
concept mapping software (e.g., Inspiration)
graphics software
Web publishing software or Web editors (optional)

SUPPLEMENTARY
RESOURCES

Web Resources

Online Dictionaries

ARTFL Project: French-English Dictionary Form:
http://humanities.uchicago.edu/orgs/ARTFL/forms_unrest/FR-ENG.html
French Dictionary Online: www.online-dictionary.net/french/index.htm

Technology Publications Online

THE Journal: Technological Horizons in Education: www.thejournal.com
Technology and Learning: www.techlearning.com

Literature Resources

Cultural Resources on Francophone Africa

Montgomery County Public Schools. (1994). *Teaching culture in Grades K–8: A resource manual for teachers of French*. Rockville, MD: Author.
Montgomery County Public Schools. (1998). *Les cultures des pays francophones de l'Afrique de l'Ouest: A resource manual and CD-ROM (Mac only) for teachers of French*. Rockville, MD: Author.

Note: The illustrations and maps used in Unit 12 activities are from the above MCPS publications. They are used by permission.

The Technology Gap in the Developing World

Coste, P. (2000, 27 avril–3 mai). Tous égaux face au Web? *L'Express*, 2547.

RESOURCES FOR
ACTIVITIES 1–2
(DAYS 1–4)

Background Information on the Francophone World

Valette, J.-P. (2000). *Discovering French—Rouge: Level 3*. Chicago: McDougal Littell/Houghton Mifflin.

Maps

Map Resources: www.mapresources.com
WorldAtlas.Com: http://worldatlas.com/webimage/testmaps/maps.htm

Nation Profiles

Abidjan.net: www.abidjan.net
BBC NEWS: Country Profiles:
    http://news.bbc.co.uk/2/hi/country_profiles/default.stm
iSenegal: http://isenegal.free.fr/senegal.htm
Library of Congress, Country Studies: Côte d'Ivoire:
    http://lcweb2.loc.gov/frd/cs/citoc.html
Le Senegal Online: http://senegal-online.com/index.html

History and Geography

Grove, A. T. (1989). *The changing geography of Africa*. Oxford: Oxford University Press. Information and maps of Africa from various time periods.

RESOURCES FOR
ACTIVITIES 3–4
(DAYS 5–7)

Banque des Etats de l'Afrique Centrale (BEAC): www.beac.int/index.html
European Central Bank (Euro Banknotes):
    www.euro.ecb.int/en/section/testnotes.nd5.html
Valette, J.-P., & Valette, R. M. (2001). *Discovering French: Europak copymasters*. Chicago: McDougal Littell. Includes explanation of designs on Euros, maps, and many activities.

RESOURCES FOR
ACTIVITIES 5–9
(DAYS 8–14)

Oral Tradition

Gambian Griot: School of Music and Dance:
    http://home.planet.nl/~verka067/Links.html
Griot: www.griot.de

African Musical Instruments

Les arts africains: www.musee-manega.bf/fr/arts/artsafricains/artsaf.htm
Guide to the Ethnomusicology LP Collection in the Oberlin College Conservatory
    Library: www.oberlin.edu/faculty/rknight/Lpcollection/Lists/5c.westafrica.html
Instruments de musique Africains (sanza, kora, balafon): http://perso.orange.fr/
    .ecole.maternelle.champigny/themes/afrique/musique/musique.htm
Les instruments de musique en Afrique de l'Ouest:
    www.artisanat-africain.com/instruments/les_instruments_de_musique.htm
Kora-music.com (MP3 sound samples and software downloads):
    www.kora-music.com
Metronimo.com (quiz: les instruments de musique africains):
    www.metronimo.com/fr/jeux/quiz/quiz64.php
La musique au Sénégal: www.senegalaisement.com/senegal/musique.html

African Music Web Sites
African Music and Drumming Resources on the Web:
http://echarry.web.wesleyan.edu/africother.html
Afropop Worldwide: www.afropop.org
African Music Home Page:
http://biochem.chem.nagoya-u.ac.jp/~endo/africa.html
Frank Bessem's Musiques d'Afrique: www.geocities.com/fbessem/musique.html

Text Sources for La Légende baoulé
Herbst, H. L., & Sturges, H. (1996). *Par tout le monde francophone: Cours intermédiaire*. New York: Longman.
Valette, J.-P. (2000). *Discovering French—Rouge: Level 3*. Chicago: McDougal Littell/Houghton Mifflin.

Audio Source for La Légende baoulé
Konté, L. (1989). *La kora du Sénégal* (Vol. 2) [CD]. Paris: Arion.

Children's Literature and Folktales (Contes)
ContesAfricains.com: Le site des contes et de la littérature orale (African folktales): www.contesafricains.com
Ocelot, M. (2001). *Kirikou et la sorcière*. Paris: Milan.
Ocelot, M., & Andrieu, P. (2002). *Kirikou et la hyène noire*. Paris: Milan.
Ocelot, M., & Andrieu, P. (2003). *Kirikou et le buffle aux cornes d'or*. Paris: Milan.
Vary, A., & Brouillet, C. (1997). *Contes et légendes du monde francophone: A collection of tales from the French-speaking world*. Chicago: National Textbook Company.
Vary, A., & Brouillet, C. (2004). *Contes et fables d'Afrique*. Columbus, OH: Glencoe-McGraw Hill.

Grammar Practice
Quia: www.quia.com

Le Pagne noir
Dadié, B. B. (1955). *Le Pagne noir*. Paris: Présence Africaine. (Out of print.)

Kirikou et la sorcière
Ocelot, M. (Director and writer). (1998). *Kirikou et la sorcière*. [74-minute animated film for children, in French with English subtitles. Original sound track by Senegal's Youssou N'Dour]. (Available from ArtMattan Productions, New York, NY; www.kirikou.net; e-mail: ArtMattan@AfricanFilm.com. Also available with 54-page French activity guide [2003] from FilmArobics, www.filmarobics.com; e-mail: film@filmarobics.com.)

Cinderella (Cendrillon)
Archivox (audio recordings of many folktales, including Cendrillon): www.archivox.com/?page=titre&catid=2&id=9
Cendrillon de Charles Perrault (Perrault version of Cendrillon): www.alalettre.com/perrault-cendrillon.htm
Les contes de Grimm (Grimm version of Cendrillon): www.chez.com/feeclochette/grimm.htm
Histoire Cendrillon: www.coindespetits.com/histoires/histcendrillon/cendrillon.html

**RESOURCES FOR
ACTIVITY 10
(DAYS 15–18)**

African Authors

Miriama Bâ

Afrik.com: www.afrik.com/article3517.html

Lire les femmes écrivains et les littératures africaines:
www.arts.uwa.edu.au/AFLIT/BaMariama.html

Literary Encyclopedia: www.litencyc.com/php/speople.php?rec=true&UID=5152

Fatou Sow Ndiaye

Lire les femmes écrivains et les littératures africaines:
www.arts.uwa.edu.au/AFLIT/NdiayeSowFatou.html

Bernard Dadié

Contes et légendes africains: www.france-mail-forum.de/dos/dos2/dos2dadie.htm

Dadié, B. B. (1955). *Le pagne noir*. Paris: Présence Africaine. (Out of print.)

Camara Laye

Résumé de *L'Enfant noir* (AP exam preparation document):
www.sonoma.edu/users/t/toczyski/camaralaye/clayeresume.html

Les Films du Paradoxe (information on the 1995 film *L'Enfant noir* by Laurent
Chevallier based on the Camara Laye novel):
www.filmsduparadoxe.com/enfantcat.html

Léopold Sédar Senghor

Académie française: www.academie-francaise.fr/immortels/base/academiciens/
fiche.asp?param=666

iSenegal: Léopold Sédar Senghor: http://isenegal.free.fr/senghor.htm

Radio France: www.radiofrance.fr/parvis/senghor.htm

Senghor au club des poètes: www.franceweb.fr/poesie/senghor2.htm

African Proverbs

Reseau Ivoire: www.rezo-ivoire.net/littérature/citation.asp

The Culture and Literature of Francophone West Africa

The following discussion summarizes 10 activities that focus on the culture and
literature of francophone West Africa. Each lesson is identified by title (e.g., Money
and Culture) and activity number (e.g., Activity 4). Complete activities, including
lesson plans, visual aids, student handouts, teacher keys, and assessment ideas, are
included on the accompanying CD. Content, language, and technology objectives are
listed for each block of activities.

**OBJECTIVES FOR
ACTIVITIES 1–2
(DAYS 1–4)**

Content

Students will be able to:

- Name the countries and capitals of francophone Africa.

- Describe an African francophone country in more detail.

Language

Students will be able to:

- Use prepositions correctly with countries, cities, and geographical places.
- Describe basic features of a country using appropriate vocabulary and structures.

Technology

Students will be able to:

- Use technology research tools (such as the Internet).
- Use technology communication tools (such as e-mail).
- Use technology productivity tools (such as word processing software, PowerPoint, or Publisher).

ACTIVITY 1 (DAY 1)

Geography of Francophone West Africa

PREVIEW

Review with students their previous knowledge of the geography of francophone West Africa and the use of prepositions with countries and cities. Remind students that they will mainly be looking for the names of francophone (rather than anglophone or lusophone) countries, although the other countries' official languages may be discussed later. These countries should have been studied before in lower levels of French, so this is considered a review.

FOCUSED LEARNING

Display Transparency 1a, a map of Africa without the names of countries. In small groups, have students write the names of the countries they know on a blank map (Handout 1a). Encourage groups to consult with one another until most countries have been identified. Then, in a whole class follow-up, display Transparency 1b with the names of each country so that students can verify their responses.

Review the names of countries and their capitals as necessary, using a large map of Africa. Then, review prepositions with countries and cities as needed. Have students complete tasks in which they identify the correct prepositions and then match West African countries with their capitals (Handout 2a). Finally, assess student knowledge of the capitals of these countries (Handout 2b).

EXPANSION

As an expansion activity, students can review French vocabulary for geographical features, such as deserts, mountains, and rivers. As an additional expansion activity, students may explore new content regarding how West Africa was divided by the colonial powers into arbitrary divisions that did not reflect existing ethnic groups and historical kingdoms. This could be an interdisciplinary activity with a social studies or world history teacher.

As a technology extension, students can be asked to find various online maps—topographical, political, population density, and so on—to provide them with more information about the region they will be studying in-depth during their individual (or small group) projects about selected African countries in Activity 2.

TEACHING TIPS

If African students are present in the classroom (or in the school), they can serve as "experts" in the small group activities or in the upcoming projects on francophone Africa.

ACTIVITY 2
(DAYS 2–4)

Country Profiles: Côte d'Ivoire and Sénégal

PREVIEW

Begin with a whole-group focus on one of the more well-known francophone countries—Côte d'Ivoire or Sénégal (usually included briefly in most French textbooks). Have students mention a few facts they know about Côte d'Ivoire or Sénégal. As a pre-assessment, have pairs or small groups of students fill in any background knowledge they possess about these countries on a country profile chart (Handout 1; see Figure 12.1). You may want to assign topics to the groups, based on the chart categories.

Figure 12.1 Excerpt from Activity 2, Handout 1.

Que savez-vous déjà au sujet de la Côte d'Ivoire ou du Sénégal?				
Géographie: Villes, Fleuves	Histoire: Indépendance	Gouvernement et Président	Economie et Produits Agricoles	Langues et Groupes Ethniques

FOCUSED LEARNING

Have groups of students report back to the class, who will take notes on the information provided. Using Web resources on Sénégal and the Background Information Sheets for Côte d'Ivoire provided on the CD, help students complete various details missing in the chart. These teacher pages can also be used as a "model report" (or anchor paper) for students. Using Handout 2 as a guide, have students practice writing paragraphs from their notes on a word processor. The result will be a short report on Côte d'Ivoire or Sénégal that serves as a model for a future research project.

EXPANSION

Have individual students or groups select another francophone African country they wish to investigate in more detail to create a country profile report. Topics explored may include geography, history, government, economics, ethnic groups, languages, and famous people, such as leaders and authors. Have student groups conduct research in the computer lab or media center to complete their reports. They may wish to consult database or encyclopedia software as research tools. If students work in groups, they should use e-mail or some other type of electronic communication to collaborate and interact with each other during the research and peer-editing processes.

Have students make presentations to other class members when the reports are completed. As oral presentations are given, students may take notes on additional copies of Handout 1 or Handout 2.

As a technology alternative, students or groups could also produce a mini-project using a presentation program such as PowerPoint, create a "country profile" brochure using software such as Publisher, or develop a Web page.

TEACHING TIPS

It could take several days in the computer lab for students to complete this research project, depending upon the required length and the technology used. If all students have access to computers at home, much of the assignment could be conducted outside of class time, which would encourage collaborative electronic communication among students.

OBJECTIVES FOR ACTIVITIES 3–4 (DAYS 5–7)

Content

Students will be able to:

- Explain the basics of the monetary system used in francophone Africa.

Language

Students will be able to:

- Expand the vocabulary needed to discuss cultural elements.
- Describe symbols found on money, including art objects, plants, people, and clothing.
- Compare and contrast cultural similarities and differences.

Technology

Students will be able to:

- Use technology research tools (such as the Internet).
- Use technology communication tools (such as e-mail).
- Use technology productivity tools (concept mapping software such as Inspiration, word processing software).

ACTIVITY 3
(DAYS 5–6)

CFA Francs

Students will study the monetary system used in the francophone African countries and examine several CFA francs (monetary units). They will discuss the various representations depicted on this currency and how these items reflect local cultures. Images of several denominations of CFA francs are provided on the CD and more can be found on the Web site listed for the Banque des Etats de l'Afrique Centrale (BEAC), www.beac.int/index.html.

PREVIEW

Read the Background Information Sheet on CFA Francs (included on the CD) aloud with students or distribute it to students as Handout 1 and have them read it at home. Go over the basic questions about CFA at the end of the article. Show pictures of the bills (Transparency 1), and introduce how CFA francs reflect the cultures of West Africa. Use the questions after the pictures of each bill to point out various items. Encourage students to answer these questions aloud during the class discussion. You may wish to show additional bills by accessing the BEAC Web site. You may also wish to distribute paper copies of the overheads to students (as Handout 2).

FOCUSED LEARNING

Brainstorm with a word splash or other activity to help students create an appropriate vocabulary list to assist them in filling out the cultural chart (Handout 3; see Figure 12.2). The exercise asks students to identify clothing styles, animals, plants, and other cultural objects depicted on various bills. Students may need a specific list of African cultural terms (see CD: Teacher Key for Handouts 3 and 4).

Discuss the cultural representations that can be found on the money bills. For example, ask students: What is depicted to represent the local lifestyle, geographic area, clothing, animals, and languages? Then have students complete Handout 3 in pairs, and afterwards, compare answers in small or large groups.

Figure 12.2 Excerpt from Activity 3, Handout 3.

Fiche d'étudiant 3 : CFA Francs : Intro-vocabulaire

Examiner les billets CFA. Avec un/une collègue, faites une liste des éléments culturels qui y sont représentés. Pensez au mode de vie, à la région géographique, aux vêtements, aux animaux, aux plantes, à la langue utilisée... Partagez les idées avec un autre groupe.

Modes de vie	Région(s) géographique(s)	Style de vêtements
Animaux	Plantes-produits agricoles	Autres objets culturels

EXPANSION

Have students draw on the previous class discussions and the completed Handout 3 to individually complete a series of questions regarding their cultural study of CFA (Handout 4). Afterward, have them discuss their answers in small groups. As an alternative, you may wish to use Handout 4 as an assessment of students' reading comprehension or as a homework assignment. (Possible answers are listed on the CD, Teacher Key for Handouts 3 and 4.)

For technology-enhanced activities, students can research the Web for information about the Zone Franc and obtain pictures of numerous bills dating back to 1919. The BCEA Web site (listed in Supplementary Resources) has a wealth of information about the choice for designs (motifs) on bills and the history of the CFA franc. Students could also investigate how the bills from one or more countries have changed over time.

TEACHING TIPS

Have native francophone speakers research the background of various CFA in different West African countries or other francophone areas (Canada, Belgium, Haiti) and report back to the class. Perhaps they could find sample bills from their country of origin to discuss with the class.

ACTIVITY 4 (DAY 7)

Money and Culture

PREVIEW

Introduce students to Euro bills. Images of Euro bills are included on the CD and can also be found at the Web site of the European Central Bank (www.euro.ecb. int/en/section/testnotes.nd5.html). You may also wish to distribute paper copies of the overheads to students (Handout 1).

FOCUSED LEARNING

Have students compare CFA bills with Euro currency and discuss what these differences indicate about Europe and West Africa. What are the major differences in money bills from these regions? What do these differences indicate culturally (and historically) about these countries? Discuss as a class or in small groups.

The next task is a formative assessment. Distribute Handout 2, which asks students to pretend they are journalists writing about cultural and historical images found on currency. They are to write an article about the cultural values portrayed on currency from francophone African countries and European countries. They should explain the following: What does a country's money imply about its cultural values? Is currency a kind of "official image" of a region or nation?

Set guidelines for the expected length of the paper, provide a rubric of criteria, and establish when first and final drafts are due. Have students begin to plan their written answer in class (using Inspiration or a different prewriting tool) so they can ask questions. Instruct them to complete their writing at home on a word processor, if available, and turn in rough drafts for peer and teacher feedback. Drafts may be submitted by e-mail, if desired.

EXPANSION

Students could examine and compare other francophone countries' currency, such as Canada or Haiti. In addition, students could examine U.S. dollar bills and reflect on American culture as portrayed by the symbols, images, and words on currency. Different groups of students could focus on just one other monetary unit and culture and compare them to the CFA francs and West African culture. Groups could then report back orally, which could be followed by a whole-class discussion.

TEACHING TIPS

Depending on the level of the class, a more in-depth discussion about symbols in general and cultural symbols in particular may be required before students begin to write. The writing prompt can also be varied according to different students' needs.

OBJECTIVES FOR
ACTIVITIES 5–9
(DAYS 8–14)

Content

Students will be able to:

- Name and describe typical African musical instruments.
- Explain the storyteller (griot) role in African oral tradition.
- State the major components of folktales.

Language

Students will be able to:

- Expand African vocabulary in French to meet content objectives.
- Compare and contrast cultural values and morals found in European and African folktales (*contes*).

Technology

Students will be able to:

- Use technology research tools.
- Use technology communication tools.
- Use technology productivity tools.

ACTIVITY 5 (DAY 8)

African Oral Tradition

PREVIEW

Introduce oral tradition storytelling, the role of the griot, and musical instruments in African cultures. Show pictures of traditional African musical instruments from the Internet. Distribute Handout 1 and have students read about the African oral tradition and discuss the poem "Le tam-tam," by Fatou-Ndiaye Sow. Discuss how poetry and music is linked in these cultures.

FOCUSED LEARNING

Distribute Handout 2 (see Figure 12.3) and have students access the Internet to find pictures and information about traditional African instruments, such as the kora, balafon, riti, or tambour, or instruct them to research a modern-day griot such as Mory Kanté. Students may complete their Web search while listening to African music on the Web or on CDs, if available. (See Supplementary Resources for African music Web sites.)

Figure 12.3. Students conduct Internet research to complete Handout 2.

Fiche d'exploration: Les instruments de musique africains et le griot

Surfez les sites Web suivants et donnez une description de chaque instrument de musique.

1. le griot—Quel est son rôle dans la société africaine? www.mali-music.com/cat/catg/griot.htm
2. la kora (cora)—Comment cet instrument est-il employé dans la musique moderne? www.mali-music.com/cat/instruments/instk/kora.htm

Nommez d'autres instruments que vous avez trouvés sur Internet: _____

e.g., www.au-senegal.com/art/musique.htm.

Trouvez un site Web avec la musique africaine traditionnelle et/ou moderne et écoutez les chansons. Mettez l'adresse du site ici et partagez-la avec un(e) camarade de classe:

www. _____

EXPANSION

Distribute Handout 3 and have students read and discuss another poem, called "Tam-Tam," by the famous author and former president of Sénégal, Léopold Sédar Senghor. Continue as a class to explore the importance of music in oral tradition and folklore.

TEACHING TIPS

If students of African origin are in the French class, they may have access to more music and actual instruments. These students could make presentations on their favorite singers.

ACTIVITY 6
(DAYS 9–10)

La Légende baoulé

PREVIEW

Have students locate Côte d'Ivoire on a map of Africa, and then show them an illustration of its major language groups (from the map used in Activity 2). Baoulé is in the Akan group of languages in the central part of the country. This activity introduces folktales, or contes. The folktale that is the focus of this activity is about *le peuple baoulé*, one of the ethnic groups in this area. The legend describes how this people got their name.

Have students read information about the author of the story, Bernard Dadié, on Handout 1, which also contains pictures of a famous ivoirian stamp of Queen Pokou. You may want to supplement the handout with information students find on the Web. Ask students to predict what Queen Pokou might have sacrificed as told in this legend.

FOCUSED LEARNING

Before reading the folktale *La Légende baoulé*, students need to review or learn African-specific vocabulary mentioned in the legend. Distribute Handout 2a, a list of vocabulary from the story, and Handout 2b, an exercise that asks students to classify this vocabulary into categories, such as animals, nature, insects, clothing, sounds, and actions. Have students work on this task in pairs. Review the answers in class (using the Teacher Key for Handout 2b, on the CD), and have students study these lexical items as homework to prepare for reading the folktale.

The class should read the entire legend aloud (taking turns) to simulate oral tradition. As an optional exercise, after the first reading, play an audio CD of Lamine Konté singing the story, while students listen and follow along, to simulate a more realistic rendering of traditional storytelling.

Discuss what students think is the message or moral contained in the story (e.g., *Il faut toujours sacrifier le bien individuel pour le bien de la société*). How does this reflect traditional African community values? As a formative assessment, have students complete the reading comprehension questions (Handout 3) for homework or as an in-class assignment.

EXPANSION

Have students read other typical African folktales, or *contes*, and determine the cultural values or traditions that are presented. What role do animals or nature play? (See Supplementary Resources for additional folktales.)

TEACHING TIPS

Make the reading of the legend as interactive as possible. The African audience often responds chorally, especially in refrains, so encourage students to join together orally in the refrain section. If a drum is available, they could lightly beat out a rhythm while the story is being read aloud.

ACTIVITY 7
(DAYS 11–12)

Structure Practice in Folktales

PREVIEW

Review the comprehension questions on *La Légende baoulé* completed for homework or as an in-class assignment (Handout 3 in Activity 6). Ask students what they think is the main message of the folktale.

FOCUSED LEARNING

Using the legend, review the use of the *imparfait* and the *passé simple*. Have students substitute the *passé composé* for verbs written in the *passé simple* in the story. Then have students complete an activity sheet on verb tenses (Handout 1). If students need more practice on verb tenses, assign activities from a grammar workbook. Additional verb drills are also available on numerous grammar practice Web sites, such as Quia (www.quia.com).

Using the legend as a basis, discuss how the author uses transition words and time words to enhance the story. In small groups, have students make a list of ones they find and then complete Handout 2. Remind students that they will need to use these words in a future writing assignment. Review the answers for Handouts 1 and 2 in class, using the teacher keys.

EXPANSION

The class can read other folktales and look for the grammatical and structural features in these stories. The moral of each tale and the traditional cultural messages it portrays should also be discussed. In addition, francophone students from other countries can share folktales from their regions. Technology-enriched activities expand students' knowledge and understanding of the genre of folktales and how culture is integral to such tales. Numerous books and Web sites are available where students can find African folktales to read. See Supplementary Resources for some ideas.

TEACHING TIPS

The verb tenses should be quite familiar by this level, but students always need practice with transition words and other discourse features found in folktales and other literature. They should apply these to their own creative writing. Students may keep a running list of such terms to help with writing activities.

ACTIVITY 8 (DAY 13)

Comparison of Folktales: *Le Pagne noir*

PREVIEW

The main objective of Activities 8 and 9 is to have students compare a similar folktale in African and European contexts. Students will read another folktale by Bernard Dadié, *Le Pagne noir*. This African tale is very similar to the Grimm version of *Cinderella*, and students should begin to look for comparisons as they read. Explain to students that *Le Pagne noir* was written down in French by Dadié and published in 1955. However, the oral tradition of this story has existed for centuries in several African languages. *Cinderella* also has hundreds of versions in various languages.

If necessary, review the use of past tenses in narratives. Using the next two stories in this unit, *Le Pagne noir* and *Cendrillon*, students should continue to practice textual cohesive devices (transition words, adverbs of time, and story formulas—once upon a time, etc.) in preparation for their summative assessment or final project.

Have students engage in a pre-reading vocabulary task to make sure the African terms found in this story are understood (Handout 1a). Introduce the main characters and their traits, which students may recognize as those of Cinderella and the wicked stepmother.

FOCUSED LEARNING

Have students read *Le Pagne noir*, preferably aloud in class in the oral tradition. (The story is included on the CD.) Assign as homework the reading comprehension questions on Handout 1b. Handout 1c can be used as a springboard for discussion after the comprehension questions are corrected in class. As a formative assessment, have students select one of the topics suggested on Handout 1c for a short writing sample (at least one paragraph). They should include new African vocabulary learned, correct verb tenses, and transition words.

EXPANSION Show the film of the African folktale *Kirikou et la sorcière*, based on the children's book (which has beautiful illustrations and music by Youssou N'Dour). A study guide is available with numerous activities, such as comparing *Kirikou* to one of the Disney films (see Supplementary Resources).

TEACHING TIPS Focus on the unfamiliar African vocabulary as necessary. Have students develop a personalized vocabulary list that they can use throughout the unit.

ACTIVITY 9 (DAY 14) ## Comparison of Folktales: *Cendrillon*

PREVIEW To start the activity, encourage students to predict the similarities to *Le Pagne noir* they will find in the Grimm brothers' version of *Cendrillon*. It is less familiar to students, but more similar to *Le Pagne noir* than the French Perrault version of *Cendrillon*, written around 1671. Explain to students that the Grimm version was written in German and published around 1812. The Grimm story is included on the CD-ROM and is also available online at www.chez.com/feeclochette/grimm.htm. The Perrault version is available at www.alalettre.com/perrault-cendrillon.htm.

You may want to prepare a pre-reading vocabulary review for antiquated or unusual words found in this version of the story.

FOCUSED LEARNING Have students read the Grimm version of *Cendrillon*. You may wish to prepare reading comprehension questions to help guide students in this task. Then brainstorm with students the similarities (and differences) of the two tales, *Cendrillon* and *Le Pagne noir*. Distribute a comparison chart (Handout 2). Have students complete the chart, working in pairs or small groups, and then report back to the whole class for discussion and observations.

EXPANSION Discuss how these stories relate to folktales from other regions of the world studied in English literature classes. Ask students to reflect on why we find wicked stepmothers, wicked stepsisters, and "good girls" in so many stories from different cultures, times, and places. What elements (such as nature and animals) are similar in folktales and oral traditions from around the world? Why?

TEACHING TIPS Before the summative assessment, it may be helpful for students to form study groups to review the essentials learned about folktales and oral tradition in this unit. Review of transition words and verb tenses is also important.

OBJECTIVES
FOR ACTIVITY 10
(DAYS 15–18)

Content

Students will be able to:

- Write an original folktale based on the elements of this genre that have been studied.
- Explain the cultural message or moral used in the folktale.

Language

Students will be able to:

- Use language appropriate to storytelling, including appropriate verb tenses, transition words, and adverbs of time.
- Describe cultural differences.

Technology

Students will be able to:

- Use technology productivity tools—concept mapping software (e.g., Inspiration) to organize ideas and a word processor for writing.
- Use technology communication tools to share their product with others.

ACTIVITY 10
(DAYS 15–18)

Conte Original (Original Folktale)

PREVIEW

As a summative assessment, students will write an original folktale that includes the cultural and structural features studied during this unit. The procedure for the entire summative assessment is provided for students in French on the CD (Handout 1).

To begin the activity, distribute Handout 1 and go over any questions. Have students read several African folktales, then meet in small groups to determine a list of traditional cultural values and/or moral messages that they believe are important to pass on to younger generations. These cultural values may be from students' own heritage groups (African, American, Chinese, Vietnamese, Hispanic, and so forth). Have student groups report to each other using a jigsaw or other grouping activity.

Students will determine which traditional value or moral message they wish to write about after listening to each other's ideas (and perhaps after checking with their families). Have each student write his or her proposed topic on an index card or e-mail and submit it to you for approval. After the topic has been approved, students can begin work on their plan, including setting, plot, and characters, using a program such as Inspiration.

Be sure to give students a writing rubric and remind them to check for the correct use of verb tenses and the inclusion of transition words and adverbs of time in their traditional story. Students must understand the story is to be original with specific cultural traits.

FOCUSED LEARNING

Instruct students to pre-write the original story in folktale format using a word processor. They can finish the first draft at home, submit it you by e-mail, and prepare (or look for) at least one illustration using a graphics program. The following day students should participate in peer-editing and a discussion of the first draft in pairs. Have students edit the work accordingly and make final revisions at home, after they have seen the teacher's feedback.

The last day of the project, have students present their original folktales orally (preferably in small groups). Direct the members of the audience to write down what they believe is the message or moral of each student's folktale.

EXPANSION

Numerous expansion activities are possible, depending on the time available and students' interests. A follow-up tech-based activity may include a joint online student publication that posts the folktales created by the class on a bulletin board or on student blogs. Students can videotape or make a sound recording of their original tale. If digital video cameras are available, students may incorporate original video clips into their presentations. They may also choose to publish a collection of the classes' tales using a word processor, presentation software, or multimedia authoring tool.

To meet Foreign Language Standard 5.1, students should use the language both within and beyond the school setting. To accomplish this, groups of students could present their stories (or dialogues created from them) to other French classes or at a French club meeting. Another idea is to have students present at a cultural evening or heritage festival organized by the school or the community.

UNIT EXTENSION ACTIVITIES

African Literature and African Proverbs

If time permits, students could explore more extended texts of African literature, such as *L'Enfant noir* (by Camara Laye) or *Une si longue lettre* (by Miriama Bâ). These works are included on the AP French literature list. Teachers will easily find these texts and study guides to accompany these works. Sources and additional authors are provided in Supplementary Resources. Technology-enriched activities could include online research about the authors and their works, followed by student oral or written presentations, using technology such as PowerPoint, if desired.

African proverbs and sayings are a rich source of cultural knowledge. Using the Réseau Ivoire Web site (www.rezo-ivoire.net/littérature/citation.asp) and others found with online searches, students may select a few African proverbs and sayings for further investigation. Students will be able to expand their understanding and knowledge of African cultural values gained by studying African folktales through the exploration and interpretation of various proverbs. Comparisons can also be made with French, Canadian, Belgian, Haitian, or Swiss proverbs.

UNIT TEACHING TIPS

The National Educational Technology Standards for Students include an important standard (2) that addresses social, ethical, and human issues. In our school, we have found a systematic way to address these issues with an official International

Baccalaureate course called Information Technology in a Global Society (ITGS). The ITGS course, taught in English, examines the social and ethical dimensions of technology use. Students work individually and in groups to find online articles about contemporary technology and social issues, such as legal and illegal music downloads; the "paralanguage" that has evolved for e-mail, chat, and instant messages; the censoring of Web content by countries such as China; and the widening technology gap in developing countries (especially those in francophone Africa).

The latter topic—the widening technology gap in the developing world—is also addressed in a unit in a French textbook we use, *Collage: Varitiés Culturelles* (2001, McGraw-Hill Higher Education). Based on an article reprinted from *L'Express*, "Tous égaux face au Web?" (Coste, 2000), this unit examines the social and human impact of the lack of technology access in poorer countries around the world. This unit engages French students in a healthy debate about the "rich" and the "poor" and how access to technology, and thus to information, leads to power. Many of our immigrant students are from these regions of the world and are concerned about this imbalance of power, and are eager to explore ways they can help bridge the gap and be advocates for the "have nots." This topic also helps students fulfill the expectations of NETS•S 6 regarding the use of technology in the development of strategies for "solving problems and making informed decisions in the real world."

While it may be difficult for content area teachers to formally assess many of the NETS•S, foreign language teachers who regularly incorporate technology into their instruction and into student projects can evaluate their students' ability to use certain technologies to complete course content and language requirements by using a technology rubric (such as that provided for this unit) as part of their assessment.

ACTFL Standard 5.2, which requires students to demonstrate evidence of becoming lifelong learners by using the language for personal enjoyment, is also typically difficult for teachers to measure. One possible way to do this is to ask students to find a French speaker in their neighborhood or online and share a personal story with that person. If students post an original story on a blog or Web site, they may also attract some "hits" from francophone readers that they can document or present anecdotally to the rest of the classroom, providing teachers with some data on this standard.

ASSESSMENT

Formative and summative assessment measures are included throughout the lesson. See the assessment materials provided on the CD.

ASSESSMENT CRITERIA

Rubrics for the assessment tasks in this unit are provided in appendix A.

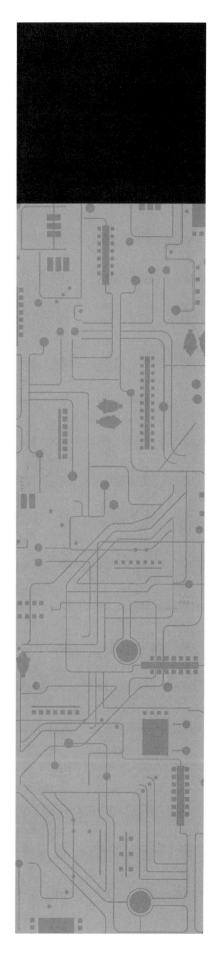

Appendixes

appendix A

Assessment Rubrics for the Resource Units

The following rubrics may be used in conjunction with the assessment ideas outlined for each unit.

Rubric for Mosaic Project ▪ Content-Based Instruction in Spanish

UNIT 1 ▪ **Introduction to Immigration: Basic Human Geography**

UNIT 2 ▪ **Basque Immigration to Oregon**

UNIT 3 ▪ **Mexican Immigration to Oregon**

The rubric on the following page contains an array of evaluation criteria, and not all may be applicable to each activity of these units. Teachers should consider the nature of the task and choose the appropriate items to evaluate. The target level of performance for these units ("meets standard") corresponds to Benchmark 5, or ACTFL Proficiency Level Intermediate Mid. Student production at a higher level exceeds the standard.

CRITERIA	IN PROGRESS	MEETS STANDARD	EXCEEDS STANDARD
TASK COMPLETION			
	Basic requirements of task are not complete; rhetorical strategies are inappropriate; information is incomplete	Basic requirements of task are complete; rhetorical strategies are appropriate; sufficient information is included	Basic requirements of task are complete; rhetorical strategies are appropriate and sophisticated; additional information is included
USE OF LANGUAGE FUNCTIONS IN TASK COMPLETION			
Describe	Includes mainly simple descriptions	Includes a combination of simple and detailed descriptions	Includes mainly detailed descriptions
Compare	Ideas are juxtaposed but not adequately expressed using target language comparative devices (más que, etc.); comparisons are inaccurate	Ideas are juxtaposed and adequately expressed using target language comparative devices (más que, etc.); comparisons are accurate and basic	Ideas are juxtaposed and well expressed using target language comparative devices (más que, etc.); comparisons are accurate and detailed
Narrate in present and past time frames	Present tense predominates; inconsistent use or distinction of two past tenses (preterit/imperfect); connectors are minimal or absent	Present and past time frames used but not always distinguished appropriately; inconsistent use or distinction of two past tenses; connectors are present but used inconsistently	Present and past time frames used and distinguished appropriately; consistent use and distinction of two past tenses (with some patterned errors); connectors are present and used consistently
Ask information questions	Consistent formation of yes/no questions; emerging ability to form information questions	Consistent and accurate formation of yes/no and information questions	Consistent and accurate formation of yes/no and information questions; appropriate use of questions as rhetorical strategy
CONTENT STANDARDS (AS OUTLINED IN THE NATIONAL GEOGRAPHY STANDARDS)			
Students demonstrate understanding of the world in spatial terms	Use of maps to represent spatial relationships is inaccurate, incomplete, or inconsistent; use of graphs and maps to represent abstract data is limited	Use of maps to represent spatial relationships is accurate; use of graphs and maps to represent abstract data is basic	Use of maps to represent spatial relationships is accurate; use of graphs and maps to represent abstract data is advanced; additional details are included
Students demonstrate understanding of places and regions	Basic descriptions of the physical and human characteristics of places	Basic descriptions of the physical, human, and cultural characteristics of places; emerging comparison of regions/cultural groups	Accurate and detailed descriptions and comparisons of the physical, human, and cultural characteristics of regions/cultural groups
Students demonstrate understanding of human systems	Descriptions of the distribution of human populations and their migrations are inaccurate or are missing crucial information	Descriptions of the distribution of human populations and their migrations are accurate and basic; push–pull factors are included	Descriptions of the distribution of human populations and their migrations are accurate and detailed; push–pull factors and the effects of migrations are included
Students demonstrate understanding of environment and society	Descriptions of the effects of the physical world on human populations (weather, economic activity, etc.) and vice versa are inaccurate or are missing crucial information	Descriptions of the effects of the physical world on human populations (weather, economic activity, etc.) and vice versa are accurate and basic	Descriptions of the effects of the physical world on human populations (weather, economic activity, etc.) and vice versa are accurate and detailed
Students demonstrate understanding of uses of geography	Use of geographical information to draw inferences, to interpret time frames, and to support cause and effect relationships is inconsistent	Use of geographical information to draw inferences, to interpret time frames, and to support cause and effect relationships is consistent and basic	Use of geographical information to draw inferences, to interpret time frames, and to support cause and effect relationships is consistent and advanced

Rubric for Mosaic Project ▪ Content-Based Instruction in Japanese

UNIT 4 ▪ **Tokugawa Japan**

UNIT 5 ▪ **Tokaido Travelers**

UNIT 6 ▪ **Kaempfer's Journal**

This rubric contains an array of evaluation criteria, and not all may be applicable to each activity of these units. Teachers should consider the nature of the task and choose the appropriate items to evaluate. The target level of performance for these units ("meets standard") corresponds to Benchmark 5, or ACTFL Proficiency Level Intermediate Mid. Student production at a higher level exceeds the standard.

CRITERIA	IN PROGRESS	MEETS STANDARD	EXCEEDS STANDARD
USE OF LANGUAGE FUNCTIONS IN TASK COMPLETION			
Describe	Includes mainly simple descriptions	Includes a combination of simple and detailed descriptions	Includes mainly detailed descriptions
Explain	Explanation is insufficient or confusing	Explanation is reasonable and basic	Explanation is reasonable and detailed
Narrate	Connectors and aspects are minimal or absent	Connectors and aspects are present but used inconsistently	Connectors and aspects are present and used consistently
Express opinions and feelings	Includes mainly simple expressions of opinions and feelings	Includes a combination of simple and detailed expressions of feelings and opinions	Includes mainly detailed expressions of feelings and opinions
HISTORICAL THINKING STANDARDS			
Chronological thinking	Understanding of the key transformations of Japan from the Edo period to current times is incomplete	Understanding of the key transformations of Japan from the Edo period to current times is basic	Understanding of the key transformations of Japan from the Edo period to current times is advanced
Historical comprehension	Comprehension of the key realities of the Edo period is incomplete; lacks ability to compare histories of Japan and the U.S.	Comprehension of the key realities of the Edo period is adequate; demonstrates basic ability to compare histories of Japan and the U.S.	Comprehension of the key realities of the Edo period is sophisticated; demonstrates advanced ability to compare histories of Japan and the U.S.
Historical analysis and interpretation	Analysis and interpretation of the social systems, the social changes, and their effects in the Edo period is inconsistent or incomplete	Analysis and interpretation of the social systems, the social changes, and their effects in the Edo period is basic	Analysis and interpretation of the social systems, the social changes, and their effects in the Edo period is extended

(Continued)

Rubric for Mosaic Project ▪ Content-Based Instruction in Japanese
(Continued)

CRITERIA	IN PROGRESS	MEETS STANDARD	EXCEEDS STANDARD
NETS•S			
Basic operations and concepts	Lacks proficiency in basic operations	Possesses proficiency in basic operations	N/A
Handling of social, ethical, and human issues	Lacks ethical and responsible manners	Demonstrates ethical and responsible manners	Promotes ethical and responsible manners of peers and/or positive attitudes toward technology
Use of technology productivity tools	Lacks minimum proficiency in using these tools	Meets minimum proficiency in using these tools	Goes beyond minimum proficiency; applies technology beyond the requirements of tasks
Use of technology communications tools	Lacks minimum proficiency in using these tools	Meets minimum proficiency in using these tools	Goes beyond minimum proficiency; applies technology beyond the requirements of tasks
Use of technology research tools	Lacks minimum proficiency in using these tools	Meets minimum proficiency in using these tools	Goes beyond minimum proficiency; applies technology beyond the requirements of tasks

Rubrics for CoBaLTT Project ▪ Content-Based Language Teaching with Technology

UNIT 7 ▪ **Le Moyen Âge en France**

Rubric for Oral Presentation

CRITERIA	EXCEEDS EXPECTATIONS (9–10)	MEETS EXPECTATIONS (8–8.9)	NEEDS IMPROVEMENT (<8)	POINTS
Content	Presentation includes all required elements as well as additional information. Examples demonstrate a depth of understanding that extends and challenges listeners' thinking. Presentation is well organized and cohesive. Presenter demonstrates in-depth knowledge of the topic.	Presentation includes all required elements. Examples include sufficient detail for listeners to grasp the ideas presented. Presentation is somewhat well organized and cohesive. Presenter demonstrates accurate knowledge of the topic.	Presentation does not include all required elements. Examples need additional detail for comprehension of the ideas presented. Presentation needs additional organization and cohesiveness. Presenter demonstrates limited knowledge of the topic.	_____ x 15 = _____ points
Language control	Language (vocabulary and linguistic structures) is consistently accurate. Vocabulary and linguistic structures are varied and sophisticated beyond the level of the class. Use of imparfait and passé composé is always accurate.	Language (vocabulary and linguistic structures) is sufficiently accurate to ensure comprehension. Vocabulary and linguistic structures are adequate for the level of the class. Use of imparfait and passé composé is accurate most of the time.	Language (vocabulary and linguistic structures) is not sufficiently accurate to ensure comprehension. Vocabulary and linguistic structures are not adequate for the level of the class. Use of imparfait and passé composé is frequently inaccurate.	_____ x 10 = _____ points
Delivery	Presentation is well rehearsed and is presented confidently. Student speaks consistently clearly with appropriate volume throughout the presentation. Speaker makes eye contact consistently. Visual enhances presentation. Notes are used as an aid, but not read. Speaker is able to elaborate examples clearly, with confidence and depth.	Presentation is rehearsed and is presented with some confidence. Student speaks consistently clearly with appropriate volume most of the time. Speaker makes eye contact some of the time. Visual is adequate. Notes are used as an aid and are occasionally read. Speaker is able to explain examples adequately.	Presentation needs additional rehearsal to be presented confidently. Student does not speak clearly with appropriate volume. Speaker does not consistently make eye contact. Visual is not adequate. Speaker depends often on notes. Speaker has difficulty explaining examples.	_____ x 5 = _____ points
GRADE: A = 94–100%; A- = 90–93%; B+ = 87–89%; B = 84–86%; B- = 80–83%; C+ = 77–79%; C = 74–76%				Total: _____/300

Rubric for Written Version of Presentation

CRITERIA	EXCEEDS EXPECTATIONS (9–10)	MEETS EXPECTATIONS (8–8.9)	NEEDS IMPROVEMENT (<8)	POINTS
Content	Speech includes all required elements as well as additional information. Examples demonstrate a depth of understanding that extends and challenges listeners' thinking. Speech is well organized and cohesive. Writer demonstrates in-depth knowledge of the topic.	Speech includes all required elements. Examples include sufficient detail for listeners to grasp the ideas presented. Speech is somewhat well organized and cohesive. Writer demonstrates accurate knowledge of the topic.	Speech does not include all required elements. Examples need additional detail for listeners to grasp the ideas presented. Speech needs additional organization and cohesiveness. Writer demonstrates limited knowledge of the topic.	_____ x 15 = _____ points
Language control	Language (vocabulary and linguistic structures) is consistently accurate. Vocabulary and linguistic structures are varied and sophisticated beyond the level of the class. Use of *imparfait* and *passé composé* is always accurate.	Language (vocabulary and linguistic structures) is sufficiently accurate to ensure comprehension. Vocabulary and linguistic structures are adequate for the level of the class. Use of *imparfait* and *passé composé* is accurate most of the time.	Language (vocabulary and linguistic structures) is not sufficiently accurate to ensure comprehension. Vocabulary and linguistic structures are not adequate for the level of the class. Use of *imparfait* and *passé composé* is frequently inaccurate.	_____ x 15 = _____ points
GRADE: A = 94–100%; A- = 90–93%; B+ = 87–89%; B = 84–86%; B- = 80–83%; C+ = 77–79%; C = 74–76%				Total: _____ /300

Rubric for Assessment of NETS•S—Technology Use for Final Project

CRITERIA	EXCEEDS EXPECTATIONS (9–10)	MEETS EXPECTATIONS (8–8.9)	NEEDS IMPROVEMENT (<8)	POINTS
Use of technology productivity tools (multimedia authoring tools)	Multimedia authoring tools were used beyond expectations. The applications of their use go beyond the requirements of the project and greatly enhanced the effectiveness of the oral presentation. Many illustrations were provided and the slides were organized in a clear and logical manner.	Multimedia authoring tools were used with the minimum proficiency required to produce an acceptable oral presentation. Some illustrations were provided and the overall presentation was easy to follow.	Multimedia authoring tools were used with an obvious lack of the proficiency required to support the oral presentation. The overall presentation suffered from the use of the tools rather than being supported by them. No illustrations were provided and the slides did not have a logical flow.	_____ x 15 = _____ points
Use of technology research tools (online search with Internet)	Students went beyond the minimum proficiency for using these tools and applied their use beyond the requirements of this project.	Students met the minimum proficiency for using these tools. Students identified useful Web sites and gathered interesting material that helped them complete their project.	Students did not meet the minimum proficiency for using these tools. Students failed to identify useful Web sites or gather interesting material that could help them complete their project.	_____ x 10 = _____ points
Use of technology communications tools (for those attempting to score extra points)	Communication tools were used beyond expectations. Students not only showed a very good control over the use of these tools but also applied their use in ways that exceed the requirements of this project. Students were successful in establishing communication with others.	Communication tools were used with the proficiency necessary to communicate with others. The use of the tools is acceptable and remains in the realm of "expected" usage. Students were not successful in establishing communication with others even though they repeatedly attempted to.	Communication tools were used unsuccessfully and their use shows a lack of the proficiency necessary to communicate with others. Students failed in their attempt to establish communication with others and abandoned their quest without further effort.	_____ x 5 = _____ bonus points
Grade: A = 94–100%; A- = 90–93%; B+ = 87–89%; B = 84–86%; B- = 80–83%; C+ = 77–79%; C = 74–76%				Total: _____/300 Bonus:_____

UNIT 8 ■ Les Stéréotypes des Français

Rubric for the Final Project

Non-negotiable items:

☐ All group members must participate in the slideshow preparation and oral presentation.

☐ All required components of the presentation must be included.

☐ A minimum of nine slides must be used.

☐ The written commentary that accompanies each slide must be turned in.

☐ A description of each individual's contribution to the group effort must be submitted (in English).

CRITERIA	4	3	2	1
Development, Organization, and Visuals	Presentation is well developed and well organized; listeners are able to follow along easily. Visuals are excellent and enhance the content of the presentation.	Presentation is somewhat developed and organized; listeners can follow most of it without difficulty. Visuals enhance the content of the presentation to some extent.	Presentation development and organization are uneven; important links may be missing and it is difficult for listeners to follow. Visuals seem peripheral and are not well integrated.	Presentation is undeveloped, unorganized, and disconnected, making it very difficult for listeners to follow. Visuals are lacking, are not integrated, or do not support the presentation.
Communication of Key Concepts	Presentation reflects strong understanding of the key concepts related to stereotypes. Examples clearly illustrate the concepts.	Presentation reflects good understanding of the key concepts related to stereotypes. Examples generally illustrate the concepts.	Presentation reflects some understanding of the key concepts related to stereotypes. Examples do not always clearly illustrate the concepts.	Presentation does not reflect understanding of the key concepts related to stereotypes. Examples are lacking.
Vocabulary and Language Use	Use of a wide range of topic-specific vocabulary; clear communication of ideas; mostly accurate use of tenses, word order. Some compound sentences included.	Use of a good range of topic-specific vocabulary; good communication of ideas; good control of tenses, word order. Some compound sentences attempted.	Lacking some critical topic-specific vocabulary; limited range of words; errors in tenses and word order at times impede understanding. Only simple sentences are included.	Vocabulary is limited and at times inappropriate, which occasionally impedes comprehension. Consistently inaccurate use of tenses and word order. Sentences are incomplete.
Pronunciation, Fluency, and Eye Contact	Pronunciation and intonation are level-appropriate. Smooth and fluent speech indicates evidence of rehearsal. Excellent eye contact with the audience.	Always intelligible, though there may be a noticeable accent and lapses in intonation. Speech mostly smooth, reflecting some rehearsal. Eyes mostly focused on audience.	Pronunciation problems partially impede comprehensibility. Speech is hesitant, showing little evidence of rehearsal (some reading of slides). Eyes focus more on notes rather than on audience.	Very difficult to follow due to pronunciation problems. Speech is slow with many pauses, showing no evidence of rehearsal (slides mostly read). Eyes focus on slides and notes.
Participation and Group Work	Each group member assumes an equal and active role in the preparation and presentation.	Each group member assumes a role, although some members appear more active or responsible for a majority of the work.	Participation among group members is uneven; some students are passive and contribute little to the presentation.	Some students hardly participate; no effort is made to distribute work among all group members.

Rubric for NETS•S Assessment—PowerPoint Multimedia Presentation Project

CRITERIA	3	2	1	SCORE
Use of technology (skills in using software, creating printed output with comments and outline format)	Students have an exceptional understanding of the technological tools, allowing them to go beyond expectations. All the required outputs were produced in the precise format requested. Students can easily answer questions about the content and procedures used to make the PowerPoint multimedia presentation.	Students have a fair understanding of the technological tools, allowing them to meet expectations. Most of the required outputs were produced although some may not have been exactly in the expected format. Students can answer most questions about the content and procedures used to make the PowerPoint multimedia presentation but may falter with some.	Students have a limited understanding of the technological tools. Few if any of the required outputs were produced and/or they were not in the expected format. Students can answer very few questions about the content and procedures used to make the PowerPoint multimedia presentation.	
Use of technology productivity tools (to enhance productivity and increase creativity)	Presentation shows considerable originality and inventiveness. The content and ideas were presented in a unique and interesting way. Students make excellent use of font, color, graphics, effects, and other elements to enhance the presentation.	Presentation shows some originality and inventiveness. The content and ideas were presented in an interesting way. Students make use of font, color, graphics, effects, and other elements to enhance the presentation but at times they fail to enhance it and seem unnecessary.	Presentation shows little or no originality and very little attempt at inventiveness. The content and ideas were not presented in an interesting way. Students make some use of font, color, graphics, effects, and other elements, but these often distract from the presentation content.	
Use of technology communications tools (using multimedia to communicate ideas better during delivery of presentation)	The PowerPoint slideshow improves the communication of ideas. Information is organized in a clear, logical way. It is easy to anticipate the type of material that might be on the next slide.	The PowerPoint slideshow supports the communication of ideas. Most information is logically sequenced though an occasional slide or item of information seems out of place.	The PowerPoint slideshow does not support the communication of ideas and actually distracts from the original content. There is no clear plan for an organized presentation of information.	
Use of technology research tools (online search with Internet)	Students went beyond the minimum proficiency for using these tools and applied their use beyond the requirements for this project.	Students met the minimum proficiency for using these tools. Students identified useful Web sites and gathered interesting material that helped them complete their project.	Students did not meet the minimum proficiency for using these tools. Students failed to identify useful Web sites or gather material that could help them complete their project.	

UNIT 9 ■ Yo Soy el Agua

Rubric for My Book on Water

CRITERIA	4	3	2	1
How do I work?	I always work hard and share my ideas with my partner.	I almost always work hard and share my ideas with my partner.	Sometimes I work hard and share my ideas with my partner.	I need a lot of help to get my work done.
How is the content in my book?	My book has more than five accurate ideas.	My book has five accurate ideas.	My book has four accurate ideas.	My book has three or fewer ideas, but they aren't all accurate.
How is the language in my book?	My ideas are stated in complete sentences with correct punctuation (capital letters and periods).	My ideas are stated in complete sentences with mostly correct punctuation (capital letters and periods).	My ideas are stated in complete sentences with some correct punctuation (capital letters and periods).	Some of my sentences are not complete and my punctuation isn't always correct.
Do my pictures support the content?	My book has many clear pictures that support the content of the book.	My book has some clear pictures that mostly support the content of the book.	My book doesn't have many clear pictures that support the content of the book.	My book doesn't have many pictures and some aren't clear or don't support the content of the book.

Rubrics for Iowa State ▪ The National K–12 Foreign Language Resource Center

UNIT 10 ▪ **Carole Fredericks: Music Is Only the Beginning**

UNIT 12 ▪ **The Culture and Literature of Francophone West Africa**

Rubric for Oral Presentation

CRITERIA	4	3	2	1
Comprehension	Student is able to accurately answer almost all questions posed by classmates about the topic.	Student is able to accurately answer most questions posed by classmates about the topic.	Student is able to accurately answer a few questions posed by classmates about the topic.	Student is unable to accurately answer questions posed by classmates about the topic.
Preparedness	Student is completely prepared and has obviously rehearsed.	Student seems pretty prepared but might have needed a couple more rehearsals.	Student is somewhat prepared, but it is clear that rehearsal was lacking.	Student does not seem at all prepared to present.
Content	Student shows a full understanding of the topic.	Student shows a good understanding of the topic.	Student shows a good understanding of parts of the topic.	Student does not seem to understand the topic very well.
Attention to Other Presentations	Student listens intently and does not make distracting noises or movements.	Student listens intently but has one distracting noise or movement.	Student sometimes does not appear to be listening but is not distracting.	Student sometimes does not appear to be listening and has distracting noises or movements.
Enunciation	Student speaks clearly and distinctly all (95–100%) the time, and mispronounces no words.	Student speaks clearly and distinctly all (95–100%) the time, but mispronounces one word.	Student speaks clearly and distinctly most (85–94%) of the time and mispronounces no more than one word.	Student often mumbles or cannot be understood or mispronounces more than one word.
Vocabulary	Student uses vocabulary appropriate for the audience. Student extends the audience vocabulary by defining words that might be new to most of the audience.	Student uses vocabulary appropriate for the audience. Student includes 1–2 words that might be new to most of the audience, but does not define them.	Student uses vocabulary appropriate for the audience. Student does not include any vocabulary that might be new to the audience.	Student uses several (5 or more) words or phrases that are not understood by the audience.
Complete Sentences	Student always (99–100% of the time) speaks in complete sentences.	Student mostly (80–98% of the time) speaks in complete sentences.	Student sometimes (70–79% of the time) speaks in complete sentences.	Student rarely speaks in complete sentences.

Rubric for Assessment of National Foreign Language Standards

CRITERIA	1 UNSATISFACTORY	2 SATISFACTORY	3 EXEMPLARY	SCORE
1.1 Students engage in conversations, provide and obtain information, express feelings and emotions, and exchange opinions.	Understanding is not in evidence.	Student demonstrates acceptable understanding within the context of the unit.	Student demonstrates exemplary understanding, making connections to personal experience through higher-level applications of thinking.	
1.2 Students understand and interpret written and spoken language on a variety of topics.	Understanding is not in evidence.	Student demonstrates acceptable understanding within the context of the unit.	Student demonstrates exemplary understanding, making connections to personal experience through higher-level applications of thinking.	
1.3 Students present information, concepts, and ideas to an audience of listeners or readers on a variety of topics.	Understanding is not in evidence.	Student demonstrates acceptable understanding within the context of the unit.	Student demonstrates exemplary understanding, making connections to personal experience through higher-level applications of thinking.	
2.1 Students demonstrate an understanding of the relationship between the practices and perspective of the culture studied.	Understanding is not in evidence.	Student demonstrates acceptable understanding within the context of the unit.	Student demonstrates exemplary understanding, making connections to personal experience through higher-level applications of thinking.	
2.2 Students demonstrate an understanding of the relationship between the products and perspectives of the culture studied.	Understanding is not in evidence.	Student demonstrates acceptable understanding within the context of the unit.	Student demonstrates exemplary understanding, making connections to personal experience through higher-level applications of thinking.	
3.1 Students reinforce and further their knowledge of other disciplines through the foreign language.	Understanding is not in evidence.	Student demonstrates acceptable understanding within the context of the unit.	Student demonstrates exemplary understanding, making connections to personal experience through higher-level applications of thinking.	
3.2 Students acquire information and recognize the distinctive viewpoints that are only available through the foreign language and its cultures.	Understanding is not in evidence.	Student demonstrates acceptable understanding within the context of the unit.	Student demonstrates exemplary understanding, making connections to personal experience through higher-level applications of thinking.	

(Continued)

Rubric for Assessment of National Foreign Language Standards *(Continued)*

CRITERIA	1 UNSATISFACTORY	2 SATISFACTORY	3 EXEMPLARY	SCORE
4.1 Students demonstrate understanding of the nature of language through comparisons of the language studied and their own.	Understanding is not in evidence.	Student demonstrates acceptable understanding within the context of the unit.	Student demonstrates exemplary understanding, making connections to personal experience through higher-level applications of thinking.	
4.2 Students demonstrate understanding of the concept of culture through comparisons of the cultures studied and their own.	Understanding is not in evidence.	Student demonstrates acceptable understanding within the context of the unit.	Student demonstrates exemplary understanding, making connections to personal experience through higher-level applications of thinking.	
5.1 Students use the language both within and beyond the school setting.	Understanding is not in evidence.	Student demonstrates acceptable understanding within the context of the unit.	Student demonstrates exemplary understanding, making connections to personal experience through higher-level applications of thinking.	
5.2 Students show evidence of becoming life-long learners by using the language for personal enjoyment and enrichment.	Understanding is not in evidence.	Student demonstrates acceptable understanding within the context of the unit.	Student demonstrates exemplary understanding, making connections to personal experience through higher-level applications of thinking.	

Rubric for Assessment of NETS•S

CRITERIA	1 UNSATISFACTORY	2 SATISFACTORY	3 EXEMPLARY	SCORE
3.1 Students use technology tools to enhance learning, increase productivity, and promote creativity.	Student shows lack of minimum proficiency in using these tools.	Student meets minimum proficiency for using these tools.	Student goes beyond minimum proficiency for using these tools, applying their use beyond the requirements of this project.	
3.2 Students use productivity tools to collaborate in constructing technology-enhanced models, preparing publications, and producing other creative works.	Student shows lack of minimum proficiency in using these tools.	Student meets minimum proficiency for using these tools.	Student goes beyond minimum proficiency for using these tools, applying their use beyond the requirements of this project.	
4.1 Students use telecommunications to collaborate, publish, and interact with peers, experts, and other audiences.	Student shows lack of minimum proficiency in using these tools.	Student meets minimum proficiency for using these tools.	Student goes beyond minimum proficiency for using these tools, applying their use beyond the requirements of this project.	
4.2 Students use a variety of media and formats to communicate information and ideas effectively to multiple audiences.	Student shows lack of minimum proficiency in using these tools.	Student meets minimum proficiency for using these tools.	Student goes beyond minimum proficiency for using these tools, applying their use beyond the requirements of this project.	
5.1 Students use technology to locate, evaluate, and collect information from a variety of sources.	Student shows lack of minimum proficiency in using these tools.	Student meets minimum proficiency for using these tools.	Student goes beyond minimum proficiency for using these tools, applying their use beyond the requirements of this project.	
5.3 Students evaluate and select new information resources and technological innovations based on the appropriateness to specific tasks.	Student shows lack of minimum proficiency in using these tools.	Student meets minimum proficiency for using these tools.	Student goes beyond minimum proficiency for using these tools, applying their use beyond the requirements of this project.	
			TOTAL POINTS	

UNIT 11 ■ A Technology-Rich Unit from *La peineta colorada*

Rubric for Cimarrones Graphic Illustration

CRITERIA	EXCELLENT	SATISFACTORY	NEEDS IMPROVEMENT
Quantity	The description contains 7–9 sentences. Some new words, some old words from previous classes, and some of the words presented in class. Creative combination of verbs, adjectives, nouns.	The description contains 4–6 sentences. Few new words. Some combination of old and new words (verbs, adjectives, nouns) but shows a tendency to use mostly what is presented in class.	The description contains 2–3 sentences. No new words. Minimal risk-taking when combining words.
Quality and Creativity	The words chosen are closely related to the topic of slavery. The description contains many creative sentences that show the author used imagination.	The words chosen are loosely related to the topic of slavery. The description contains some creative sentences (1–2) that show the author used imagination.	The words chosen do not seem to be related to the topic of slavery. The description lacks creative sentences, indicating the author did not use much imagination.
Mechanics	1–3 errors in spelling. Careful use of dictionary and class notes to write the poem.	4–6 errors in spelling. Some use of dictionary and class notes to write the poem.	7 or more errors in spelling. Little use of any aid to write the poem.
Neatness	The final draft of the description is readable, clean, neat, and attractive. It is free of erasures and crossed-out words. It looks like the author took pride in the work.	The final draft of the description is readable. It may have one or two erasures, but they are not distracting. It looks like the author rushed through parts of it.	The final draft is not neat or attractive. It looks like the author rushed through it to get it done and neglected the presentation.

Rubric for Oral Presentation

CRITERIA	EXCELLENT	SATISFACTORY	NEEDS IMPROVEMENT
Comprehensibility	Student speaks clearly, moves at a good pace, and mispronounces few to no words. The mispronunciations do not get in the way of understanding.	Student speaks clearly, moves at a fast pace, and mispronounces several words. The mispronunciations do not get in the way of understanding.	Student often mumbles, moves either too fast or too slow, and mispronounces many words. Some of the mispronunciations get in the way of understanding.
Comprehension	Student is able to accurately answer almost all questions about words that might be new to the audience.	Student is able to accurately answer a few questions about words that might be new to the audience.	Student is unable to accurately answer questions about words that might be new to the audience.
Preparedness and Enthusiasm	Student has obviously rehearsed and the body language shows strong enthusiasm and interest in the presentation. Student made eye contact and used a loud and clear voice.	Student is somewhat prepared but rehearsal is lacking. The body language shows some interest in the presentation. Student made some eye contact and used a clear voice.	Student does not seem prepared and the body language does not show involvement or interest in the presentation. Student made little or no eye contact and used a low and unclear voice.

Rubric for Assessment of National Foreign Language Standards

CRITERIA	1 UNSATISFACTORY	2 SATISFACTORY	3 EXEMPLARY	SCORE
1.1 Students engage in conversations, provide and obtain information, express feelings and emotions, and exchange opinions.	Understanding is not in evidence.	Student demonstrates acceptable understanding within the context of the unit.	Student demonstrates exemplary understanding, making connections to personal experience through higher-level applications of thinking.	
1.2 Students understand and interpret written and spoken language on a variety of topics.	Understanding is not in evidence.	Student demonstrates acceptable understanding within the context of the unit.	Student demonstrates exemplary understanding, making connections to personal experience through higher-level applications of thinking.	
1.3 Students present information, concepts, and ideas to an audience of listeners or readers on a variety of topics.	Understanding is not in evidence.	Student demonstrates acceptable understanding within the context of the unit.	Student demonstrates exemplary understanding, making connections to personal experience through higher-level applications of thinking.	
2.2 Students demonstrate an understanding of the relationship between the products and perspectives of the culture studied.	Understanding is not in evidence.	Student demonstrates acceptable understanding within the context of the unit.	Student demonstrates exemplary understanding, making connections to personal experience through higher-level applications of thinking.	
3.1 Students reinforce and further their knowledge of other disciplines through the foreign language.	Understanding is not in evidence.	Student demonstrates acceptable understanding within the context of the unit.	Student demonstrates exemplary understanding, making connections to personal experience through higher-level applications of thinking.	
			TOTAL POINTS	

Rubric for Assessment of NETS•S

CRITERIA	1 UNSATISFACTORY	2 SATISFACTORY	3 EXEMPLARY	SCORE
3.1 Students use technology tools to enhance learning, increase productivity, and promote creativity.	Student shows lack of minimum proficiency in using these tools.	Student meets minimum proficiency for using these tools.	Student goes beyond minimum proficiency for using these tools, applying their use beyond the requirements of this project.	
4.2 Students use a variety of media and formats to communicate information and ideas effectively to multiple audiences.	Student shows lack of minimum proficiency in using these tools.	Student meets minimum proficiency for using these tools.	Student goes beyond minimum proficiency for using these tools, applying their use beyond the requirements of this project.	
5.1 Students use technology to locate, evaluate, and collect information from a variety of sources.	Student shows lack of minimum proficiency in using these tools.	Student meets minimum proficiency for using these tools.	Student goes beyond minimum proficiency for using these tools, applying their use beyond the requirements of this project.	
5.2 Students use technology tools to process data and report results.	Student shows lack of minimum proficiency in using these tools.	Student meets minimum proficiency for using these tools.	Student goes beyond minimum proficiency for using these tools, applying their use beyond the requirements of this project.	
			TOTAL POINTS	

appendix B

National Educational Technology Standards

National Educational Technology Standards for Students (NETS•S)

The National Educational Technology Standards for students are divided into six broad categories. Standards within each category are to be introduced, reinforced, and mastered by students. Teachers can use these standards as guidelines for planning technology-based activities in which students achieve success in learning, communication, and life skills.

1. **Basic operations and concepts**
   - Students demonstrate a sound understanding of the nature and operation of technology systems.
   - Students are proficient in the use of technology.

2. **Social, ethical, and human issues**
   - Students understand the ethical, cultural, and societal issues related to technology.
   - Students practice responsible use of technology systems, information, and software.
   - Students develop positive attitudes toward technology uses that support lifelong learning, collaboration, personal pursuits, and productivity.

3. **Technology productivity tools**
   - Students use technology tools to enhance learning, increase productivity, and promote creativity.
   - Students use productivity tools to collaborate in constructing technology-enhanced models, preparing publications, and producing other creative works.

4. **Technology communications tools**

   - Students use telecommunications to collaborate, publish, and interact with peers, experts, and other audiences.

   - Students use a variety of media and formats to communicate information and ideas effectively to multiple audiences.

5. **Technology research tools**

   - Students use technology to locate, evaluate, and collect information from a variety of sources.

   - Students use technology tools to process data and report results.

   - Students evaluate and select new information resources and technological innovations based on the appropriateness to specific tasks.

6. **Technology problem-solving and decision-making tools**

   - Students use technology resources for solving problems and making informed decisions.

   - Students employ technology in the development of strategies for solving problems in the real world.

National Educational Technology Standards for Teachers (NETS•T)

All classroom teachers should be prepared to meet the following standards and performance indicators.

I. Technology Operations and Concepts

Teachers demonstrate a sound understanding of technology operations and concepts. Teachers:

A. demonstrate introductory knowledge, skills, and understanding of concepts related to technology (as described in the ISTE National Educational Technology Standards for Students).

B. demonstrate continual growth in technology knowledge and skills to stay abreast of current and emerging technologies.

II. Planning and Designing Learning Environments and Experiences

Teachers plan and design effective learning environments and experiences supported by technology. Teachers:

A. design developmentally appropriate learning opportunities that apply technology-enhanced instructional strategies to support the diverse needs of learners.

B. apply current research on teaching and learning with technology when planning learning environments and experiences.

C. identify and locate technology resources and evaluate them for accuracy and suitability.

D. plan for the management of technology resources within the context of learning activities.

E. plan strategies to manage student learning in a technology-enhanced environment.

III. Teaching, Learning, and the Curriculum

Teachers implement curriculum plans that include methods and strategies for applying technology to maximize student learning. Teachers:

A. facilitate technology-enhanced experiences that address content standards and student technology standards.

B. use technology to support learner-centered strategies that address the diverse needs of students.

C. apply technology to develop students' higher-order skills and creativity.

D. manage student learning activities in a technology-enhanced environment.

IV. Assessment and Evaluation

Teachers apply technology to facilitate a variety of effective assessment and evaluation strategies. Teachers:

A. apply technology in assessing student learning of subject matter using a variety of assessment techniques.

B. use technology resources to collect and analyze data, interpret results, and communicate findings to improve instructional practice and maximize student learning.

C. apply multiple methods of evaluation to determine students' appropriate use of technology resources for learning, communication, and productivity.

V. Productivity and Professional Practice

Teachers use technology to enhance their productivity and professional practice. Teachers:

A. use technology resources to engage in ongoing professional development and lifelong learning.

B. continually evaluate and reflect on professional practice to make informed decisions regarding the use of technology in support of student learning.

C. apply technology to increase productivity.

D. use technology to communicate and collaborate with peers, parents, and the larger community in order to nurture student learning.

VI. Social, Ethical, Legal, and Human Issues

Teachers understand the social, ethical, legal, and human issues surrounding the use of technology in PK–12 schools and apply that understanding in practice. Teachers:

A. model and teach legal and ethical practice related to technology use.

B. apply technology resources to enable and empower learners with diverse backgrounds, characteristics, and abilities.

C. identify and use technology resources that affirm diversity.

D. promote safe and healthy use of technology resources.

E. facilitate equitable access to technology resources for all students.

National Educational Technology Standards for Administrators (NETS•A)

All school administrators should be prepared to meet the following standards and performance indicators. These standards are a national consensus among educational stakeholders regarding what best indicates effective school leadership for comprehensive and appropriate use of technology in schools.

I. **Leadership and Vision—Educational leaders inspire a shared vision for comprehensive integration of technology and foster an environment and culture conducive to the realization of that vision. Educational leaders:**

   A. facilitate the shared development by all stakeholders of a vision for technology use and widely communicate that vision.

   B. maintain an inclusive and cohesive process to develop, implement, and monitor a dynamic, long-range, and systemic technology plan to achieve the vision.

   C. foster and nurture a culture of responsible risk taking and advocate policies promoting continuous innovation with technology.

   D. use data in making leadership decisions.

   E. advocate for research-based effective practices in use of technology.

   F. advocate, on the state and national levels, for policies, programs, and funding opportunities that support implementation of the district technology plan.

II. **Learning and Teaching—Educational leaders ensure that curricular design, instructional strategies, and learning environments integrate appropriate technologies to maximize learning and teaching. Educational leaders:**

   A. identify, use, evaluate, and promote appropriate technologies to enhance and support instruction and standards-based curriculum leading to high levels of student achievement.

   B. facilitate and support collaborative technology-enriched learning environments conducive to innovation for improved learning.

   C. provide for learner-centered environments that use technology to meet the individual and diverse needs of learners.

   D. facilitate the use of technologies to support and enhance instructional methods that develop higher-level thinking, decision-making, and problem-solving skills.

   E. provide for and ensure that faculty and staff take advantage of quality professional learning opportunities for improved learning and teaching with technology.

III. **Productivity and Professional Practice**—Educational leaders apply technology to enhance their professional practice and to increase their own productivity and that of others. Educational leaders:

   A. model the routine, intentional, and effective use of technology.

   B. employ technology for communication and collaboration among colleagues, staff, parents, students, and the larger community.

   C. create and participate in learning communities that stimulate, nurture, and support faculty and staff in using technology for improved productivity.

   D. engage in sustained, job-related professional learning using technology resources.

   E. maintain awareness of emerging technologies and their potential uses in education.

   F. use technology to advance organizational improvement.

IV. **Support, Management, and Operations**—Educational leaders ensure the integration of technology to support productive systems for learning and administration. Educational leaders:

   A. develop, implement, and monitor policies and guidelines to ensure compatibility of technologies.

   B. implement and use integrated technology-based management and operations systems.

   C. allocate financial and human resources to ensure complete and sustained implementation of the technology plan.

   D. integrate strategic plans, technology plans, and other improvement plans and policies to align efforts and leverage resources.

   E. implement procedures to drive continuous improvements of technology systems and to support technology-replacement cycles.

V. **Assessment and Evaluation**—Educational leaders use technology to plan and implement comprehensive systems of effective assessment and evaluation. Educational leaders:

   A. use multiple methods to assess and evaluate appropriate uses of technology resources for learning, communication, and productivity.

   B. use technology to collect and analyze data, interpret results, and communicate findings to improve instructional practice and student learning.

   C. assess staff knowledge, skills, and performance in using technology and use results to facilitate quality professional development and to inform personnel decisions.

   D. use technology to assess, evaluate, and manage administrative and operational systems.

VI. **Social, Legal, and Ethical Issues—Educational leaders understand the social, legal, and ethical issues related to technology and model responsible decision making related to these issues. Educational leaders:**

A. ensure equity of access to technology resources that enable and empower all learners and educators.

B. identify, communicate, model, and enforce social, legal, and ethical practices to promote responsible use of technology.

C. promote and enforce privacy, security, and online safety related to the use of technology.

D. promote and enforce environmentally safe and healthy practices in the use of technology.

E. participate in the development of policies that clearly enforce copyright law and assign ownership of intellectual property developed with district resources.

This material was originally produced as a project of the Technology Standards for School Administrators Collaborative.

appendix C

The Standards for Foreign Language Learning

The national standards for foreign language education center around five goals: Communication, Cultures, Connections, Comparisons, and Communities—the five C's of foreign language education.

Communication

Communicate in Languages Other Than English

Standard 1.1: Students engage in conversations, provide and obtain information, express feelings and emotions, and exchange opinions

Standard 1.2: Students understand and interpret written and spoken language on a variety of topics

Standard 1.3: Students present information, concepts, and ideas to an audience of listeners or readers on a variety of topics

Cultures

Gain Knowledge and Understanding of Other Cultures

Standard 2.1: Students demonstrate an understanding of the relationship between the practices and perspectives of the culture studied

Standard 2.2: Students demonstrate an understanding of the relationship between the products and perspectives of the culture studied

Connections

Connect with Other Disciplines and Acquire Information

Standard 3.1: Students reinforce and further their knowledge of other disciplines through the foreign language

Standard 3.2: Students acquire information and recognize the distinctive viewpoints that are only available through the foreign language and its cultures

Comparisons

Develop Insight into the Nature of Language and Culture

Standard 4.1: Students demonstrate understanding of the nature of language through comparisons of the language studied and their own

Standard 4.2: Students demonstrate understanding of the concept of culture through comparisons of the cultures studied and their own.

Communities

Participate in Multilingual Communities at Home and Around the World

Standard 5.1: Students use the language both within and beyond the school setting

Standard 5.2: Students show evidence of becoming life-long learners by using the language for personal enjoyment and enrichment.

Reprinted with permission from the National Standards in Foreign Language Education Project.